Automated Security Management

Ehab Al-Shaer • Xinming Ou • Geoffrey Xie
Editors

Automated Security Management

 Springer

Editors
Ehab Al-Shaer
Department of Software and
    Information Systems
University of North Carolina Charlotte
Charlotte, NC, USA

Xinming Ou
Computing and Information Sciences
Kansas State University
Manhattan, KS, USA

Geoffrey Xie
Department of Computer Science
Naval Postgraduate School
Monterey, CA, USA

References to various copyrighted trademarks, servicemarks, marks and registered marks owned by the respective corporations and/or connected subsidiaries may appear in this book. We use the names, logos, and images only in an editorial fashion with no intention of infringement of the trademark.

ISBN 978-3-319-34536-9   ISBN 978-3-319-01433-3 (eBook)
DOI 10.1007/978-3-319-01433-3
Springer Cham Heidelberg New York Dordrecht London

Printed on acid-free paper

Springer is part of Springer Science+Business Media (www.springer.com)

Preface

With the increasing trend of cyber attacks, more security technologies and devices have been developed. A typical enterprise network might have hundreds of security devices such as firewalls, IPSec gateways, IDS/IPS, authentication servers, authorization/RBAC servers, and crypto systems. However, each security device might contain thousands of security configuration variables and rules that must be set correctly and consistently across the entire network in order to enforce end-to-end security properties. Moreover, security configuration must be constantly changing to optimize protection and block prospective attacks. Tuning configuration to balance security, flexibility, and performance is another major challenging task. This is extremely burdensome not only for regular users but also for experienced administrators, who have to be very lucky to get things working right all the time. The resulting security configuration complexity places a heavy burden on both regular users and experienced administrators and dramatically reduces overall network assurability and usability.

Automated Security Management presents a number of topics in the area of configuration automation. This book is based on papers published at the fifth Symposium on Configuration Analytics and Automation (SafeConfig 2012). It is a source of information for IT security configuration automation for both researchers and practitioners. Part introduces modeling and validation of configurations based on high-level requirements. Part II discusses how to manage the security risk as a result of configuration settings of network systems. Part III introduces the concept of configuration analysis and why it is important in ensuring the security and functionality of a properly configured system. Part IV presents ways to identify problems when things go wrong. We would like to thank all the chapter authors for contributing such a diverse collection of timely and interesting research results.

Charlotte, NC, USA   Ehab Al-Shaer
Manhattan, KS, USA   Xinming Ou
Monterey, CA, USA   Geoffrey Xie

Contents

Part I
Configuration Modeling and Checking

Chapter 1
Towards a Unified Modeling and Verification of Network and System Security Configurations

Mohammed Noraden Alsaleh, Ehab Al-Shaer, and Adel El-Atawy

Abstract Systems and networks access control configuration are usually analyzed independently although they are logically combined to define the end-to-end security property. While systems and applications security policies define access control based on user identity or group, request type and the requested resource, network security policies uses flow information such as host and service addresses for source and destination to define access control. Therefore, both network and systems access control have to be configured consistently in order to enforce end-to-end security policies. Many previous research attempt to verify either side separately, but it does not provide a unified approach to automatically validate the logical consistency between both of them.

In this paper, we introduce a cross-layer modeling and verification system that can analyze the configurations and policies across both application and network components as a single unit. It combines policies from different devices as firewalls, NAT, routers and IPSec gateways as well as basic RBAC-based policies of higher service layers. This allows analyzing, for example, firewall polices in the context of application access control and vice versa providing a true end-to-end configuration verification tool. Our model represents the system as a state machine where packet header, service request and location determine the state and transitions that conform with the configuration, device operations, and packet values are established. We encode the model as Boolean functions using binary decision diagrams (BDDs). We used an extended version of computational tree logic (CTL) to provide more useful operators and then use it with symbolic model checking to prove or find counter examples to needed properties.

M.N. Alsaleh (✉) • E. Al-Shaer
University of North Carolina at Charlotte, Charlotte, NC, USA
e-mail: malsaleh@uncc.edu; ealshaer@uncc.edu

A. El-Atawy
Google Inc, Mountain View, CA, USA
e-mail: aelatawy@google.com

E. Al-Shaer et al. (eds.), *Automated Security Management*,
DOI 10.1007/978-3-319-01433-3_1, © Springer International Publishing Switzerland 2013

1.1 Introduction

Users inadvertently trigger a long sequence of operations in many locations and devices by just a simple request. The application requests are encapsulated inside network packets which in turn are routed through the network devices and subjected to different types of routing, access control and transformation policies. Misconfigurations at the different layers in any of the network devices can affect the end to end connection between the hosts them selves and the communicating services running on top of them. Moreover, applications may require to transform requests to another one or more requests with different characteristics. This means that the network layer should guarantee more than one packet flow at the same time in order for the application request to be successful. Although it is already very hard to verify that only the legitimate packets can pass through the network successfully, the consistency between network and application layer access configuration adds another challenge. The different natures of policies from network layer devices to the logic of application access control makes it more complex.

In this paper we have extended ConfigChecker [3] to include application layer access control. The ConfigChecker is a model checker for network configuration. It implemented many network devices including: routers, firewalls, IPSec gateways, hosts, and NAT/PAT nodes. ConfigChecker models the transitions based on the packet forwarding at the network layer where the packet header fields along with the location represent the variables for the model checker. We define application layer requests following a loose RBAC model: a 4-tuple of <user, role, object, action>. The request can be created by users or services running on top of hosts in the network. The services in our model can also transform a request into another one or more requests and forward them to a different destination. We have implemented a parallel model checker for application layer configuration. The transitions in the application layer model is determined by the movement of the requests between different services. However, the network and application layer model checkers are not operating separately. Requirements regarding both models can be verified in a single query using our unified query interface. Moreover, inconsistency between network configuration and application layer configuration can be detected.

The nature of the problem of verifying network-wide configurations necessitate having a very scalable system in terms of time and space requirements. Larger networks, more complex configurations, and richer variety of devices are all dimensions over which the system should handle gracefully. The application-layer access control depends on different variables than most of network layer policies. We chose to implement a parallel model checker for application access control rather than adding the application layer variables (which correspond to request fields) to the network model checker itself. This can decrease the number of system states and improve the performance. As the case in ConfigChecker, both model checkers are represented as state machines and encoded as boolean function using Binary Decision Diagrams (BDDs). We use an extended version of computational tree logic (CTL) to provide more useful operators and then use it with symbolic model checking to prove or find counter examples for needed properties regarding both models.

The rest of this paper is organized as follows. We first briefly describe our framework components in Sect. 1.2. We then present the model used for capturing the network and application layer configuration in Sects. 1.3 and 1.4 respectively. Section 1.5 shows how to query the model for properties, and lists some sample queries. In Sect. 1.6 we report the performance evaluation of the proposed approach. The related work is presented in Sect. 1.7. We finally present our conclusion and future remarks in Sect. 1.8.

1.2 Framework Overview

The framework consists of a few key components: configuration loader, model compiler, and query engine. The duty of each component is described briefly below (Fig. 1.1):

- The *Configuration Loader* parses the main configuration file that points out to the configuration files of network devices. Each file represents a device or entity (e.g. firewall, router, application-layer service, etc.). Each configuration file consists mainly of two sections: meta-data directives, and policy. The initial directives act as an initialization step to configure the device properties like default gateway, service port, host address, etc. The policy is listed afterwards as a simple list of rules.
- The *Model Compiler* translates the configuration into a Boolean expressions for each policy rule and builds a single expression for each device. These expressions are then combined into a single expression representing the whole network.
- The *Query Engine* is responsible for verifying properties of the system by executing simple scripts based on CTL expressions. Scripts is written using a very limited set of primitives for refining the user output, and for defining the property itself.

The model compiler component builds two separate expressions. The first represents the network layer configuration that reflects the packets forwarding and transformation through the network core and end points as described in Sect. 1.3.

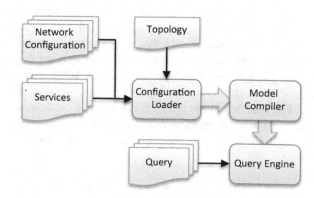

Fig. 1.1 A simple overview of the framework design and flow

The other expression represents the application layer configuration including services and users. This reflects how requests are forwarded and transformed in the service level. Section 1.4 describes this process in more details. Although we can integrate the two expressions and build only one expression that accommodates for both the network and application layer configuration, we chose to split them into two expressions. The variables used on each of them are generally independent except for the location variable. Building one expression takes more space because the network configuration will be duplicated for each different combination of application layer variables generating more and more states. This helps our model to scale and avoid state explosion.

1.3 Network Model

We model the network as a single finite state machine. The state space is the cross-product of the packet properties by its possible locations in the network. The packet properties include the header information that determines the network response to a specific packet.

1.3.1 State Representation

Initially, the information we need about the packet is its header. Therefore, we can encode the state of the network with the following characteristic function:

$$\sigma_n : \mathbf{IP_s} \times \mathbf{port_s} \times \mathbf{IP_d} \times \mathbf{port_d} \times \mathbf{loc} \rightarrow \{\mathbf{true, false}\}$$

$\mathbf{IP_s}$ the 32-bit source IP address
$\mathbf{port_s}$ the 16-bit source port number
$\mathbf{IP_d}$ the 32-bit destination IP address
$\mathbf{port_d}$ the 16-bit destination port number
$\mathbf{loc}$ the 32-bit IP address of the device currently processing the packet

The function σ_n encodes the state of the network by evaluating to true whenever the parameters used as input to the function correspond to a packet that exists in the network and false otherwise. If the network contains five different packets and one location, then exactly five assignments to the parameters of the function σ_n will result in true. Note that because we abstract payload information, we cannot distinguish between two packets that are at the same device if they also have the same IP header information.

Each device in the network can then be modeled by describing how it changes packets. For example, a firewall might remove the packet from the network or it might allow it to move on to the device on the other side of the firewall.

A router might change the location of the packet but leave all the header information unchanged. A device performing network address translation might change the location of the packet as well as some of the IP header information. The behavior of each of these devices can be described by a list of rules. Each rule has a condition and an action. The rule condition can be described using a Boolean formula over the bits of the state (the parameters of the characteristic function σ_n). If the packet at the device matches a rule condition, then the appropriate action is taken. As described above, the action could involve changing the packet location as well as changing IP header information. In all cases, however, the change can be described by a Boolean formula over the bits of the state. Sometimes the new values are constant (completely determined by the rule itself), and sometimes they may depend on the values of some of the variables in the current state. In either case, a transition relation can be constructed as a relation or characteristic function over two copies of the state bits. An assignment to the bits/variables in the transition relation yields true if the packet described by the first copy of the bits will be transformed into a packet described by the second copy of the bits when it is at the device in question.

1.3.2 Network Devices

We integrate the policies of different network devices including firewalls, routers, NAT and IPSec gateways. The details of their policies and how they are encoded into BDDs are discussed thoroughly in [3]. However, we have modified the encoding of hosts to reflect the request transformation performed by the services running on top of each host. The host may be configured to run one or multiple services. Each of which has its own access-control list as will be discussed in Sect. 1.4. The service configuration may also specify a set of possible request transformations where the incoming request is transformed into another (sometimes completely new) request. For example, a request to a web server can be translated into an NFS request to load a user's home page. The new request will be carried through the network over packets. In our initial model the host receives packet and then forward them into the application layer within the host itself and it cannot forward it to another host. We modified this model so that the host will be able to forward packets to other hosts in order to support the requests transformation performed by the services running on top of it.

1.4 Application Layer Model

We also model the application layer as a finite state machine. The state space is the cross-product of the application layer request attributes by its possible locations in the network. The request properties include the fields that determine the service action that should be applied to a specific request.

$$\sigma_p : \textbf{usr} \times \textbf{role} \times \textbf{obj} \times \textbf{act} \times \textbf{loc} \times \textbf{srv} \rightarrow \{\textbf{true}, \textbf{false}\}$$

usr   the 32-bit user ID
role the 32-bit role ID which the user belongs to
obj   the 32-bit object ID
act   the 16-bit action ID
loc   the 32-bit IP address of the device currently processing the request
srv   the 16-bit service ID

In the application layer model only the devices that operates on the application level are considered (i.e. the devices who has a defined users list or services running on top of them). Here, we describe how we define access-control rights for service requests, and how we model these services and integrate them into the application layer state transition diagram.

1.4.1   Application Layer Access-Control

In order to have a homogeneous policy definition across applications, we use a simplified RBAC model as a way to specify all application requests and consequently the access-control policy. As in firewall policy, the access-control list of application layer services is defined by specifying an action like (permit or deny) to the requests satisfying certain criteria. This criteria is defined using the request attributes $< user, role, object, action >$ or $< u, r, o, a >$ for short. We assume that each host has a list of potential users who can use it. This list can simply be set to "any", to indicate that all defined users can access the host which enables a more powerful model for an adversary against which we want to verify the robustness of the policy. It is even possible to use one of the request attributes in a slightly different meaning. For example, in a web server model; an action can be a POST or GET, the role can be a logged in versus guest visitor and the object and user will have their obvious meanings. On the other hand, for database servers, we might have users, roles, actions, and resources used in their original meaning.

When a service receives a request from other device it first verifies it against its access-control policy. If it satisfies the access-control policy it will be forwarded to the service to be executed or transformed as shown in Fig. 1.2. If the request does not satisfy the access policy it will be dropped. A policy typically is defined as a list of tuples with an assigned action:

```
user       role      resource      action       decision
;user black listing
1          *         *             *            deny
2          *         *             *            deny
;admin account
100        1         *             *            permit
;guests can only read
*          guest     1--50         3            permit
;a read only resource
*          *         60            4            permit
*          *         60            *            deny
```

Fig. 1.2 Service model. S_1, S_2, S_3, and S_4 represent services running on different hosts. The *dashed lines* represent application requests. Requests are subjected to the access control list of the target service

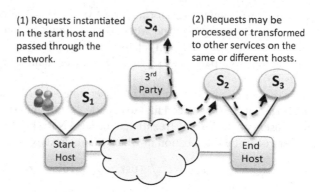

(1) Requests instantiated in the start host and passed through the network.

(2) Requests may be processed or transformed to other services on the same or different hosts.

As in firewall policies, we use a first-match semantic. For example, the last two rules allow read access, and then deny every other action. Also, the first few black-listing rules do not conflict with the guest account rule that appears later in the policy. From the common practices in the area of application level and RBAC policies, we believe that it should never be the case that a user or a role be specified as a range. Although, this fact does not affect our implementation (i.e. we support single values, ranges, or "any" values in all four fields of the access-control rules).

1.4.2   State Representation

Requests that pass the access-control phase are forwarded to the execution phase of the service. We have simplified the execution phase to one of two options as suggested in Fig. 1.2. A request can be executed on the service itself, which means that the request life-time ends at this phase, and no further events are triggered. The other possibility is that the service transforms the request into another form by modifying one or more fields (i.e. user, role, object or action) and sends it to another service running on the same or a different host. For example, a request to a web server can be translated into an NFS request to load a user's home page. Each request transformation is associated with a packet flow in the network level, the host should be able to send the appropriate packet to its gateway based on the service transformation.

Only the network devices that support application layer services represented by hosts in our model are included in the application layer model. The requests that leave a host may come from two sources: either a user operating directly on the host or through a service, or a request is transformed from another one. We do not require the destination of each request to be defined in the configuration. We assume that any request instantiated in any host can be directed to any service in the network. To build the transition relation for each host in the network we need the following inputs. (1) The set U of users who can access the host. Each user is represented by its unique ID in the system. It can also be expressed as a <user, role> pair. (2) The set

T of possible request transformations. (3) The set P of access control policies for each service running in the network. These policies are encoded as BDD expressions before building the transition relation of the application layer. Each policy in the set corresponds to a particular service ID (the port number of the service can be used as its ID).

Lets assume that the list U_H of <user, role> pairs represents the users who can access the host H. We need first to encode the possible states that result from having these users on the host H (recall that the state is the product of the request properties <user, role> by the location in which the request exists).

$$U_{BDD} = \bigvee_{i \in U_H} (\mathbf{usr} = u_i \wedge \mathbf{role} = r_i \wedge \mathbf{loc} = H) \tag{1.1}$$

where u_i and r_i are the user and role IDs of the item i in the users list U_H. To find the transitions we need to find out which services can be reached starting from the states defined in the expression U_{BDD} (i.e. any service whose access-control policy allows defined requests to pass).

$$T_u = \bigvee_{i \in indices(P)} (U_{BDD} \wedge P(i) \wedge \mathbf{loc}' = l_i \wedge \mathbf{srv}' = s_i) \tag{1.2}$$

where $P(i)$, l_i, and s_i are the policy, location, and the service ID respectively of the target service i. The variables $\mathbf{loc}'$ and $\mathbf{srv}'$ represents the location and service ID variables in the next state of the transition.

The expression T_u does not include the transitions that result from request transformations. The following represents the transition that result from one transformation performed by the service i.

$$\mathbf{usr} = u_i \wedge \mathbf{role} = r_i \wedge \mathbf{obj} = o_i \wedge \mathbf{act} = a_i \wedge \mathbf{loc} = H \wedge \mathbf{srv} = s_i$$
$$\mathbf{usr}' = u_i' \wedge \mathbf{role}' = r_i' \wedge \mathbf{obj}' = o_i' \wedge \mathbf{act}' = a_i' \wedge P'(s_i') \wedge \mathbf{loc}' = l_i' \wedge \mathbf{srv} = s_i'$$
$$\tag{1.3}$$

The values $< u_i, r_i, o_i, a_i >$ are the attributes of the initial request and the values $< u_i', r_i', o_i', a_i' >$ represent the attributes of the transformed packet. The values $P'(s_i')$, l_i' and s_i' are the policy, location and the service ID of the target service to which the request is transformed. Note that we use $P'(s_i')$ instead of $P(s_i')$ to indicate that the transformed request (and not the initial request) should pass the target service access-control policy in order to complete the transition. The disjunction of all the transitions caused by all the possible transformations along with the expression T_u calculated earlier formulate the final transition relation of the host H.

1.5 Querying the Model

A query in our system takes the form of a Boolean expression that specifies some properties over packet flows, requests and locations, with temporal logic criteria specified using CTL operators. By evaluating the given expression in the context of the state machine (i.e. states and transitions), we obtain the satisfying assignments to that expression represented in the same symbolic representation as the model itself. The simplest form for the result can be the constant expression "true" (e.g. the property is always satisfied), or "false" (e.g. no one violates the required property), or can be any subset of the space that satisfies the property (e.g. only flows with port 80, or traffic that starts from this location, etc.).

1.5.1 Model Checking

We have described how to construct a transition relation for each device in the network. Each transition relation describes a list of outgoing packets for the device it models. The formulas are constructed with the requirement that the current location be equal to the device being modeled, so these transitions can only be taken when a packet or a request is at the device. To get the transition relation for the entire network, we simply take the disjunction of the formulas for the individual devices. This is applied on both models (the network and the application layer models). Recall that this global transition relation is a characteristic function for transitions in the model. If we substitute the values for a packet that is in the system into the current state variables of the transition relation, what we are left with is a formula describing what the possible next states of that packet. We have all the machinery to perform symbolic model checking. We use BDDs for all the formulas described above and we use standard model checking algorithms to explore the state space and compute states that satisfy various CTL properties. The BuDDy BDD package provides all the required operations. For a much more complete description of symbolic model checking, the reader is encouraged to see [7].

The network layer model checker and the application layer model checker are encoded separately. Each of them is working on different variables. However, we may need to verify some requirements using both of them together. Although the application layer requests are transmitted from an application to another, the requests are encapsulated inside network packets. We do not require to have static one-to-one mapping between each request and the packet flow used to transfer the request. The mapping can be expressed in the query itself by specifying precise network packet characteristics <protocol, source ip, destination ip, source port, destination port>. Figure 1.3 shows how the two models are used together to verify the requirements.

1.5.2 Query Structure and Features

The query in our model checker retrieves the states that satisfy a given condition. The condition is expressed by restricting some variables in the model checker to a given value or using CTL operators to express a temporal condition. We also need

Fig. 1.3 Using two models
to run a query

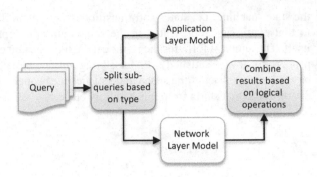

to specify what information to be retrieved about the states which satisfy the query
(i.e. a list of variables to be retrieved). An example query can look like this:

$$Q3 = [loc(10.12.13.14) \wedge EF((\neg loc(10.0.0.0/8)) \wedge (\neg Q2))]$$

$$Q3 : extractField\ loc\ dport$$

$$Q3 : listBounded\ 20\ loc\ dport$$

The query $Q3$ is defined by the given expression (i.e. what flows are in a given
location (10.12.13.14) and in the future will be outside of the domain (10.0.0.0/8)
and do not satisfy a previously defined query ($Q2$). The second and third lines are
used to format the result of the query. The second line tells the query engine that we
are only interested in the variables loc and $dport$. The third line specifies that we
need to display only the first 20 satisfying assignments. If there is no satisfying
assignment for the given query nothing will be returned. To handle the queries
on both the network layer and application layer models, we use the concept of
sub-query. Each sub-query is applied on one model. The application-layer sub-
query should not include variables related to network layer model such as source
or destination addresses and port numbers and vice versa. A query can include one
or more sub-queries based on the following cases.

- It can include only one sub-query. In this case the query is applied on the
  appropriate model.
- It can include more than one sub-query of the same type linked by the logical
  operators such as $AND, OR, IMPLIES$, etc. In this case all the sub-queries are
  executed on the appropriate model and the final result is calculated by applying
  the specified operations.
- It can include multiple sub-queries of different types linked by logical operators.
  In this case, the results of the different types of sub-queries have different
  variables and we cannot apply the linking operation directly. However, the
  location variable (**loc**) is common between the two models and it has the same
  meaning and value for the same device. For different types of sub-queries we
  apply the logical operations based on the location variable only. For example,
  if an application-layer sub-query is combined with a network-layer sub-query by

Table 1.1 Examples for reachability and security properties

Property	Query expression form
P1 (a):	*Requests reaching the host but not the service it is running.*
	$loc(user\_addr) \land [src(user\_addr) \land dest(server) \land dport(port') \land EF(loc(server))] \land [usr(userID) \land \neg EF(loc(server) \land srv(port'))]$
P1 (b):	*Requests reaching the service but can't reach the host itself.*
	$loc(user\_addr) \land [usr(userID) \land EF(loc(server) \land srv(port'))] \land [src(user\_addr) \land dest(server) \land dport(port') \land \neg EF(loc(server))]$
P2:	*Backdoor: A user is denied direct access to a service, but can use another service to indirectly access it.*
	$loc(user\_addr) \land [usr(userID) \land \neg EF(usr(userID) \land obj(o) \land loc(server) \land srv(port')) \land EF(usr(\neg userID) \land obj(o) \land loc(server) \land srv(port')] \land [EF(loc(server) \land dport(port'))]$
P3 (a):	*What roles and actions can a user use to access a specific object from outside the server domain?*
	$\neg loc(server) \land [EF(loc(server) \land srv(port') \land usr(u) \land obj(o))] \land [\neg src(server) \land EF(loc(server) \land dport(port'))]$
P3 (b):	*What users can access a given object?*
	$\neg loc(server) \land [\neg src(server) \land EF(loc(server) \land dport(port'))] \land [EF(loc(server) \land srv(port') \land role(r) \land obj(o) \land act(a))]$
P4:	*Is there any inconsistency between rights of low and high privilege requests?*
	$EF(loc(server) \land srv(port') \land [high\ security\ requirements])$
	$\land \neg EF(loc(server) \land srv(port') \land [low\ security\ requirements])$

the AND operation, we calculate the result of both sub-queries and then calculate the intersection between the *location* values in both results. Only requests and packet flows whose location falls within the intersection are returned.

The result of a query is a list of states that satisfy the query expression. In our model we may have two types of results. The first is a set of network-layer states each represented as a packet flow characteristics and location. The second is a set of application-layer states each represented as a request characteristics and location. The existence of these two types depends on the types of sub-queries included within the query script.

1.5.3   Example Properties

Property 1: Conflicting network and application access-control
(a): Given a user location and userID, does the current configuration allows the user to access the server machine, while the application layer access-control blocks the connection?
The query shown in the Table 1.1 specifies the initial properties of flows with certain user information (e.g. a specific source IP "*user_addr*", and user identifier in the application layer request) and targeted towards a service residing elsewhere (i.e.

server, port'). If there is an inconsistency in the configuration the query returns a list of requests that cannot access the specified service and another list of packet flows that can eventually reach the host network layer. We can see that the query combines two different types of sub-queries and restricts the location to a particular source machine. Each sub-query is surrounded by angle brackets "[ ]".

(b): Does the current configuration blocks the user's access to the server machine through network layer filtering, while the application's access-control layer permits such connection?

As in the pervious property (a), we try to see if a request that is permitted by the application layer access control will never reach the service. This means that somewhere before reaching the server hosting the service there is a network layer device blocks the traffic, or fails to route it correctly. We use the application layer model to find those requests that can pass from the source to a particular service, and we use the network model to find if the underlaying packet flows who should carry the requests are allowed to flow from the source to the appropriate destination.

Property 2: Can a user access a resource under different credentials, if he is prohibited from accessing it under his original identity?

In this property, we check if a certain user can masquerade under another identity to access a resource. This forms a back-door to this specific object-action pair. A straight forward example can be a user accessing an NFS server for which he does not have access via a web-server who can retrieve the content in the form of web pages. This can be achieved by an improper request transformation in a service which should not be reachable by the specified user. This is defined formally by evaluating the expression specifying which users cannot access an object, while it can be accessed eventually if the constraint on the user identity is removed.

Property 3: What access rights does an object require?

(a): What roles can user u use to access object o?

It is sometimes essential to know what roles can a user manifest when accessing a specific object, or a group of objects. The query consists of checking the space of requests that can pass through the network and RBAC filtering to reach our object of interest. By restricting the user part of the space, we get the possible roles that can be used. We can also, restrict the action if needed. An addition that can prove practically useful is to add another restriction of origin of request: by filtering the location and source address from which the request originated from other than that of the server. In Table 1.1 we show only the condition part of the query neglecting the result format part, we can specify to return only the roles and/or any other fields in the results.

(b): Which users can access object o via a role r?

This is a similar query to the previous one. This query concerns the different users who can access a given object in a certain capacity. For example, we might want to know who can access a critical file as an administrator. Also, we can add extra restrictions to see who can access this object for writing rather than just reading.

Property 4: Is there any conflicts within the application layer access-control?
(a): Is there any inconsistencies in allowed actions for a specific object?
Such conflicts can arise within the same policy or cross policies. For example, if a user is granted the write access to an object then, most probably, read access should be allowed as well. This query is application dependent, and priority between actions has to be specified explicitly (e.g. 'delete' > 'write' > 'read'). We write the query for a service to check if it is possible for some user/role to reach the service via a higher action, but not with a lower one. We represent the general form for such query in Table 1.1, the profiles $[high\ security\ requirements]$ and $[low\ security\ requirements]$ can be replaced with any combination of constraints on the request fields. For example, to compare rights for reading and writing, the high security profile may be $[obj(o) \land act(wr)]$ and the low security profile may be represented as $[obj(o) \land act(rd)]$ for the particular object (o).
(b): Are role-role relations consistent?
As in the pervious property (a), we might need to verify that the order of role privileges is maintained. In other words, a more powerful role should be always capable of performing all actions possible for a weaker role. For example, an administrator should perform at least everything doable by a staff member, and guests should never have more access to other roles. It is defined by checking if the space of possible actions-over-objects that can be performed by $role1$ but not $role2$ is empty (given that $role1 < role2$). In this case the high and low security profiles can be represented as $[role(role1) \land obj(o) \land act(a)]$ and $[role(role2) \land obj(o) \land act(a)]$ respectively.

1.6   Evaluation

An extensive evaluation have been performed for the network model construction in [3]. In our evaluation we focus on comparing the performance of the two aforementioned architectures: (1) using single transition relation for both network and application access control configurations by appending the application access control variables to the network model variables, and (2) using two transition relations for each of application and network models. In the following discussion, we refer to these two architectures by *Single* and *Parallel* respectively. Our evaluation includes space and time requirements to construct the state machines. We have randomly generated a number of networks with varying sizes. The generated configuration includes the topology of the network, the configuration of network devices, and the allocation and configuration of services on top of hosts. In the synthesized networks the number of services is roughly equal to 50 % of the number of network devices and the average service policy size is 500 rules.

Space Requirements. Space requirements are measured by the number of BDD nodes used for the model. This includes variable information and links between

Fig. 1.4 Space requirements

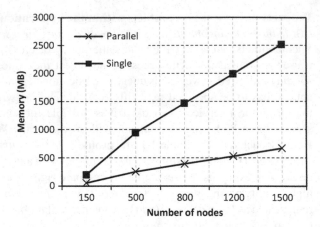

Fig. 1.5 Time requirements

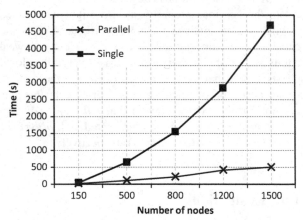

nodes. In Fig. 1.4, we can see that for both architectures the space required to compile a network is linear in its size. The reported space requirement for the parallel architecture represents the sum of space required to build both models. We can see in Fig. 1.4 that the required space for *Parallel* architecture is almost 25 % of that required for the *Single* architecture.

Time Requirements. Figure 1.5 shows the time required to build the BDD expression for the test networks. The reported time for the parallel architecture represents the total time required to build both models. We can see that the *Parallel* architecture outperforms the *Single*. There is a big difference in time requirement especially as the network gets larger. In the *Single* architecture there is a big portion of states that will be replicated due to the addition of application access control variables. This increases the time required to build the exponentially increasing transitions and optimize the structure of the BDD.

1.7 Related Work

There have been significant research effort in the area of configuration verification and management in the past few years. We can classify the work in this area into two main approaches: top-down and bottom-up. The top-down approaches [5, 20] create clean-slate configurations based on high-level requirements. However, the bottom-up approaches [1,13,24] analyze the existing configuration to verify desired properties. We focus our discussion on bottom-up approach as it is closer to our work in this paper.

There has been considerable work recently in detecting misconfiguration in routing and firewall. Many of these approaches are specific for BGP misconfiguration [4, 9, 11, 17]. Yang et al. [23], Hamed et al. [13], Al-Shaer and Hamed [1], and Yuan [24] focused on conflict analysis of firewalls configuration. A BDD-based modeling and taxonomy of IPSec configuration conflicts was presented in [2, 13]. FIREMAN [24] uses BDD to show conflicts on Linux©iptables configurations. In [19] and [21], the authors developed a firewall analysis tool to perform customized queries on a set of filtering rules of a firewall. But no general model of network connections is used in this work.

In the field of distributed firewalls, current research mainly focuses on the management of distributed firewall policies. The first generation of global policy management technology is presented in [12], which proposes a global policy definition language along with algorithms for verifying the policy and generating filtering rules. In [6], the authors adopted a better approach by using a modular architecture that separates the security policy and the underlying network topology to allow for flexible modification of the network topology without the need to update the security policy. Similar work has been done in [14] with a procedural policy definition language, and in [16] with an object-oriented policy definition language. In terms of distributed firewall policy enforcement, a novel architecture is proposed in [15] where the authors suggest using a trust management system to enforce a centralized security policy at individual network endpoints based on access rights granted to users or hosts. We found that none of the published work in this area addressed the problem of discovering conflicts in distributed firewall environments.

A variety of approaches have been proposed in the area of policy conflict analysis. The most significant attempt for IPSec policy analysis is proposed in [10]. The technique simulates IPSec processing by tracking the protection applied on the traffic in every IPSec device. At any point in the simulation, if packet protection violates the security policy requirements, a policy conflict is reported. Although this approach can discover IPSec policy violations in a certain simulation scenario, there is no guarantee that it discovers every possible violation that may exist. In addition, the proposed technique only discovers IPSec conflicts resulting from incorrect tunnel overlapping, but do not address the other types of conflicts that we study in this research.

Other works attempt to create general models for analyzing network configuration [8, 22]. An approach for formulating and deriving of sufficient conditions of connectivity constraints is presented in [8]. The static analysis approach [22] is one of the most interesting work that is close to ConfigChecker. This work uses graph-based approach to model connectivity of network configuration and use set operations to perform static analysis. The transitive closure, as apposed to a fixed point in our approach, is computed. Thus, it seems that all possible paths are computed explicitly. In addition, considering security devices and properties, providing a rich query interface based on our CTL extension, and utilizing BDDs optimization are major advantages of our work. Anteater [18] is another interesting tool for checking invariants in the data plane. It checks the high-level network invariants represented as instances of boolean satisfiability problems (SAT) against network state using a SAT solver, and reports counterexamples for violations, if exist.

Thus, in conclusion, although this body of work has a significant impact on the filed, it is either provide limited analysis due to restriction on specific network or application. Unlike the previous work, our work offers a global configuration verification that is comprehensive, scalable and highly expressive.

1.8 Conclusion

We presented an extension to the ConfigChecker tool to incorporate both network and application configurations in a unified system across the entire network. Our extended system models the configuration of various devices in the network layer (hubs, switches, routers, firewalls, IPsec gateways) and access control of application layer services including multiple-level of request translation. Network and system configuration can be modeled together and used to verify properties using CTL-embedded functions translated into Boolean operations. We show that we can separate variables in two model checkers to reduce the state space and required resources. Yet, both models can be used to run combine queries.

Our future work includes enhancements in the model's performance for even faster execution and lower the construction time. Also, we plan to extending the supported devices, and node types to add more virtual devices and compound devices that can incorporate multi-node functionality as in some modern network-based devices. Moreover, a user interface for facilitating interactive execution of queries as well as updating and editing the configurations for a more practical deployment patterns for the tool. We will also try to find a practical mapping scheme between application requests and corresponding packet flows to automatically detect the flows required to communicate a request between different services.

References

1. Al-Shaer, E., Hamed, H.: Discovery of policy anomalies in distributed firewalls. In: Proceedings of IEEE INFOCOM'04, Hong Kong (2004)
2. Al-Shaer, E., Hamed, H.: Taxonomy of conflicts in network security policies. IEEE Commun. Mag. **44**(3), 134–141 (2006)

3. Al-Shaer, E., Marrero, W., El-Atawy, A., Elbadawi, K.: Network configuration in a box: towards end-to-end verification of network reachability and security. In: ICNP, Princeton, pp. 123–132 (2009)
4. Alimi, R., Wang, Y., Yang, Y.R.: Shadow configuration as a network management primitive. In: SIGCOMM'08: Proceedings of the ACM SIGCOMM 2008 Conference on Data Communication, Seattle, pp. 111–122. ACM, New York (2008)
5. Ballani, H., Francis, P.: Conman: a step towards network manageability. SIGCOMM Comput. Commun. Rev. 37(4), 205–216 (2007)
6. Bartal, Y., Mayer, A., Nissim, K., Wool, A.: Firmato: a novel firewall management toolkit. ACM Trans. Comput. Syst. 22(4), 381–420 (2004)
7. Burch, J., Clarke, E., McMillan, K., Dill, D., Hwang, J.: Symbolic model checking: 10^{20} states and beyond. J. Inf. Comput. 98(2), 1–33 (1992)
8. Bush, R., Griffin, T.: Integrity for virtual private routed networks. In: Proceedings of IEEE INFOCOM'03, San Franciso, vol. 2, pp. 1467–1476 (2003)
9. Feamster, N., Balakrishnan, H.: Detecting BGP configuration faults with static analysis. In: NSDI, Boston (2005)
10. Fu, Z., Wu, F., Huang, H., Loh, K., Gong, F., Baldine, I., Xu, C.: IPSec/VPN security policy: correctness, conflict detection and resolution. In: Policy'01 Workshop, Bristol, pp. 39–56 (2001)
11. Griffin, T.G., Wilfong, G.: On the correctness of IBGP configuration. In: SIGCOMM'02: Proceedings of the ACM SIGCOMM 2002 Conference on Data Communication, Pittsburgh, pp. 17–29 (2002)
12. Guttman, J.: Filtering posture: local enforcement for global policies. In: IEEE Symposium on Security and Privacy, Oakland, pp. 120–129 (1997)
13. Hamed, H., Al-Shaer, E., Marrero, W.: Modeling and verification of IPSec and VPN security policies. In: IEEE International Conference of Network Protocols (ICNP'05), Boston (2005)
14. Hinrichs, S.: Policy-based management: bridging the gap. In: 15th Annual Computer Security Applications Conference (ACSAC'99), Phoenix, pp. 209–218 (1999)
15. Ioannidis, S., Keromytis, A., Bellovin, S., Smith, J.: Implementing a distributed firewall. In: 7th ACM Conference on Computer and Comminications Security (CCS'00), Athens, pp. 190–199 (2000)
16. Luck, I., Schafer, C., Krumm, H.: Model-based tool assistance for packet-filter design. In: IEEE Workshop on Policies for Distributed Systems and Networks (POLICY'01), Bristol, pp. 120–136 (2001)
17. Mahajan, R., Wetherall, D., Anderson, T.: Understanding BGP misconfiguration. In: SIGCOMM'02: Proceedings of the ACM SIGCOMM 2002 Conference on Data Communications, Pittsburgh, pp. 3–16. ACM, New York (2002)
18. Mai, H., Khurshid, A., Agarwal, R., Caesar, M., Godfrey, P.B., King, S.T.: Debugging the data plane with anteater. SIGCOMM Comput. Commun. Rev. 41(4), 290–301 (2011)
19. Mayer, A., Wool, A., Ziskind, E.: Fang: a firewall analysis engine. In: IEEE Symposium on Security and Privacy (SSP'00), Berkeley, pp. 177–187 (2000)
20. Narain, S.: Network configuration management via model finding. In: LISA, San Diego, pp. 155–168 (2005)
21. Wool, A.: A quantitative study of firewall configuration errors. IEEE Comput. 37(6), 62–67 (2004)
22. Xie, G.G., Zhan, J., Maltz, D.A., Zhang, H., Greenberg, A., Hjalmtysson, G., Rexford, J.: On static reachability analysis of IP networks. In: IEEE INFOCOM, Miami, vol. 3, pp. 2170–2183 (2005)
23. Yang, Y., Martel, C.U., Wu, S.F.: On building the minimum number of tunnels: an ordered-split approach to manage ipsec/vpn tunnels. In: 9th IEEE/IFIP Network Operation and Management Symposium (NOMS'04), Seoul, pp. 277–290, (2004)
24. Yuan, L., Mai, J., Su, Z., Chen, H., Chuah, C., Mohapatra, P.: FIREMAN: a toolkit for firewall modeling and analysis. In: IEEE Symposium on Security and Privacy (SSP'06), Berkeley/Oakland (2006)

Chapter 2
Modeling and Checking the Security of DIFC System Configurations

Mingyi Zhao and Peng Liu

Abstract Decentralized information flow control (DIFC) systems provide strong protection for data secrecy and integrity. However, the complicated configuration of information flow between system objects increases the chance of misconfiguration, making the system vulnerable to attackers. In this paper we first present a systematic analysis of misconfigurations and their security threats for DIFC systems. Then we define the security analysis problem for DIFC configurations based on a formal state-transition model, which allows model checkers to prove a configuration is secure or detect misconfigurations that violate the desired security goal. The experiment shows that bounded model checking techniques plus a novel preprocessing algorithm are effective in solving this problem.

2.1 Introduction

Decentralized information flow control (DIFC) systems [1–4] are recent innovations aimed at protecting data secrecy and integrity. DIFC systems allow applications to express their security policies by assigning secrecy and integrity labels to their objects. Application developers can also configure the rules of changing labels, delegating privileges, and declassifying confidential data to satisfy advanced security and functionality requirements. These configurations are faithfully enforced by the kernel or the user-level reference monitor.

DIFC systems have four main advantages. First, they have better support for the least privilege principle (e.g. an untrusted program can process confidential data, but not leak it). Second, with decentralized policy management and better

M. Zhao (✉) • P. Liu
College of Information Sciences and Technology, The Pennsylvania State University,
University Park, PA 16802, USA
e-mail: muz127@ist.psu.edu; pliu@ist.psu.edu

E. Al-Shaer et al. (eds.), *Automated Security Management*,
DOI 10.1007/978-3-319-01433-3_2, © Springer International Publishing Switzerland 2013

compatibility with existing software, DIFC systems are more practical compared to previous information flow control solutions. Third, the size of trusted components in a DIFC system is greatly reduced, making verification easier. Fourth, the effects of covert channels are limited in DIFC systems.

In order to utilize these advantages, however, application developers or system administrators must properly configure labels, capabilities, etc., which is a complicated task. Configurations of individual applications might also have inconsistency upon interaction due to the decentralized nature of configuration management in DIFC systems. Therefore, misconfigurations might occur and make the system insecure. Thus malicious processes can leak confidential information or hamper the integrity of data by exploiting misconfigurations in different ways. One possible attack is *information laundering*: the misuse of declassification channel to leak confidential data. For example [5], suppose a declassification rule stipulates that only four digits of a credit card can be released. Then an attacker can encode confidential information into these four digits and declassify any information he wants with the control of this channel. In addition, a successful attack typically contains several steps such as privilege escalation, privilege delegation and information laundering by multiple processes. As the number of steps grow exponentially, it is impossible for the software developer or the system administrator to manually find them. Therefore, ensuring the correctness of configurations can be as challenging as faithfully enforcing them. Without the capability to prove that the system configuration is compliant with the desired security policy, or to show that the configuration is vulnerable by finding a counter-example, the DIFC technology, though disruptive, cannot be widely deployed in the real world.

Previous works [6, 7] have made significant steps in addressing this challenge, but a comprehensive modeling of DIFC configuration is missing. For example, these works have incompletely modeled several important components of DIFC such as declassification and capability grant mechanisms. Without a comprehensive configuration model, the security analysis of DIFC will be incomplete. Aimed to fill this gap, we systematically model the DIFC configuration and analyze misconfigurations and their security threats for DIFC systems. Inspired by access control policy analysis [8], we show that the DIFC configuration can be represented in a state-transition model and the security properties can be expressed as temporal logic formulas. Although the security analysis problem proposed here is intractable in general [7, 9], we are still able to show that bounded model checking techniques can handle considerably large cases.

The remainder of this paper is organized as follows. Section 2.2 gives an overview of important concepts in DIFC. Section 2.3 analyzes the threat model against DIFC systems. Section 2.4 provides a formal model of the DIFC configuration and the security policy. The model checking approach we use is explained in Sect. 2.5. The experiment is presented in Sect. 2.6. We discuss implications and possible extensions of our work in Sect. 2.7. Related works are presented in Sect. 2.8. Finally, we conclude our work in Sect. 2.9.

2.2 Preliminaries

In this paper, we will primarily focus on Flume [3], a DIFC system for standard OS abstractions. But our method could be extended to analyze other DIFC systems without significant change, for they fundamentally share the same idea. There are three rationales behind the choice of Flume. First, Flume is implemented as a user-level reference monitor which is more retrofittable to legacy code and hardware support than kernel-level implementation. Second, labels defined in Flume are easy to use and understand compared to other systems like Asbestos [1] or HiStar [2]. Third, Flume's noninterference property is formally proved in [10]. In the remainder of this section, we will give an overview of the Flume model.

2.2.1 Tags and Labels

In Flume, each object (i.e., process or file) is attached with two labels, secrecy label Ls_o and integrity label Li_o. A *label* is a set of tags. Each tag represents a category of secrecy or integrity. For example, tag a represents Alice's private data. The information flow control is embodied in the partial order of the subset relation [11] between labels, which is defined as:

Definition 1. *(safe information flow)* Information flow from o_i to o_j is safe iff $Ls_{oi} \subseteq Ls_{oj}$ and $Li_{oi} \supseteq Li_{oj}$.

This rule ensures that confidential information will never be leaked to untrusted objects, and similarly, untrusted objects will never hamper high integrity objects.

2.2.2 Capabilities

To support advanced functionalities and security requirements, Flume allows processes to change their labels dynamically using *capabilities* denoted as a set C_p (we will use Cs_p and Ci_p to represent the capabilities for secrecy tags and integrity tags, respectively). For each tag t, Flume has two capabilities t^+ and t^-. If $t^+ \in C_p$, then process p has the right to add t to its labels. This capability enables the *transitive closure*: to read from an object whose Ls has t, p needs first to add t to Ls_p; but after that p cannot send information to objects without tag t. Such transitive closure is important for the protection of confidentiality. Similarly, $t^- \in C_p$ gives p the right to remove t from its labels. With t^-, p can export (declassify) information to objects without t in their secrecy labels. As we will see, this declassification privilege is critical for the safety of the system. The requirement of safe label change is defined as:

Definition 2. *(safe label change) For a process p, let L be Ls_p or Li_p, and let L' be the new value of the label. The change from L to L' is safe iff: $\{L' - L\}^+ \cup \{L - L'\}^- \subseteq C_p$.*

A process can get a capability through three ways: (1) Any process can create a new tag t and update its capability sets by $C_p \leftarrow C_p \cup \{t^+, t^-\}$. (2) Capabilities can be delegated through message sending between processes. (3) In Flume, a central tag registry will grant capabilities to a process with the correct token. Each token is an opaque byte string, which can be used to get a particular capability. This last mechanism is primarily designed to support persistent privileges so that a process can regain its privileges after reboot. It is also an alternative method to transfer capabilities between processes.

2.2.3 Declassification

It is well known that an information control system cannot function properly without *declassification*: the deliberate release of confidential information. For example, when a user provides a password to the login service, it has to declassify at least one bit of information, i.e., whether the password is correct. Since declassification is the only channel for releasing confidential information (we leave out the modeling of covert channels in this work), processes that own such privileges are usually included in the trusted computing base (TCB), which is expected to be verified.

The capability t^- is a basic approach for declassification (*direct declassify*). To support advanced functionalities, Flume also allows certain processes to launch declassifier without the corresponding tag t^- by using setlabel file or privileged filters (*indirect declassify*). A *setlabel file* contains a token and a command to start a declassifier, and access to this facility is controlled by the labels of the setlabel file. A *privileged filter* is another way to automatically endorse or declassify a file. A process with an activated filter could temporarily change its label before reading the file in order to declassify it. In addition, Flume also allows a process to bundle several capabilities together as a *group* to provide a simpler capability management mechanism. Please note that this facility is not unique for Flume. HiStar, for example, allows such declassification through a mechanism called *gate*. In general, we believe that these facilities are inevitable for DIFC systems to support complex real world applications. Since malicious processes can utilize declassification channels in a way that violates the security policy, these channels are critical for the safety of DIFC system, as we shall see in Sect. 2.3.

2.2.4 Configuration and Security Policy

In summary, a *DIFC system configuration* contains three parts: (1) initial labels for each system object and capabilities for each process, (2) rules for granting capabilities (token files) and (3) rules for declassifying information (setlabel files).

A software developer enforces the configuration in the program source code, and previous works [12,13] can largely make this process automatic. In addition, system administrators will also manage configurations at the whole-system level. And for both developers and administrators, the challenge is to make sure that these configurations comply with high level security policies [3] such as *export protection*, i.e., confidential information in a confinement will not be leaked to outside, *read protection*, i.e., confidential information cannot be read by untrusted processes, and *integrity protection*, i.e., high integrity objects cannot receive information from low integrity objects. For simplicity, we primarily focus on export protection, a main goal of ensuring information confidentiality.

2.3 Threat Model

Information flow control mechanisms mentioned above not only enhance the system security, but also increase the difficulty of configuration, due to at least four major reasons. First, the information flow relationship between labels (a lattice) is complex when multiple security levels and categories exist. The fact that a tag can have one of the several possible meanings (e.g. content of information, ownership, etc.) also aggravates the problem. Second, the capability transfer makes the information flow relationship dynamic and thus hard to predict. Third, because most software systems require declassification channels to leak certain information, these "legitimate violations" of the information flow relationship are hard to manage. Fourth, DIFC allows an application to configure labels and capabilities of its own objects. These application-wide configurations interacting with each other often lead to inconsistencies. Therefore, misconfigurations can easily occur and render the whole system vulnerable.

We will explain this threat in detail. Suppose several malicious processes are installed in the system. A malicious process might be a software component easy to be compromised, or a program downloaded from untrusted websites. Ideally, the DIFC system could "tolerate" them since they will only get minimal privileges for their tasks and not enough for harming the information confidentiality or integrity. For example, the configuration of a browser will give third party plug-ins the privilege to read and process users' sensitive data, but not to leak them to the network. However, this conclusion will not be true if some misconfigurations exist. We provide a simple running example (revised from a case in [3]) to illustrate this threat. Figure 2.1 shows the configuration of a simple web server scenario with two users, Alice and Bob. Alice owns four files: a secret, a calendar file, a token file that helps Alice to regain the control of the declassifer after logout, and the setlabel file which could launch the declassification channel. In addition, Both Alice and Bob have installed the same editor program, which happens to be a Trojan horse with the goal of leaking Alice's data. The desired security policy for Alice is to keep all files secret but enable the sharing of a portion of the calendar file to Bob through a declassification channel. To implement this policy, Alice has configured the system as Fig. 2.1 shows. .

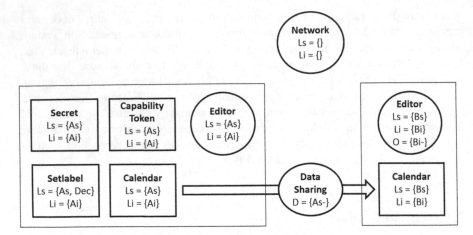

Fig. 2.1 The DIFC configuration for a simple web server

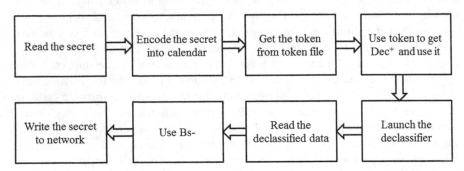

Fig. 2.2 The attack sequence for Fig. 2.1. The first five operations is carried out by Alice's editor. The last three steps are executed by Bob's editor

It looks like Alice's secret cannot be leaked to either Bob or others on the network because the malicious editor is confined by its secrecy label $\{As\}$. However, misconfigurations exist and Alice's policy could be violated. The first one is *under protective label*: an object does not get sufficient secrecy tags. For example, the token file which can be used to acquire capability Dec^+ is somehow accessible for the editor. The second misconfiguration is *extra privilege*: a process gets extra tags or capabilities for its task. Bob's editor process, which does not need to communicate with the network, accidentally gets the privilege Bs^- of declassifying Bob's data (probably for convenience). With these misconfigurations, malicious processes now can achieve their goals, as Fig. 2.2 shows.

Please note that the order of operations in Fig. 2.2 matters. If Alice's editor uses Dec^+ before encoding confidential information to the calendar (i.e. putting step 2 after step 4), the attack will not be successful because with Dec in the secrecy label, the editor cannot write to the calendar file anymore.

We can summarize the threat model against DIFC system as follows. The goal of the attacker is to export confidential information or hamper data integrity. A set of malicious processes controlled by the attacker are allowed to perform any operations permitted by the configuration to achieve the goal. Usually, a successful attack is composed of several steps, which is defined as an *attack sequence*. Finding a successful attack sequence under a complex configuration is impossible for human, because the number of possible attack sequences grows exponentially. Therefore we need to have some automatic and efficient approaches to either find valid attack sequences or prove they do not exist. We will address this challenge in the following sections.

2.4 Formal Model

2.4.1 DIFC Configuration Schemes

To reason the security of a configuration, we need to abstract it into a formal model. Here, we use a method derived from role-based access control policy analysis [8,14]. We first define the general scheme of a DIFC configuration as:

Definition 3. *(DIFC Configuration Schemes) A DIFC configuration scheme is a state-transition system* $< \Gamma, \Psi, \Delta >$*, where* Γ *is a set of DIFC states,* Ψ *is a set of state-transition rules and* Δ *is a set of security properties.*

In addition, we assume that there are five finite sets: F (the set of files), P (the set of processes), $T_{s/i}$ (the set of tags for secrecy/integrity), I (the set of information) and D (the set of all declassifier). The set I mainly contains two types of information: confidential information and tokens for getting capabilities. D is actually a set of trusted processes that are dedicated to declassification. From these five sets we can further derive several additional sets: $O = F \cup P$ (the set of system objects), $L_{s/i} = powerSet(T_{s/i})$ (the set of secrecy/integrity labels) and $C = \{t^{+/-} | t \in T\}$ (the set of all capabilities). Next, we will define each component of DIFC configuration scheme in detail.

2.4.1.1 States

Γ is the set of DIFC states. Each DIFC state $\gamma \in \Gamma$ is a 5-tuple $< OL_{s/i}, PC, OI, IC, OA >$. $OL_{s/i} \subseteq O \times L_{s/i}$ specifies the secrecy/integrity label of each object. Based on existing DIFC mechanisms, file labels ($FL_{s/i}$) will not be changed after creation. $PC \subseteq P \times C$ specifies the capabilities of each process. $OI \subseteq O \times I$ describes the information contained in each object. An object can have one or multiple pieces of information. Intuitively, this relation is used to track information flow. Although tags in DIFC system can be regarded as a way of information flow tracking, we still need to explicitly define OI, for the tag tracking will stop at the point of declassification. $IC \subseteq I \times C$ is the mapping between a token and the corresponding capability stored in the central tag registry. Finally, $OA \subseteq O \times A$ assigns security related attributes to each object. A is an attribute set which has the following values: *malicious*, *sink*, and *protected*. *Malicious* is the attribute only for process, while *sink* and *protected* could be assigned to both file and process. We use *sink* to denote the destination of leaked confidential information and *protected* to mark the object with integrity requirement.

Essentially, each state holds two meanings. First, since DIFC configuration is dynamic, a state represents one possible configuration starting from the initial one. Second, it also reflects the progress of the attack. For example, OI records how information has been propagated by the malicious processes. PL and PC tell what privileges the malicious processes own.

2.4.1.2 State Transition Rules

Ψ is the set of state-transition rules. A state-transition rule $\psi \in \Psi$ determines how the system state changes from one to another. ψ essentially is a set of actions and each transition is an action preformed by a process (we will use action and state transition interchangeably). Each action $\sigma \in \psi$ has four components: initiator, targets, pre-condition and consequence. If the pre-condition holds, a state transition $\gamma \rightarrow \gamma'$ will occur. $\gamma \rightarrow_{\sigma*} \gamma'$ means that γ can reach γ' after finite transitions (we will call γ' a reachable state for γ). In this work, we define six types of actions:

- *Read.* The action of process p reading information from object o is represented as $read(p, o)$. This action will be successful in state γ that meets the safe information flow condition (Definition 1):

  - $(p, Ls_p), (o, Ls_o) \in OL_s \wedge (p, Li_p), (o, Li_o) \in OL_i$.
  - $(Ls_p \supseteq Ls_o) \wedge (Li_p \subseteq Li_o)$.

  The consequence is a new state γ' that is different with γ only by $OI' = OI \cup \{(p, I_p \cup I_o)\}$, that is, p gets "tainted" by all information in o after the read action is successfully preformed. For the example in Fig. 2.1, $read(editor, secret)$ will be successful because the pre-condition $(\{a_s\} \supseteq \{a_s\}) \wedge (\{a_i\} \subseteq \{a_i\})$ holds. Thus the editor gets tainted by the confidential information, $OI' = OI \cup \{(editor, I_{editor} \cup \{i_{confidential}\})\}$.

- *Write.* The definition of $write(p, o)$ is in duality with $read(p, o)$. For the pre-condition part:

  - $(p, Ls_p), (o, Ls_o) \in OL_s \wedge (p, Li_p), (o, Li_o) \in OL_i$.
  - $(Ls_p \subseteq Ls_o) \wedge (Li_p \supseteq Li_o)$.

  And the consequence is a new state γ' whose $OI' = OI \cup \{(o, I_p \cup I_o)\}$.

- *Use capability.* Process p can add/remove tag t from its secrecy/integrity label by taking the action $useCapability(p, t^{+/-})$. Here, we will only take positive capabilities and secrecy labels as example for this and the following action definitions. The pre-condition is the safe label change (Definition 2):

- $(t \notin Ls_p) \wedge (t^+ \in C_p^+)$.

And the state after this action will have $OL' = OL \cup \{(p, Ls_p \cup \{t\})\}$.
- *Delegate capability.* The form of this action is $delegate\text{-}Capability(p, q, t^+)$. It means that process p sends the capability t^+ to process q. The pre-condition is still the safe information flow condition:

- $(p, Ls_p), (q, Ls_q) \in OL_s \wedge (p, Li_p), (q, Li_q) \in OL_i$.
- $(Ls_p \subseteq Ls_q) \wedge (Li_p \supseteq Li_q)$.

After this action, the next state will not only have $PC'^+ = PC^+ \cup \{t^+\}$, but also $OI' = OI \cup \{(q, I_p \cup I_q)\}$, for the capability delegation could be used as a implicit information channel. So the receiver q will be automatically tainted.
- *Grant capability.* As we have discussed in Sect. 2.2, a central tag registry will grant capability to a process that has the right token i. Therefore, the pre-conditions of $grantCapability(p, i)$ are:

- $(p, i) \in OI \wedge (i, t^+) \in IC$.
- $(t^+ \notin Cs_p)$.

The result of a successful action is $PC' = PC \cup \{(p, Cs_p^+ \cup \{t^+\})\}$.
- *Indirect declassify.* Finally, we define the action for indirect declassification, $declassify(p, d)$. Each declassification channel $d \in D$ has four parts, $(o_{from}, o_{to}, Ls_d, Li_d)$, where o_{from}, o_{to} are the source and destination of the declassification, and Ls_d, Li_d are the protection labels. We didn't define the direct declassify as a unique action because it is simply a combination of $useCapability(p, t^-)$ and $write(p, o)$. To launch an declassifier from a setlabel file, the initiator shall meet the label requirement:

- $(Ls_p \subseteq Ls_d) \wedge (Li_p \supseteq Li_d)$.

A successful indirect declassification will result in an information flow from o_{to} to o_{from}, i.e., $OI' = OI \cup \{(o_{to}, I_{from} \cup I_{to})\}$.

2.4.1.3 Properties

Each property $\delta \in \Delta$ states a security policy for the DIFC system. Here we assume that γ is the configuration to be checked (initial state). We have identified several possible properties:

- *Confidentiality protection.* Confidential information i will never flow to objects with attribute $sink$. Formally, the property is:

- $\nexists \gamma' \, s.t. \, \gamma \rightarrow_{\sigma*} \gamma' \wedge (o, i) \in OI' \wedge (o, sink) \in OA'$.

- *Integrity protection.* Information from malicious processes will never flow to objects with attribute *protected*. Formally, the property is:

  - $\nexists \gamma' \, s.t. \, \gamma \rightarrow_{\sigma*} \gamma' \wedge (o, i_{malicious}) \in OI' \wedge (o, protected) \in OA'$.

  Here, $i_{malicious}$ is used to represent the integrity damage caused by malicious processes.
- *Privilege protection.* Capability $t^{+/-}$ will never be acquired by processes with attribute *malicious*. Formally, the property is:

  - $\nexists \gamma' \, s.t. \, \gamma \rightarrow_{\sigma*} \gamma' \wedge (p, t^{+/-}) \in PC'^{+/-} \wedge (p, malicious) \in OA'$.

Above properties are all security-related. However, δ could also be functionality-related. For example, we might want to make sure that a configuration does not block the legitimate information flow:

- *Flow protection.* Information i should be able to flow to object o. Formally, the property is:

  - $\exists \gamma' \, s.t. \, \gamma \rightarrow_{\sigma*} \gamma' \wedge (o, i) \in OI'$.

We didn't list all possible properties due to space limitation. But we believe that the above properties are most interesting for the security analysis.

2.4.2 Security Analysis Problem for DIFC Configuration

Finally, we will give a formal definition of the security analysis problem. A DIFC configuration is in the form of (γ, ψ) where $\gamma \in \Gamma$ and $\psi \in \Psi$. γ is the initial state (configuration) which will transit to next state under the state-transition rule ψ. Suppose we have a property $\delta \in \Delta$, the definition of the security analysis problem (SAP) is:

Definition 4. *(SAP-DIFC) An instance of SAP for a DIFC configuration is given by a configuration (γ, ψ) and a security property δ. It asks whether δ holds for (γ, ψ), that is, $(\gamma, \psi) \vdash \delta$.*

In addition, if the security analysis falsifies a property, it is often useful to get a counter-example in order to analyze the root cause and debug the configuration. A counter-example is a state-transition sequence σ^* s.t. $\gamma \rightarrow_{\sigma*} \gamma'$, where γ' is the state violating the property. The attack sequence in Fig. 2.2 is a counter-example for the configuration in Fig. 2.1. Please note that for certain properties such as the flow protection, counter-examples do not exist.

The complexity of the security analysis for system configuration in general is showed to be in intractable [9]. Yang et al. [7] also proved that the problem of DIFC policy verification is NP-Hard. Since their problem can be reduced to the SAP-DIFC, the security analysis problem presented in this paper is intractable in general.

Nevertheless, we are able to show that the existing model checking techniques can handle considerably large cases and have the potential to be used in practice.

2.5 Our Approach

2.5.1 Model Checking

We use model checking to solve the security analysis problem. Model checking is a technique to determine whether system model M satisfies a temporal logic property δ. If the property holds for M, then the model checker will return true; otherwise it will return false plus a counter-example (if it exists). For our problem, M is an instance of the configuration (γ, ψ). A DIFC configuration can be directly translated to model checking code and Fig. 2.3 gives a short example. It is also straightforward to express the security property of DIFC configuration into temporal logic formula, as Fig. 2.4 shows.

Since writing complex model checking code could be time-consuming and error-prone, we will first describe a DIFC configuration in the configuration description language (Fig. 2.5) and then automatically translate it into the model checking code. In addition, previous works [15] can be used to automatically extract the model from a DIFC system. We leave this as a future work.

Another challenge for applying model checking is the state explosion problem. To combat it, the *bounded model checking* approach is often used. Bounded model checking verifies the property in only k or fewer steps, i.e., the model checker only examines $\{\gamma'|\gamma \rightarrow_{\sigma*} \gamma' \wedge \sigma^* \leq |k|\}$. We choose model checking primarily for its efficiency. However, the problem proposed in this paper can also be solved by other approaches, such as Datalog (e.g. [6]) or Prolog (e.g. [16]).

```
init(info[2][1]) := FALSE;
next(info[2][1]) := case
    read2_6 & info[6][1] : TRUE;
    read2_7 & info[7][1] : TRUE;
    TRUE : info[2][1];
esac;
```

Fig. 2.3 An example of state transition rule in NuSMV. Here, we use a distinct number to represent each object and information. info[objectID][infoID] is equivalent to OI

Fig. 2.4 An example of LTL specification

```
LTLSPEC
    G (info[7][1] = FALSE);
```

Fig. 2.5 The CDL for the
example in Fig. 2.1

Objects:
secret, $\{As\}$, $\{Ai\}$, confidential
token, $\{As\}$, $\{Ai\}$, $Dec+$
calendarA, $\{As\}$, $\{Ai\}$
calendarB, $\{Bs\}$, $\{Bi\}$
setlabel, $\{As, Dec\}$, $\{Ai\}$
network, $\{\}$, $\{\}$, sink
editorA, $\{As\}$, $\{Ai\}$, $\{\}$, malicious
editorB, $\{Bs\}$, $\{Bi\}$, $\{Bs-\}$, malicious
Declassification:
De1, calendar file (Alice), calendar file (Bob), $(\{As, Dec\}, \{\})$
Capability Transfer Rules:
Ca1, $\{Dec+\}$,$\{token\}$
Security Property:
confidential, !network

2.5.2 Preprocessing

The efficiency of model checking is determined by the number of states and state-transition rules of the model $M : (\gamma, \psi)$. For $SAP - DIFC$, the number of state variables N_s is roughly equal to the sum of $|OI|$, $|PL|$ and $|PC|$, while the number of state-transition rules N_t is approximately $N_a \times |P| \times |O|$, where N_a is the number of action types. However, some state variables can be deleted, for they are fixed in all reachable states or not related to the property at all. Many state-transition rules are also removable, because their pre-condition will never be triggered by any process. For the configuration in Fig. 2.1, $read(editorA, editorB)$ can be removed because these two processes can never communicate. Therefore, we prune M before applying model checking. Algorithm 2.1 is a simple yet effective algorithm for preprocessing. The basic intuition is to first calculate the upper and lower bound of labels an object could possibly get, and then use them to prune actions whose pre-condition cannot be satisfied even in boundary conditions. In addition, before running the preprocessing, we will aggregate files with the same secrecy label and integrity label.

This algorithm works as follows:

- First, we get the upper and lower bound of each process p's secrecy label and integrity label, $maxLs_p$, $minLs_p$, $maxLi_p$ and $minLi_p$, in line 1–16. $maxLs_p$ is the set of secrecy labels that p could get. $minLs_p$ is the set of secrecy labels that p cannot get rid of. The definitions for $maxLi_p$ and $minLi_p$ are same. For p, transitions that beyond these four bounds will never be triggered. $maxCs_p^{+/-}$ are the upper bound of p's secrecy capabilities. They are set to $p's$ capabilities at the initialization, but will be updated in each iteration by checking whether new capabilities can be acquired from tokens or transfers.
- Then, we prune state transitions and state variables by label bounds in line 17–26. Line 17–21 prune state transitions (actions) if they will not be triggered. Line 22–26 prune object o if it does not belong to any transition's initiator or targets. The prune process for other state variables are similar.

```
 1  while M is not fixed do
 2      foreach process p in M do
 3          maxLs_p ← Ls_p ∪ maxCs_p^+ ;
 4          minLs_p ← Ls_p − maxCs_p^- ;
 5          maxLi_p ← Li_p ∪ maxCi_p^+ ;
 6          minLi_p ← Li_p − maxCi_p^- ;
 7      end
 8      foreach process p in M do
 9          maxCs_p^+ ← maxCs_p^+ ∪ capabilityFromToken(p);
10          foreach process pair (p, p') in M do
11              if canWriteBound(p', p) then
12                  maxCs_p^+ ← maxCs_p^+ ∪ maxCs_p^+ ;
13              end
14          end
15      end
        /* The code for updating maxCs_p^+ and maxCi_p^{+/-} is
           omitted.                                              */
16  end
17  foreach state transition σ in M do
18      if !matchBound(init(σ), target(σ), precond(σ)) then
19          delete(σ, M);
20      end
21  end
22  foreach object o in M do
23      if ∄σ s.t. o ∈ init(σ) ∨ o ∈ targets(σ) then
24          delete(o, M);
25      end
26  end
    /* The code for pruning sets T, I, D, is omitted.           */
```

Algorithm 2.1: Preprocessing algorithm

Although our preprocessing algorithm is effective in experiment (see Sect. 2.6), it is not optimal. Improving the preprocessing algorithm is an interesting work for future.

2.6   Experiment and Evaluation

We have conducted an experiment to test the efficiency of model checking in handling cases of different scales. Five DIFC configuration cases were created in total. Each case has two versions: a safe version in which the property is true, and a vulnerable version in which the property does not hold and a counter-example exists. Among the five cases, two of them are manually-created cases with long attack sequences, which enables us to evaluate how well the model checker detects

Table 2.1 Experiment Result. In this table, (AP) means after prune. The Runtime (FALSE) row displays the analysis time for the vulnerable version of each cases. Runtime (TRUE) row displays the analysis time of the safe version. If an experiment runs longer than 2 h or out of memory, the result would be N/A

	man1	man2	rand1	rand2	rand3
Num. of tags	7	10	20	40	60
Num. of malicious processes	3	6	6	13	20
Num. of declassification rules	2	3	10	20	30
Num. of capability rules	2	3	12	22	36
Attack sequence length	9	18	6	6	6
Num. of state variables	40	210	2,265	10,479	25,031
Num. of state variables (AP)	40	205	351	3,339	7,898
Num. of state transitions	108	1,067	23,217	229,019	847,758
Num. of state transitions (AP)	78	639	839	35,301	147,410
Runtime (FALSE)	0.065 s	0.997 s	0.940 s	1 min13 s	7 min25 s
Runtime (TRUE)	6 min57 s	1 h09 min37 s	N/A	N/A	N/A

these deep hidden vulnerabilities. Other cases are randomly generated and their key parameters are displayed in Table 2.1.

The model checker we choose is NuSMV2.5.4 [17]. Specifically, we use iterative bounded model checking (check_ltlspec _bmc_inc, k = 20) to find a counter-example for the vulnerable configuration. Then we use unbounded model checking (with parameters -coi -df -dcx) to prove the property of the safe version. The experiment was performed on a Linux workstation with an Intel Xeon 3.06 GHz CPU and 2 GB memory. We put the results in Table 2.1.

Several interesting discoveries can be found in Table 2.1. First, our preprocessing algorithm effectively reduces the number of state variables and state transitions, particularly for the randomly generated cases. Second, even for large-scale cases, it is efficient to prove a property to be *false* and to find a counter-example by bounded model checking. However, proving a property to be *true* is very time-consuming, and we didn't even get a result with cases having 20 or more tags in the time span of the experiment. Nevertheless, we can use bounded model checking to partially prove a configuration's safety by setting a large bound k, because the longer an attack sequence is, the harder it can be found and exploited by malicious processes.

2.7 Discussion

Since our goal is to provide a foundation for analyzing DIFC configuration, we only capture necessary components in the formal model. Several extensions can be made. First, we can describe *endorsement* (the deliberate upgrade of low integrity information) in the similar way as modeling declassification due to the duality between confidentiality and integrity. Second, we can add more actions to the state-transition rules. An important action missing from our current model is object creation. Since existing model checkers can only verify properties over bounded set of objects, it is not straightforward to do this extension. We believe that the work of verifying DIFC program with unbounded processes [15] could be a promising approach. Third, the current characterization of declassification rule is rather simple: we have only used labels as the pre-condition. However, a truly robust declassification channel will have other pre-conditions to prevent information laundering, so the security analysis needs to capture these pre-conditions. Fourth, to make our approach more useful, the low level state-transition formulation needs to be transformed into a higher level abstraction. Locating the root cause of a misconfiguration and automatically fixing the vulnerabilities are also interesting extensions.

2.8 Related Works

2.8.1 Decentralized Information Flow Control

The idea of DIFC is initially applied in programming language design [18, 19]. Asbestos [1] was the first DIFC operating system, followed by HiStar [2] that implements a Unix-like environment with almost entirely untrusted user-level libraries. Flume [3], on the other hand, is a user-level implementation atop stock operating systems like Linux. Thus, Flume is more portable and can benefit from existing kernel support for hardware, but has a much larger TCB. DIFC also inspires the design of new secure distributed systems such as DStar [4] and Aeolus [20]. In addition, Laminar [21] is a hybrid system inspired by both language-based DIFC and operating system-based DIFC. Extending the configuration analysis to these DIFC systems is an interesting future work.

Previous works already noticed the challenge of creating and managing DIFC configurations. There are two lines of research on this issue. The first line is to improve the usability of DIFC systems. For example, Efstathopoulos and Kohler [12] provided a high-level policy description language and debugging mechanisms to simplify the programming in Asbestos. Harris et al. [13] created a tool that can automatically instrument DIFC code to "DIFC-unaware" programs. These works could help software developers make less mistakes in configuration. However, the mis-configuration problem could not be eliminated for two reasons. First, these assistant tools cannot construct all of the configurations required. Second, using these tools could also be complex, for they still need users to specify the security requirement of each object. In addition, they only benefit application developers without considering the demand of system administrator.

Our work falls into the second line: verifying the safety of DIFC system. Krohn and Tromer [10] prove that the Flume model has the noninterference property: "that unprivileged user processes cannot leak data from the system, whether via explicit communication or implicit channels." However, an assumption of this work is that the DIFC system should be properly implemented and configured, so our work is complementary to this proof. Harris et al. [15] use model checking and random isolation to prove the correctness of DIFC code with unbounded processes. Chaudhuri et al. [6] and Yang et al. [7] verify DIFC configuration at system object-level. Chaudhuri et al. reduce the safety analysis problem to query satisfiability in Datalog. Yang et al. propose an rigorous formalization of DIFC policies and also prove that the complexity of DIFC policy verification problem is NP-Complete. They use model checking to verify whether a set of processes can keep a security property. Our work goes beyond them by providing a more comprehensive threat model and formal model. In addition, we use bounded model checking to handle large cases.

2.8.2 Security Analysis of Access Control

Our work is also highly related to the security analysis of access control. The landmark paper [9] by Harrison et al. models the configuration of an operating system as access matrix and further shows that the problem of determining whether a process can acquire a particular right to an object in a given situation is intractable in general [9]. Since then, there has been significant amount of research in this direction. Among them, security analysis of the role-based access control (RBAC) [8, 14, 22] is a very active area, thanks to the wide usage of RBAC in real world. These works [8, 22] demonstrate the efficiency of model checking in verifying the security of a RBAC policy (e.g. a untrusted user cannot acquire sensitive roles). Some advanced techniques such as abstraction-refinement based approach [22] have significantly increased the efficiency of RBAC analysis and also have the potential to accelerate DIFC configuration analysis. In addition, the formal model used in this paper is directly inspired by the work of Li and Tripunitara [14]. The roles in RBAC has similar effects as the labels and capabilities in DIFC. The decentralization of user-role assignment and revocation in administrative RBAC also resembles the decentralization in DIFC. However, significant differences exist between DIFC and these access control schemes. For example, access control systems prevent untrusted subjects from reading confidential information, while DIFC allows them to access sensitive data as long as they cannot leak it. In addition, DIFC configuration analysis is closer to the underlying system, resulting in a larger state space and more complex state-transition rules. These differences provide new challenges for the formal analysis of DIFC system.

Researchers have also designed tools to analyze the safety of access control in commodity operating system such as Windows [6,16] and Unix-like systems [23,24] based on model checking or logic programing. In addition, verifying information flow goals for other security systems have been studied by Focardi and Gorrieri [25] and Guttman et al. [24].

2.9 Conclusion

In this paper, we provide a systematic analysis of misconfigurations and their security threats for DIFC systems. We formulate the security analysis problem for DIFC configurations in a state-transition model, which allows model checkers to prove a configuration is secure or detect misconfigurations that violate the desired security goal. The experiment shows that the preprocessing algorithm and bounded model checking techniques are effective in fulfilling the task. In sum, this approach could be a framework to analyze the security of DIFC configurations.

Acknowledgements This work was supported by AFOSR FA9550-07-1-0527 (MURI), ARO W911NF-09-1-0525 (MURI), NSF CNS-0905131, NSF CNS-1223710, ARO W911NF1210055, and U.S. ARL and U. K. MoD W911NF-06-3-0001. The authors would like to thank Yue Zhang, Jun Wang, William Robert Grace and Eunsuk Kang for their valuable feedbacks. The authors would also like to thank all the anonymous reviewers for their detailed comments and suggestions.

References

1. Efstathopoulos, P., Krohn, M., VanDeBogart, S., Frey, C., Ziegler, D., Kohler, E., Mazieres, D., Kaashoek, F., Morris, R.: Labels and event processes in the asbestos operating system. In: Proceedings of the Twentieth ACM Symposium on Operating Systems Principles, Brighton, pp. 17–30. ACM (2005)
2. Zeldovich, N., Boyd-Wickizer, S., Kohler, E., Mazières, D.: Making information flow explicit in histar. In: Proceedings of the 7th Symposium on Operating Systems Design and Implementation, Seattle, pp. 263–278. USENIX Association (2006)
3. Krohn, M., Yip, A., Brodsky, M., Cliffer, N., Kaashoek, M., Kohler, E., Morris, R.: Information flow control for standard os abstractions. In: Proceedings of Twenty-First ACM SIGOPS Symposium on Operating Systems Principles, Stevenson, pp. 321–334. ACM (2007)
4. Zeldovich, N., Boyd-Wickizer, S., Mazieres, D.: Securing distributed systems with information flow control. In: Proceedings of the 5th USENIX Symposium on Networked Systems Design and Implementation, San Francisco, pp. 293–308. USENIX Association (2008)
5. Sabelfeld, A., Sands, D.: Dimensions and principles of declassification. In: 18th IEEE Computer Security Foundations Workshop (CSFW-18 2005), Aix-en-Provence, pp. 255–269. IEEE (2005)
6. Chaudhuri, A., Naldurg, P., Rajamani, S., Ramalingam, G., Velaga, L.: Eon: modeling and analyzing dynamic access control systems with logic programs. In: Proceedings of the 15th ACM Conference on Computer and Communications Security, Alexandria, pp. 381–390. ACM (2008)
7. Yang, Z., Yin, L., Jin, S., Duan, M.: Towards formal security analysis of decentralized information flow control policies. Int. J. Innov. Comput. Inf. Control **8**(11), 7969–7981 (2012)
8. Jha, S., Li, N., Tripunitara, M., Wang, Q., Winsborough, W.: Towards formal verification of role-based access control policies. IEEE Trans. Dependable Secur. Comput. **5**(4), 242–255 (2008)
9. Harrison, M., Ruzzo, W., Ullman, J.: Protection in operating systems. Commun. ACM **19**(8), 461–471 (1976)
10. Krohn, M., Tromer, E.: Noninterference for a practical difc-based operating system. In: 30th IEEE Symposium on Security and Privacy, Oakland, pp. 61–76. IEEE (2009)

11. Denning, D.: A lattice model of secure information flow. Commun. ACM **19**(5), 236–243 (1976)
12. Efstathopoulos, P., Kohler, E.: Manageable fine-grained information flow. ACM SIGOPS Oper. Syst. Rev. **42**(4), 301–313 (2008)
13. Harris, W., Jha, S., Reps, T.: DIFC programs by automatic instrumentation. In: Proceedings of the 17th ACM Conference on Computer and Communications Security, Chicago, pp. 284–296 (2010)
14. Li, N., Tripunitara, M.: Security analysis in role-based access control. ACM Trans. Inf. Syst. Secur. **9**(4), 391–420 (2006)
15. Harris, W., Kidd, N., Chaki, S., Jha, S., Reps, T.: Verifying information flow control over unbounded processes. In: FM 2009: Formal Methods, Eindhoven, pp. 773–789 (2009)
16. Chen, H., Li, N., Gates, C., Mao, Z.: Towards analyzing complex operating system access control configurations. In: Proceeding of the 15th ACM Symposium on Access Control Models and Technologies, Pittsburgh, pp. 13–22. ACM (2010)
17. Cimatti, A., Clarke, E., Giunchiglia, E., Giunchiglia, F., Pistore, M., Roveri, M., Sebastiani, R., Tacchella, A.: Nusmv 2: an opensource tool for symbolic model checking. In: Computer Aided Verification, Copenhagen, pp. 241–268. Springer (2002)
18. Myers, A., Liskov, B.: A decentralized model for information flow control. In: ACM SIGOPS Oper. Syst. Rev. **31**, 129–142 (1997)
19. Myers, A.: Jflow: practical mostly-static information flow control. In: Proceedings of the 26th ACM SIGPLAN-SIGACT Symposium on Principles of Programming Languages, San Antonio, pp. 228–241. ACM (1999)
20. Cheng, W., Ports, D., Schultz, D., Popic, V., Blankstein, A., Cowling, J., Curtis, D., Shrira, L., Liskov, B.: Abstractions for usable information flow control in aeolus. In: Proceedings of the 2012 USENIX Annual Technical Conference, Boston. USENIX Association (2012)
21. Roy, I., Porter, D., Bond, M., McKinley, K., Witchel, E., Laminar: practical fine-grained decentralized information flow control. ACM SIGPLAN Not. **44**(6), 63–74 (2009)
22. Jayaraman, K., Ganesh, V., Tripunitara, M., Rinard, M., Chapin, S.: Automatic error finding in access-control policies. In: Proceedings of the 18th ACM Conference on Computer and Communications Security, Chicago, pp. 163–174. ACM (2011)
23. Ramakrishnan, C., Sekar, R., et al.: Model-based analysis of configuration vulnerabilities. J. Comput. Secur. **10**(1/2), 189–209 (2002)
24. Guttman, J., Herzog, A., Ramsdell, J., Skorupka, C.: Verifying information flow goals in security-enhanced linux. J. Comput. Secur. **13**(1), 115–134 (2005)
25. Focardi, R., Gorrieri, R.: The compositional security checker: a tool for the verification of information flow security properties. IEEE Trans. Softw. Eng. **23**(9), 550–571 (1997)

Part II
Vulnerability and Risk Assessment

Chapter 3
Increasing Android Security Using a Lightweight OVAL-Based Vulnerability Assessment Framework

Martín Barrère, Gaëtan Hurel, Rémi Badonnel, and Olivier Festor

Abstract Mobile computing devices and the services offered by them are utilized by millions of users on a daily basis. However, they operate in hostile environments getting exposed to a wide variety of threats. Accordingly, vulnerability management mechanisms are highly required. We present in this paper a novel approach for increasing the security of mobile devices by efficiently detecting vulnerable configurations. In that context, we propose a modeling for performing vulnerability assessment activities as well as an OVAL-based distributed framework for ensuring safe configurations within the Android platform. We also describe an implementation prototype and evaluate its performance through an extensive set of experiments.

3.1 Introduction

The overwhelming technological advances in the broad sense of mobile computing have made end users to experience real computers in their pockets. Android[1] [2], a Linux-based operating system for mobile devices, is nowadays the election of millions of users as the platform for governing their mobile devices. Only in the first quarter of 2012, worldwide sales of smartphones to end users reached 144.4 million units where Android-based devices leaded the market share owning the 56.1 % followed by iOS[2] with 22.9 % [15]. However, despite of the many security improvements that have been done since Android's creation, the underlying

---

[1] Android is developed by Open Handset Alliance, led by Google [22]
[2] Apple iOS [4]

M. Barrère (✉) • G. Hurel • R. Badonnel • O. Festor
INRIA Nancy Grand Est – LORIA – University of Lorraine, Nancy Cedex, France
e-mail: barrere@inria.fr; hurel@inria.fr; badonnel@inria.fr; festor@inria.fr

E. Al-Shaer et al. (eds.), *Automated Security Management*,
DOI 10.1007/978-3-319-01433-3_3, © Springer International Publishing Switzerland 2013

operating system as well as services and applications have also evolved providing room for new vulnerabilities. Moreover, the open and barely protected mobile environment facilitates attackers to take advantage of such vulnerabilities. Sensitive data handled by mobile users becomes easily exposed. Under this perspective, managing vulnerabilities is a crucial and challenging task that must be addressed in order to ensure safe configurations and to increase the overall security of the system.

Once a vulnerability is discovered in almost any typical software product, its patch cycle normally describes a time gap until the vulnerability is disclosed, another time span until the patch is available and yet another time span until the end user applies the patch [14]. It is usually during this period that attackers activity takes place. Within the Android environment, this issue gets worse. Android is distributed as open source and device manufacturers and telecommunications carriers customize it in order to provide specific services as well as added value to their customers. When a patch is released by Google, an extra time gap will occur until the manufacturer adapts it to work with its own hardware and another time span will pass until the patch is released by the carrier [29]. In addition to this problem, several application markets allow to fast distribute third party applications with only some security checks expecting that the community identifies and reports malicious software. With thousands of applications in the market, Android users are very likely to encounter malware[3] on their devices [18].

Such scenario imperatively requires solutions for rapidly identifying new vulnerabilities and minimizing their impact. Even though no patch might be available for a new vulnerability at a given time, countermeasures can be taken in order to mitigate the problem until the disclosure of an official patch. In that context, vulnerability assessment mechanisms are highly required in order to increase the vulnerability awareness of the system. In addition, mobile devices usually have limited resources thus optimized lightweight tools should be developed to ensure efficiency without losing functionality. Moreover, there are no current solutions built over solid foundations as well as open and mature standards that foster its adoption and speed up general vulnerability information exchange.

In light of this, we propose a novel approach for increasing the security of the Android platform, though it could be applied over other mobile platforms as well, using the OVAL[4] language [26] as a means for describing Android vulnerabilities. We put forward a mathematical model that supports the assessment strategy and a lightweight framework that efficiently takes advantage of such knowledge in order to detect and prevent configuration vulnerabilities. We also present an implementation prototype as well as an extensive set of experiments that shows the feasibility of our solution.

Finally, the remainder of this paper is organized as follows. Section 3.2 describes existing work and their limits. Section 3.3 presents our approach for modeling

---

[3]Malicious software including viruses, worms and spyware among others
[4]Open Vulnerability and Assessment Language

the vulnerability assessment process. Section 3.4 details the proposed framework describing its architecture and the proposed strategy for performing self-assessment activities. Section 3.5 depicts the internals of our implementation prototype. Section 3.6 shows an extensive set of experiments and the obtained results. Section 3.7 presents conclusions and future work.

3.2   Related Work

Android is an open source operating system that integrates some security features by design. It uses the Dalvik virtual machine [10] for executing end user applications written in Java [25]. It is not the same standard Java virtual machine used in most popular platforms such as Linux, Mac OS X or Windows. It has its own API[5] that is almost the same as the standard one. The Dalvik virtual machine takes the Java application classes and translates them into one or more *.dex* (Dalvik Executable) files generating optimized and smaller code. The internal design of the Android platform provides important security features such as the sandbox execution approach [29]. Such approach executes Android applications within separate instances of the Dalvik virtual machine that in turn are represented by different Linux kernel processes. In order to manage the underlying system resources, Android uses an access control policy based on unique identifiers for each application to ensure that they cannot interfere between each other.

Despite of the many security features provided by the Android platform [11,27], end users still face security threats due to existing vulnerabilities within the system itself, misuse of personal data performed by applications and malicious third party software [12, 13]. Several approaches have been proposed for analyzing Android applications and their risks [9, 17]. These contributions provide a strong support for increasing the security of the Android platform. Nevertheless, vulnerability assessment mechanisms have been barely or not at all discussed. Currently, dozens of security applications exist for the Android platform developed by different providers [18, 21, 31]. However, they generally use private knowledge sources as well as their own assessment techniques, and they do not provide standardized and open means for describing and exchanging vulnerability descriptions within the community.

Much of the work done in vulnerability analysis has defined the assessment infrastructure using its own vulnerability specification language arising compatibility and interoperability problems. Languages such as VulnXML [30] have been developed as an attempt to mitigate these problems and to promote the exchange of security information among applications and security entities. However, these languages are only focused on web applications covering a subset of the existing vulnerabilities in current computer systems. In order to cope with these problems, the MITRE corporation [19] has introduced the OVAL language [26],

---

[5]Application Programming Interface

an information security community effort to standardize how to assess and report upon the machine state of computer systems. OVAL is an XML-based language that allows to express specific machine states such as vulnerabilities, configuration settings, patch states. Real analysis is performed by OVAL interpreters such as Ovaldi [24] and XOvaldi [7]. Several related technologies have evolved around the OVAL language. NIST [20] is responsible for the development of emerging technologies including the SCAP[6] protocol [5] and the XCCDF[7] language [32]. The SCAP protocol is a suite of specifications that includes OVAL and XCCDF, and it can be used for several purposes, including automating vulnerability checking, technical control compliance activities, and security measurement. XCCDF is a language for authoring security checklists/benchmarks and for reporting results of checklist evaluation. The use of SCAP, particularly OVAL and XCCDF, not only allows to specify vulnerabilities, but also to bring a system into compliance through the remediation of identified vulnerabilities or misconfigurations. While OVAL provides means for describing specific machine states, XCCDF allows to describe certain actions that should be taken when these states are present on the system under analysis.

Several previous contributions have taken advantage of public vulnerability databases [1] and the use of the OVAL language for performing vulnerability assessment activities in large scale networks [23]. Currently, OVAL repositories offer a wide range of vulnerability descriptions though Android is not yet an official supported platform. In this work, we have instrumented our approach with an experimental OVAL extension for Android within the OVAL Sandbox project [26]. Such extension enables practitioners and experts within the field to specify known vulnerabilities for Android in a machine-readable manner and at the same time, it promotes the exchange and enrichment of Android security information within the community. Our work aims at defining a solution for increasing the security of Android devices by capitalizing Android vulnerability descriptions specified with the OVAL language. Such security advisories are automatically integrated in a distributed architecture where self-assessment activities are performed in order to ensure safe mobile configurations.

3.3   Vulnerability Assessment Process Model

The process by which vulnerabilities are assessed is critical for efficiently analyzing a target system and minimizing computation costs at the same time. In this section we present a mathematical model that defines and efficiently supports the vulnerability assessment process. Usually, a vulnerability can be understood as a logical combination of properties that if observed in a target system, the security problem associated with such vulnerability is present on that system. Properties can

---

[6]Security Content Automation Protocol

[7]eXtensible Configuration Checklist Description Format

vary depending on the nature of the vulnerability being described, some examples are: a specific process is running (e.g., httpd), a specific port is open (e.g., 80), the system has a specific version (e.g., 2.6.10.rc). Frequently, one property is required by several vulnerability descriptions and naturally one vulnerability description may require several properties. Under this perspective, the set of vulnerability descriptions that constitutes a knowledge base can be compactly represented by using a boolean pattern matrix PM defined as follows:

$$PM = \begin{array}{c} \\ v_1 \\ v_2 \\ \vdots \\ v_m \end{array} \begin{pmatrix} a_{1,1} & a_{1,2} & \cdots & a_{1,n} \\ a_{2,1} & a_{2,2} & \cdots & a_{2,n} \\ \vdots & \vdots & \ddots & \vdots \\ a_{m,1} & a_{m,2} & \cdots & a_{m,n} \end{pmatrix} \quad a_{i,j} \in \{0,1\}$$

Each matrix row encodes the properties required to be observed for the vulnerability v_i to be present. Thus, each entry $a_{i,j}$ denotes if the vulnerability v_i requires the property p_j. Considering for instance a scenario with three vulnerabilities v_1, v_2 and v_3, a pattern matrix PM can be built as follows:

$$\left. \begin{array}{l} v_1 = (p_1, p_3, p_5) \\ v_2 = (p_2, p_4) \\ v_3 = (p_1, p_2, p_5) \end{array} \right\} \quad PM_{3,5} = \begin{pmatrix} 1 & 0 & 1 & 0 & 1 \\ 0 & 1 & 0 & 1 & 0 \\ 1 & 1 & 0 & 0 & 1 \end{pmatrix}$$

The pattern matrix can also provide useful information for performing statistics. The $vflatten$ operation aggregates the number of times that each property occurs within the whole set of known vulnerabilities. The resulting vector provides an indicator that helps to identify most common properties involved in vulnerabilities. Such indicator provides valuable information that can be used for closer monitoring and controlling critical components changes.

$$vflatten(PM) = (\sum_{i=1}^{m} a_{i1}, \sum_{i=1}^{m} a_{i2}, \ldots, \sum_{i=1}^{m} a_{in})$$

Other useful metric can be extracted from the pattern matrix when the aggregation operation is performed horizontally, as indicated by $hflatten$. A column vector is obtained from its application where each entry j denotes the amount of properties required by each vulnerability v_j. This metric can be utilized, among other uses, for identifying those vulnerabilities that are most likely affected by changes performed in the environment, thus assessment activities should be taken into account as well.

$$hflatten(PM) = (\sum_{j=1}^{n} a_{1j}, \sum_{j=1}^{n} a_{2j}, \ldots, \sum_{j=1}^{n} a_{mj})^T$$

The state of a system can be encoded in the same manner as done with vulnerabilities, indicating for those properties under control, which ones are present and which ones are not. Thus, a system state is a boolean vector s defined as follows:

$$s = (s_1, s_2, \ldots, s_n) \quad s_i \in \{0, 1\}$$

Each entry s_i takes the value 1 if the property p_i is present in the system and 0 if it is not. Considering these constructs, the results of performing the vulnerability assessment process over a given system is defined by the following equation:

$$w = hflatten(PM) - [PM * s^T]$$

$$\Downarrow$$

$$w = \begin{pmatrix} \sum_{j=1}^{n} a_{1j} \\ \sum_{j=1}^{n} a_{2j} \\ \vdots \\ \sum_{j=1}^{n} a_{mj} \end{pmatrix} - \left[\begin{pmatrix} a_{1,1} & a_{1,2} & \cdots & a_{1,n} \\ a_{2,1} & a_{2,2} & \cdots & a_{2,n} \\ \vdots & \vdots & \ddots & \vdots \\ a_{m,1} & a_{m,2} & \cdots & a_{m,n} \end{pmatrix} \times \begin{pmatrix} s_1 \\ s_2 \\ \vdots \\ s_n \end{pmatrix} \right] \quad (3.1)$$

The resulting assessment vector $w = (w_1, w_2, \cdots, w_m)$ denotes the status of each vulnerability v_i in the target system. The semantic of the vector w is given by the *Kronecker delta* function as follows:

$$\delta_i = \begin{cases} 0, \text{ if } i \neq 0 \\ 1, \text{ if } i = 0 \end{cases}$$

A null entry w_i indicates that the vulnerability v_i is present in the system while non null values denotes the absence of the corresponding vulnerability. This fact can be understood as a distance metric where a positive value indicates a positive distance between the vulnerability and the target system, and a null distance indicates that the vulnerability is actually in the system. Computing matrix operations in optimized manners constitutes a field that has been studied for years [28]. The integration of the proposed model into real computing systems can take advantage of such expertise providing a compact and efficient representation for performing vulnerability assessment activities.

3.4 An OVAL-Based Framework for Assessing Android Vulnerabilities

The previous model establishes a well-founded process for assessing vulnerabilities in an efficient manner. By taking advantage of OVAL security advisories, such model can be used for efficiently increasing the security of mobile computing devices. Mobile devices have become a daily useful resource for connecting people, entertainment, working, managing personal data and much more. This fact attracted

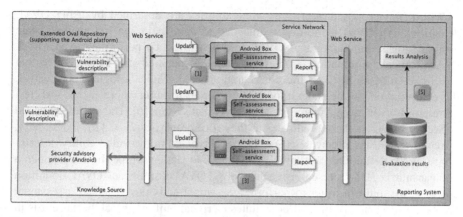

Fig. 3.1 OVAL-based vulnerability assessment framework for the Android platform

the attention of legitimate users of these pocket-computers but also from attackers. In only the first semester of 2011, malware for the Android platform has grown at 250 % [18]. It is critical to develop open security frameworks that can speed up the knowledge exchange among community users and also being able to take advantage of such information in order to augment their own security. In this section we present our approach for efficiently increasing the security of Android-based devices by automatically evaluating OVAL-based vulnerability descriptions and reporting analysis results.

3.4.1   Architecture and Main Components

We have designed the proposed architecture illustrated in Fig. 3.1 as a distributed infrastructure composed of three main building blocks: (1) a knowledge source that provides existing security advisories, (2) Android-based devices running a self-assessment service and (3) a reporting system for storing analysis results and performing further analysis. The overall process is defined as follows. Firstly at step 1, the Android device periodically monitors and queries for new vulnerability descriptions updates. This is achieved by using a web service provided by the security advisory provider. At step 2, the provider examines its database and sends back new found entries. The updater tool running inside the Android device synchronizes then its security advisories. When new information is available or configuration changes occur within the system, a self-assessment service is launched in order to analyze the device at step 3. At step 4, the report containing the collected data and the results of the analyzed vulnerabilities is sent to a reporting system by means of a web service request. At step 5, the obtained results are stored and analyzed to detect potential threats within the Android device. In addition, this information can also be used with different purposes such as forensic activities or statistical analysis.

Within the proposed approach, vulnerabilities are described by using OVAL definitions. An OVAL definition is intended to describe a specific machine state using a logical combination of OVAL tests that must be performed over a host. If such logical combination is observed, then the specified state is present on that host (e.g. vulnerability, specific configuration) [26]. Under a logical perspective, this combination can be understood as a first order formula where each OVAL test corresponds to an atomic unary predicate over that system [6]. The model presented in Sect. 3.3 denotes these predicates as the set of properties $P = \{p_1, p_2, \ldots, p_n\}$. P represents all the predicates (OVAL tests) involved in the vulnerability descriptions (OVAL definitions) available within our knowledge source. In this manner, a boolean matrix PM representing each involved OVAL test for each OVAL definition can be easily built in order to perform assessment activities. The self-assessment component depicted in Fig. 3.1 constitutes a critical building block because it is in charge of orchestrating the entire lifecycle of the framework in an automatic manner. Hence, optimized algorithms for performing self-assessment activities are highly required. In order to achieve this objective, we have designed and implemented a strategy that uses the model presented in Sect. 3.3 for minimizing the system components required to be assessed.

3.4.2 Optimized Assessment Strategy

Due to the limited resources provided usually by mobile devices, it is important to optimize the use of such elements without losing functionality and performance. The proposed assessment strategy takes this issue into account and minimizes computation costs by using a boolean pattern matrix PM that represents known vulnerabilities and a system state vector s that holds the current system properties. The overall assessment is then efficiently performed using both the pattern matrix and the system vector defined in Sect. 3.3. Within our approach, two types of events can trigger self-assessment activities: (i) when changes occur in the system and (ii) when new vulnerability definitions are available. Algorithm 3.1 depicts the overall strategy for treating such events and minimizing the number of OVAL tests to be re-evaluated. In order to explain the proposed algorithm, we put forward an illustrative example that considers both situations and uses the matrix $PM_{3,5}$ illustrated in Sect. 3.3. Let consider the property $p_2 = \{Package\ X\ has\ version\ Y\}$ and the system state $s = (1, 0, 0, 0, 1)$ meaning that only the properties p_1 and p_5 are present in the system. Within the OVAL language, p_2 is described using an OVAL test that involves an OVAL *package_object* with its attribute *name* $= X$ and an OVAL *package_state* with its attribute *version* $= Y$.

Let suppose now that an event of type *package_updated* has occurred in the system affecting the package X (line 1). Usually, a complete evaluation of each OVAL definition involving the OVAL test that describes the property p_2 should be carried out. However, only the truth value of the involved OVAL test for p_2 is required for recomputing the results of all the descriptions affected. In order to

---

Input: Event event, PatternMatrix matrix, SystemState state
Output: VulnerabilityList list

1 **if** *event is of type SystemChange* **then**
2 $\quad$ $objs \leftarrow getAffectedObjectsByEvent(e)$;
3 $\quad$ **foreach** *Property $p \in state$* **do**
4 $\quad\quad$ $o \leftarrow getObjectFromProperty(p)$;
5 $\quad\quad$ **if** $o \in objs$ **then**
6 $\quad\quad\quad$ $result \leftarrow evaluateProperty(p)$;
7 $\quad\quad\quad$ $updateSystemState(state, p, result)$;
8 $\quad\quad$ **end**
9 $\quad$ **end**
10 **end**
11 **if** *event is of type DefinitionUpdate* **then**
12 $\quad$ $defs \leftarrow getDefinitionsFromEvent(e)$;
13 $\quad$ $props \leftarrow getPropertiesFromDefinitions(defs)$;
14 $\quad$ **foreach** *Property $p \in props$* **do**
15 $\quad\quad$ **if** $p \notin state$ **then**
16 $\quad\quad\quad$ $addEmptyPropertyColumn(matrix, p)$;
17 $\quad\quad\quad$ $addEmptyPropertyColumn(state, p)$;
18 $\quad\quad\quad$ $result \leftarrow evaluateProperty(p)$;
19 $\quad\quad\quad$ $updateSystemState(state, p, result)$;
20 $\quad\quad$ **end**
21 $\quad$ **end**
22 $\quad$ **foreach** *Definition $d \in defs$* **do**
23 $\quad\quad$ $addAndLoadDefinitionRow(matrix, d)$;
24 $\quad$ **end**
25 **end**
26 $w \leftarrow hSumMatrix(matrix) - (matrix * state)$;
27 $index \leftarrow 0$;
28 **foreach** *Entry $v \in w$* **do**
29 $\quad$ **if** $v = 0$ **then**
30 $\quad\quad$ $vulnDef \leftarrow getVulnDef(index)$;
31 $\quad\quad$ $addToOutputList(list, vulnDef)$;
32 $\quad$ **end**
33 $\quad$ $index \leftarrow index + 1$;
34 **end**

Algorithm 3.1: Event-based vulnerability assessment algorithm

achieve this, the objects affected by the event are retrieved (line 2) and compared with the objects related to the system properties (lines 3–4). If the object of one property is seen to be affected (line 5), the property represented by an OVAL test is re-evaluated and reflected in the system state (lines 6–7). Within our example, such optimization point will only assess and change the second entry of the system state s. Due to both events are disjoint (system changes at line 1 and definition update at line 11), we now explain the end of the algorithm for the first case and then we discuss the behavior for the second case. Let suppose that the new value for the package version is Y thus the new system state becomes $s = (1, 1, 0, 0, 1)$. Once the assessment of the OVAL test for p_2 has been done, the overall assessment result is achieved by performing two operations between boolean matrices (line 26), within our example, as given by Eq. 3.2.

$$
w = \begin{pmatrix} 3 \\ 2 \\ 3 \end{pmatrix} - \left[\begin{pmatrix} 1\ 0\ 1\ 0\ 1 \\ 0\ 1\ 0\ 1\ 0 \\ 1\ 1\ 0\ 0\ 1 \end{pmatrix} \times \begin{pmatrix} 1 \\ 1 \\ 0 \\ 0 \\ 1 \end{pmatrix} \right] = \begin{pmatrix} 1 \\ 1 \\ 0 \end{pmatrix} \tag{3.2}
$$

For each entry in the result vector w (line 28), we use the *Kronecker delta* function (line 29) in order to detect if the vulnerability represented by that entry is present in the target system. If it is the case, the vulnerability definition is added in the output detected vulnerability list (lines 30–31). Within our example, it can be observed that the change performed in the system has exposed itself to new security risks due to the presence of the vulnerability v_3.

The second situation involves the arrival of new vulnerability descriptions (line 11). In this case, both the pattern matrix PM and the system state s have to be extended so as to cover the new properties involved in the OVAL definitions. In order to achieve this, the new definitions are retrieved from the event (line 12), and the properties involved within such definitions are analyzed (lines 13–14). For each uncovered property (line 15), an extension process must be applied. The extension process for the pattern matrix PM will include new columns with null entries for the new properties within existing vulnerability definitions (line 16). The system state s is extended (line 17) and updated as well with the result of the property assessment (lines 18–19). It is important to notice that the arrival of new vulnerability definitions does not imply changes on the system and that the assessment results for known properties are already loaded in the system state, thus there is no need to re-evaluate them again. Finally, for each new vulnerability definition (line 22), a new row is added in the pattern matrix PM indicating the required properties for that vulnerability to be present (line 23). The final assessment procedure is then performed in the same manner as explained in the first situation (lines 26–34). The proposed strategy constitutes a critical part of our framework and it has been integrated into our implementation prototype, which is the heart of the next section.

3.5   Implementation Prototype

In order to provide a computable infrastructure to the proposed approach, a running software component inside Android capable of performing self-assessment activities is required. Currently, 60.3 % of Android users operate their devices using *Gingerbread* (versions 2.3.3–2.3.7, API level 10) and a total of 79.3 % operate versions starting at 2.3.3 until its last release *Jelly Bean* (version 4.1, API level

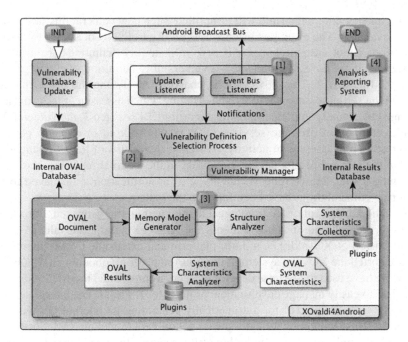

Fig. 3.2 Self-assessment service high-level operation

16) [3]. Our implementation prototype has been developed to be compliant with Android platforms starting at version 2.3.3, thus covering almost 80 % of the Android market share. In this section, we describe the prototyping of our solution as well as the high-level operation performed during the assessment activity.

The implementation prototype has been purely written in Java [25] and is composed of four main components: (1) an update system that keeps the internal database up-to-date, (2) a vulnerability management system in charge of orchestrating the assessment activities when required, (3) an OVAL interpreter for the Android platform and (4) a reporting system that stores the analysis results internally and sends them to an external reporting system. Figure 3.2 depicts the main operational steps performed during the self-assessment activity and the connection with the mentioned four main components. The prototype is executed as a lightweight service that is running on background and that can be awakened by two potential reasons. The first one is that the update system in charge of monitoring external knowledge sources has obtained new vulnerability definitions; the second one is that changes in the system have occurred hence it is highly possible that some vulnerability definitions need to be re-evaluated. The prototype is still in an early development phase so we only cover some system events such as when a package has been installed.

In order to be aware of these two potential self-assessment triggers, two listeners remain active as shown at step 1. The updater listener listens the vulnerability database updater component and will be notified when new vulnerability definitions become available. The event bus listener uses the Android broadcast bus to capture notifications about system changes. If new vulnerability definitions are available or system changes have been detected, a vulnerability definition selection process is launched at step 2. This process is in charge of analyzing the cause that has triggered the self-assessment activity and deciding which assessment tasks must be performed by actually implementing the Algorithm 3.1. At step 3, the vulnerability manager component uses the services of XOvaldi4Android in order to perform the corresponding assessment activity. At step 4, the results of the assessment are stored in the internal results database and sent to the external reporting system by performing a web service request. Finally, a local notification is displayed to the user if new vulnerabilities have been found in the system.

XOvaldi4Android plays a fundamental role within the proposed framework because it is in charge of actually assess the Android system. XOvaldi4Android is an extension of XOvaldi [7], a multi-platform and extensible OVAL interpreter. We have ported the XOvaldi system to the Android platform obtaining a 94 KB size library. We have used the Eclipse development environment and the ADT plugin [3] for Eclipse to easily manage development projects for Android. The interpreter uses the JAXB[8] technology [16] for automatically generating its internal OVAL-based data model. This technology provides means not only for modeling XML documents within a Java application data model but also for automatically reading and writing them. Such feature provides to the interpreter the ability to evolve with new OVAL versions as well as extensions, in this work for the Android platform, with almost no developing cost. As shown in Fig. 3.2, the high-level operation performed by XOvaldi4Android follows the same assessment process proposed by OVAL. In order to provide extensibility features, the interpreter decouples the analysis of the OVAL structure from the actual collection and evaluation activities by using a plugin repository. While the former is implemented as the core of the interpreter, each plugin provides injectable functionality (collection and evaluation) for the specific type of OVAL test it was built for. In this manner, declarative extensibility of the interpreter is achieved by automatic code generation using the JAXB technology and functional extensibility is supported by its plugin-based architecture.

3.6   Performance Evaluation

Devices with limited resources imperatively require well-designed and optimized software that take care of such elements. In this section we present an analytical evaluation of the proposed mathematical model as well as a technical evaluation that involves a comprehensive set of experiments showing the feasibility and scalability of our solution.

---

[8]Java Architecture for XML Binding

3.6.1   Analytical Evaluation

Within the proposed approach, the vulnerability assessment process is governed by Eq. (3.3). Given n as the number of system properties being monitored and m the number of available vulnerability definitions, the complexity of computing the result vector w is $n \times m$. Considering the worst case ($n = m$), the complexity is $O(n^2)$. Being $hflatten(PM)$ a known value, the number of operations performed during the process are n boolean multiplications plus $n - 1$ integer sums for each vulnerability definition. Then, the total number of boolean multiplications is $m \times n$ and the total number of integer sums is $m \times (n - 1)$. Hence, $m \times (n + (n - 1)) \approx n^2$ arithmetic operations are performed for assessing the entire knowledge repository in the worst case.

Considering a knowledge repository with 1,000 vulnerability definitions involving 1,000 different system properties, the size of the pattern matrix PM is 10^6. This means that the assessment process defined by the model will perform 10^6 arithmetic operations for assessing the entire knowledge base. Considering MFLOPS[9] as the performance measure, though boolean and entire operations are cheaper than floating point operations, the assessment requires 1 MFLOP. Within our experimental devices *Samsung Galaxy Gio* running Android 2.3.3, we have measured an average of 8.936 MFLOPS. With this information, we can infer that a dedicated application of our strategy over a 10^6 size matrix takes less than 1 s in almost any standard Android-based device.

Moreover, latest models may achieve more than 100 MFLOPS meaning that a knowledge source of 10,000 vulnerability definitions involving 10,000 different properties could be mathematically assessed in less than 1 s. Currently, the OVAL repository [26] offers 8747 UNIX vulnerability definitions including all versions and families after years of contributions made by the community. Such scenario provides real facts making the proposed approach highly suitable for efficiently performing vulnerability assessment activities.

3.6.2   Technical Experimentation

We have performed several experiments in order to analyze the behavior of our implementation prototype. The proposed methodology cyclically tests the framework without other applications running in foreground. The OVAL definitions set is increased by 5 each time until a set of 100 definitions is evaluated. The used OVAL definitions are similar in size containing on average two OVAL tests. For instance, the vulnerability with the *CVE-2011-3874* id permits a locally installed application to gain root privileges by causing a buffer overflow within

---

[9]Million Floating Point Operations Per Second

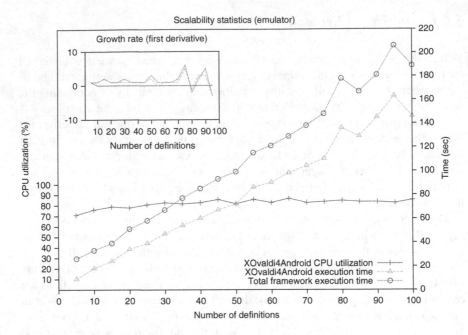

Fig. 3.3 Scalability statistics in a simulated environment

libsysutils. This vulnerability only affects specific Android versions (first OVAL test) and requires the existence of the library *libsysutils* (second OVAL test). Figure 3.3 illustrates the behavior of our implementation prototype over the emulated Android device. We analyze three performance dimensions: (1) the CPU utilization when XOvaldi4Android is executed (red solid line with crossings), (2) the XOvaldi4Android execution time (green dashed line with triangular points) and (3) the total framework execution time (blue dashed line with rounded points). During the XOvaldi4Android execution, we have observed a stable and linear behavior in terms of CPU utilization, consuming 80 % on average. Its execution time is also stable as shown by the first derivative within the inner graph. While assessing 50 definitions takes about 72 s, 100 definitions takes almost twice the time. The overall execution time across the framework, including database updates and reporting results, shows the same behavior though slightly increased in time due to the sequential execution of its components. It is important to notice that these experiments consider extreme cases. As a matter of fact, only new definitions or a small set of definitions affected by system changes will be evaluated in most situations.

In order to analyze the framework behavior using a real device, we have performed the same experiments using a standard smartphone *Samsung Galaxy Gio S5660* (CPU 800 MHz, 278 MB of RAM, Android 2.3.3). Figure 3.4 illustrates the obtained results. We can observe the same behavior on each curve as with the emulated device, describing a linear growth for each analysis dimension as

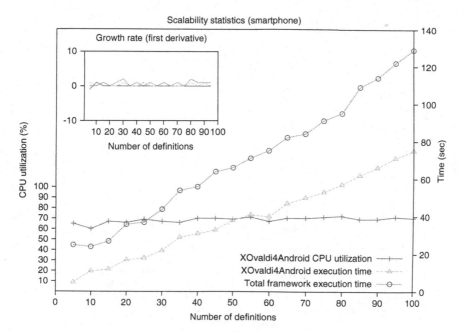

Fig. 3.4 Scalability statistics in a real device

shown in the inner graph. Nevertheless, we have also detected an improvement in terms of speed and resource usage. The average value for the CPU utilization is now about 65 %. In addition, the execution time of XOvaldi4Android is almost half the emulator execution time, taking 38 s for analyzing 50 vulnerabilities and 75 for 100 vulnerabilities. This is probably due to a slower emulated CPU. The overall execution time is also reduced due to the faster execution of the vulnerability assessment process. However, its growth rate, though linear, is faster because the internetwork connections are real in this case.

As a final but not less important dimension to analyze, we have experimented with the memory load. Within this analysis, we have considered the allocated memory required by XOvaldi4Android when it is executed. The system classifies the allocated memory in two categories, native and Dalvik, taking on average 40 % for native memory and 60 % for Dalvik memory. Figure 3.5 illustrates the total memory load considering both, the emulator and the smartphone. We have observed an almost constant utilization of the RAM memory. Within the emulator (blue solid line with rounded points), XOvaldi4Android requires 12 MB on average (4.8 MB of native memory, 7.2 MB of Dalvik memory). Within the smartphone (red dashed line with rhomboid points), XOvaldi4Android requires a little less memory, 11 MB on average (4.4 MB of native memory, 6.6 MB of Dalvik memory).

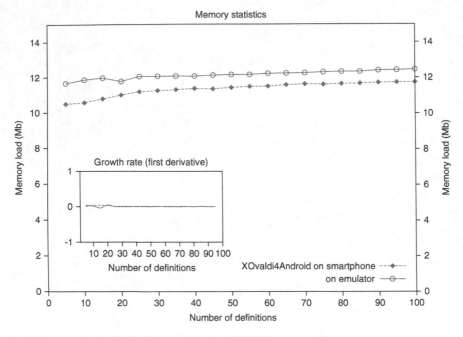

Fig. 3.5 Memory load in both emulated and real device

3.7 Conclusions and Future Work

Vulnerability management constitutes a complex activity that must be addressed in order to increase the overall security of computing devices. In that context, we have proposed an approach for supporting vulnerability assessment tasks as the first key step for integrating this activity within the Android platform. We have put forward a mathematical model as well as an optimized strategy that provides solid foundations for its instantiation on this platform. We have proposed a lightweight framework that enables the integration of OVAL security knowledge into the management plane of mobile Android-based devices. By maintaining low-consumption services monitoring the system, the proposed approach minimizes heavy task executions by only triggering assessment activities when configuration changes are detected or new vulnerability definitions are available. In light of this, we have developed an implementation prototype that efficiently performs self-assessment activities by following the proposed optimized strategy. We have also performed an analytical evaluation of the proposed model as well as an extensive set of technical experiments that shows the feasibility of our solution.

For future work we plan to analyze protection mechanisms of the assessment framework itself as well as collaborative techniques for exchanging security information among neighboring devices over secure channels. We aim at distributing the resulting improved implementation prototype within the community as open source.

In addition, botnets such as the one built by the *DroidDream* malware in 2011 are an emerging mobile trend [18]. We also aim at extending our previous work [8] for quantifying compliant network nodes involved in distributed vulnerabilities in order to describe massive attack scenarios within mobile environments. Finally, we state that real autonomy can be achieved if mobile devices are capable of closing the vulnerability lifecycle by performing corrective tasks as well. In that context, we also plan to analyze remediation strategies for correcting vulnerable configurations, leading us closer to get real autonomic solutions.

Acknowledgements This work was partially supported by the EU FP7 Univerself Project and the FI-WARE PPP.

References

1. Ahmed, M.S., Al-Shaer, E., Taibah, M.M., Abedin, M., Khan, L.: Towards autonomic risk-aware security configuration. In: Proceedings of the IEEE Network Operations and Management Symposium (NOMS'08), Salvador, Apr 2008, pp. 722–725
2. Android: http://www.android.com/. Cited Aug 2012
3. Android Developers: http://developer.android.com/. Cited Aug 2012
4. Apple iOS: http://www.apple.com/ios/. Cited Aug 2012
5. Banghart, J., Johnson, C.: The Technical Specification for the Security Content Automation Protocol (SCAP). NIST Special Publication. U.S. Department of Commerce, National Institute of Standards and Technology, Gaithersburg (2009)
6. Barrère, M., Badonnel, R., Festor, O.: Supporting vulnerability awareness in autonomic networks and systems with OVAL. In: Proceedings of the 7th IEEE International Conference on Network and Service Management (CNSM'11), Paris, Oct 2011
7. Barrère, M., Betarte, G., Rodríguez, M.: Towards machine-assisted formal procedures for the collection of digital evidence. In: Proceedings of the 9th Annual International Conference on Privacy, Security and Trust (PST'11), Montreal, July 2011, pp. 32–35
8. Barrère, M., Badonnel, R., Festor, O.: Towards the assessment of distributed vulnerabilities in autonomic networks and systems. In: Proceedings of the IEEE/IFIP Network Operations and Management Symposium (NOMS'12), Maui, Apr 2012
9. Bartel, A., Klein, J., Monperrus, M., Traon, Y.L.: Automatically securing permission-based software by reducing the attack surface: an application to Android. CoRR abs/1206.5829 (2012)
10. Dalvik Virtual Machine: http://www.dalvikvm.com/. Cited Aug 2012
11. Enck, W., Ongtang, M., McDaniel, P.: Understanding Android security. IEEE Secur. Priv. 7(1), 50–57 (2009)
12. Enck, W., Octeau, D., McDaniel, P., Chaudhuri, S.: A study of Android application security. In: Proceedings of the 20th USENIX Conference on Security (SEC'11), San Francisco. USENIX Association (2011)
13. Felt, A.P., Finifter, M., Chin, E., Hanna, S., Wagner, D.: A survey of mobile malware in the wild. In: Proceedings of the 1st ACM Workshop on Security and Privacy in Smartphones and Mobile Devices (SPSM'11), Chicago, Oct 2011
14. Frei, S., Schatzmann, D., Plattner, B., Trammel, B.: Modelling the security ecosystem – the dynamics of (In)Security. In: Proceedings of the Workshop on the Economics of Information Security (WEIS'09), London, June 2009
15. Gartner: http://www.gartner.com/. Cited Aug 2012

16. Java Architecture for XML Binding: http://java.sun.com/developer/technicalArticles/\WebServices/jaxb/. Cited Aug 2012
17. Li, S.: Juxtapp and DStruct: detection of similarity among Android applications. Master's thesis, EECS Department, University of California, Berkeley, May 2012
18. Lookout Mobile Security: https://www.mylookout.com/mobile-threat-report. Cited Aug 2012
19. MITRE Corporation: http://www.mitre.org/. Cited Aug 2012
20. NIST, National Institute of Standards and Technology: http://www.nist.gov/. Cited Aug 2012
21. Norton Mobile Security: http://us.norton.com/norton-mobile-security/. Cited Aug 2012
22. Open Handset Alliance: http://www.openhandsetalliance.com/. Cited Aug 2012
23. Ou, X., Govindavajhala, S., Appel, A.W.: MulVAL: a logic-based network security analyzer. In: On USENIX Security, Baltimore, 2005
24. Ovaldi: The OVAL Interpreter Reference Implementation. http://oval.mitre.org/language/interpreter.html. Cited Aug 2012
25. The Java Platform: http://www.oracle.com/technetwork/java/. Cited Aug 2012
26. The OVAL Language: http://oval.mitre.org/. Cited Aug 2012
27. Shabtai, A., Fledel, Y., Kanonov, U., Elovici, Y., Dolev, S., Glezer, C.: Google Android: a comprehensive security assessment. IEEE Secur. Priv. **8**(2), 35–44 (2010)
28. Strassen, V.: Gaussian elimination is not optimal. Numer. Math. **13**, 354–356 (1969). doi:10.1007/BF02165411
29. Vidas, T., Votipka, D., Christin, N.: All your droid are belong to Us: a survey of current Android attacks. In: Proceedings of the 5th USENIX Conference on Offensive Technologies (WOOT'11), San Francisco, pp. 10–10. USENIX Association (2011)
30. VulnXML:http://www.oasis-open.org/committees/download.php/7145/AVDL\protect\kern+.1667em\relax%20\Specification\protect\kern+.1667em\relax%20V1.pdf. Cited Aug 2012
31. X-Ray for Android: http://www.xray.io/. Cited Aug 2012
32. Ziring, N., Quinn, S.D.: Specification for the Extensible Configuration Checklist Description Format (XCCDF). NIST Special Publication. U.S. Department of Commerce, National Institute of Standards and Technology, Gaithersburg (2012)

Chapter 4
A Declarative Logic-Based Approach for Threat Analysis of Advanced Metering Infrastructure

Mohammad Ashiqur Rahman and Ehab Al-Shaer

Abstract The Advanced Metering Infrastructure (AMI) is the core component in a smart grid. It exhibits highly complex heterogeneous network configurations comprising of different cyber-physical components. These components are inter-connected through different communication media, protocols, and secure tunnels, and are operated using different modes of data delivery and security policies. The inherent complexity and heterogeneity in AMI significantly increase the potential of security threats due to misconfiguration or attacks, which can cause devastating damage to AMI. Therefore, creating a formal model that can represent the global behavior based on AMI configuration is evidently essential to verify, evaluate and harden its capabilities against dormant security threats. In this paper, we present a novel declarative logic approach for analyzing AMI configurations against various security threats. We develop a tool, called *AMISecChecker*, which offers manifold contributions: (i) modeling of AMI components' configurations and their interactions based on property level abstraction; (ii) modeling of AMI topology and communication properties; and (iii) verifying the compliance of AMI configuration with security control guidelines. The efficacy and scalability of the tool have been evaluated in real and synthetic test networks.

4.1 Introduction

Smart grid provides many innovative energy management services that offer efficiency, reliability, and cost-reduction both customers and providers. Considering the potential market of smart grid, it is likely to be the most widely deployed critical infrastructures in the twenty-first century. The advent and use of advanced smart metering infrastructure (AMI) [3] in smart grid enable energy service providers as

M.A. Rahman (✉) • E. Al-Shaer
University of North Carolina at Charlotte, Charlotte, NC, USA
e-mail: mrahman4@uncc.com; ealshaer@uncc.com

E. Al-Shaer et al. (eds.), *Automated Security Management*,
DOI 10.1007/978-3-319-01433-3_4, © Springer International Publishing Switzerland 2013

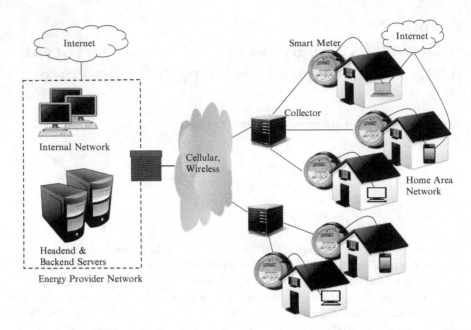

Fig. 4.1 A typical smart grid network

well as end-users to monitor and control power consumption remotely via smart meters and intelligent collectors. Unlike traditional networks, the operations and controls in AMI depends on a highly complex network configuration comprising varieties of heterogeneous wired/wireless networks, different modes of data deliveries, and alternative security polices. In addition, AMI can be connected to the Internet via headend system and home area network (HAN) to allow energy service providers and users, respectively, to program smart grid features. Figure 4.1 shows a typical AMI network. Security attacks on such networks have the potential to cause critical damages including power outages and destruction of electrical equipments [9, 11].

From the perspective of security, AMI smart grid networks are complex, because they require integration/interdependencies of multiple heterogeneous components with different security requirements. These networks may involve potential misconfigurations and different security threats (like denial of service, jamming, violation of boundary protection, etc.) depending on new critical services and cross-network inter-dependencies. Thus, there is a need of an automated security analysis and verification tool for identifying various misconfiguration problems and security threats in AMI smart grid. The verification of AMI configuration is complicated due to the large size of the network. Thus, an efficient formal abstraction model should include only the necessary details to verify the desired safety and security properties avoiding state explosion. In this paper, we present a declarative tool, called *AMISecChecker* that offers the following:

- Providing a model abstraction capable of representing millions of heterogeneous AMI devices' configurations and their dependencies.
- Comprehensive identification and analysis of different devices and flow level misconfigurations.
- Systematic analysis of various potential security threats (e.g., denial of service) to AMI.

We use the declarative logic framework, Prolog to build our tool. Declarative representation of the reasoning logic allows us to understand and apply the logic easily. The review and extension, if necessary, of declarative specification are simple and uncomplicated. The efficacy of the tool has been evaluated by deploying it in real smart grid enterprise network. The reports generated by the tool can be used to correct the system operations and security for the future provable threats. To achieve better scalability, our model will be devised based on property level abstraction.

The rest of the paper is organized as follows: Sect. 4.2 describes the background and security challenges of AMI smart grid. We present the architecture and functional description of AMISecChecker tool in Sect. 4.3. The declarativemodeling of AMI components, network topology, and data delivery modes is presented in Sect. 4.4. The next section presents the modeling and analysis of various security controls in smart grid network. The evaluation of our tool is presented in Sect. 4.6. The related works on smart grid security modeling and analysis are describe in Sect. 4.7. Finally conclusion and future work are presented in Sect. 4.8.

4.2 Background and Challenges

4.2.1 AMI System Complexity

AMI exhibits highly complex heterogeneous configurations. AMI comprises of a large number of heterogeneous physical components, such as smart meters (SM), intelligent data collectors (IC), and cyber components, such as headend management systems (HS), firewall, IPSec, and IDS devcies, etc. These components are interconnected through heterogeneous communication media (e.g., wireless, wire, power line, etc.) and different protocols (e.g., TCP/IP, LonTalk, etc.). An AMI network involves many data stream types, such as power usage data, control commands, alarms, s/w patches that exhibit different priority and resource requirements. Unlike Internet forwarding, AMI components usually follow different modes of time-driven data delivery. Moreover, AMI network is required to be accessible from the utility network, home area network (HAN), or even from Internet.

Meters, collectors, and headend systems are the major components of AMI. Smart meters must be configured to perform security pairing with a specific data collector, establish a secure connection, monitor and report energy usage periodically, and accept control commands from headend systems to shut or limit power usage. Collectors are more complex and they are configured to collect

Meter Class	ID	Type	Patch Info	Sampling Info	Reporting Mode (to Collector)	Push Report Schedule	Ports in Service	Comm Protocol
meter	m00003	ge	pm011, pm115	s	push	15,40	nil	lontalk
meter	m00123	echelon	pm115	15, 30	push	20,30	nil	lontalk
meter	m00129	echelon	pm0115	20, 30	push	20,60	nil	lontalk

Collector Class	ID	Type	Patch Info	Buffer Info	Buffer Allocation	Reporting Mode (to Headend)	Push Schedule (to headend)	Pull Schedule (from meter)
collector	c0003	rev03	pc213, pc012	data, 9000, 1	nil	pull	nil	nil
collector	c0005	rev02	pc012	data, 8000, 1	nil	push	300, 14400	nil

Collector Class	ID	Connected Meters	Connected Headend	Link (to Meter)	Ports in Service	Comm Protocol
collector	c0003	m00003,5; m00123,4	hs001	powerline1	22, 53, 161, 222	lontalk, ip
collector	c0005	m00003,5; m00129,5	hs001	powerline1	22, 53, 161, 222	lontalk, ip

Headend Class	ID	Type	OS	Patch Info	Pull Schedule (from Collector)	Ports in Service	Comm Protocol
headend	hs001	nil	win2010	p357, p254	180, 2880	22, 53, 161	ip

Zone	ID	IP Address	Members	Gateway
zone	zc101	150.24.1.0/24	c0003,200; c0005,220	v1
zone	zc102	150.24.2.0/24	c0003, 400	v1
zone	zhs101	172.16.0.0/16	hs001, 2	r2

Fig. 4.2 An example data of AMI topology configuration

data report from a group of smart meters, establish secure connection with a headend, forward data to the headend. On the other way, they forward commands to the smart meters from the headend. There are two data delivery modes used between meter and collector, and between collector and headend: (i) *Pull-driven* in which meter or collector only reports data upon request, and (ii) *Push-driven* in which meter or collector reports data periodically based on pre-configured delivery schedule. In the first case, requests are usually sent periodically following some schedules. In AMI network different security devices, such as firewall, IPSec, and IDS devices are deployed to control flow of traffics throughout the network. Firewall can be configured to limit the traffic flows to some bounds. An example of AMI configuration is presented in Fig. 4.2, which shows the operational and security properties of different AMI components.

4.2.2   Potential Threats in AMI

The inherent complexity of integrating multiple heterogeneous systems in AMI significantly increases the potential of network security threats, which can cause massive and extremely devastating damage. There are two main sources of threats in AMI [3, 12]. First is the *misconfiguration* that might cause inconsistency, unreachability, broken secure tunnels, improper data scheduling, improper boundary protection and traffic access control. Recent studies show that 65–70 % of security vulnerabilities are due to misconfiguration errors in traditional networks. Second is the *weak (or absence of) security controls* that can cause cascaded cyber attacks, such as scanning, denial of service (DoS), jamming, etc. Threats might come due to *operational errors*, which are similar to misconfiguration. As an example of physical misconfigurations that might lead to cyber breakdown is inappropriate data delivery scheduling of millions of smart meters. If the data delivery is request-driven rather than time-driven, then operational error, such as requesting of data from a large number of collectors at once or sending patch data at the time of requesting report, can create problems too. These may, in turn, result flooding on headend or communication links. Cyber attacks can propagate to physical AMI components causing massive power instability and outages.

Researchers have proposed different network security analysis tools [1, 13] using formal methods. These tools concentrate on misconfiguration problems in traditional networks and do not model complex heterogeneous configurations like time-driven data forwarding and different security controls in smart grid. Again, the manual enforcement or compliance analysis of a large number of security controls is overwhelming and can be potentially inaccurate due to human errors. Hence, the objective of this work is to build an automated tool for analyzing various security threats and misconfiguration problems in AMI smart grid.

4.3   AMISecChecker Architecture

The AMISecChecker is an automated security analysis tool for verifying AMI smart grid configurations. The basic architecture of the tool has been presented in Fig. 4.3. Firstly, the tool takes the *AMI configuration* and *security guidelines* as inputs to generate a declarative model of the global AMI configuration and various security controls. The users can input the *configuration* based on AMI device profiles, topology, abstraction, communication media, security properties,

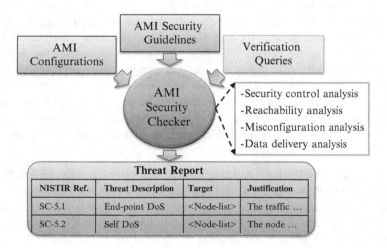

Fig. 4.3 AMISecChecker architecture

and traffic scheduling. Here, we apply property-level abstraction that exploits
the correlations between the configuration parameters of different AMI devices.
Figure 4.2 shows an example of AMI configuration. The tool then checks for any
violation of different security controls in the network. These security controls follow
NISTIR 7628 security guidelines [12]. AMISecChecker also allows administrators
to verify different misconfiguration problems (such as, reachability under different
constraints, flow scheduling, etc.) depending on organizational security policy.

The tool finally generates a report based on the analysis describing the attack
targets and sources, and the reasonings of the attacks. This will in turn help the
administrators in debugging complex AMI configurations and allow selectively
performing penetration tests on AMI network.

4.4 AMI Configuration Model

AMI network consists of different types of terminal devices (e.g., meters, collectors,
headend systems, and backend servers), routing and security devices (e.g., routers
and firewalls), communication links, etc. In this section, we formalize these
components according to their configurations using Prolog declarative logic. Since
the number of terminals is very large, we formalize these devices using abstraction
to make the model scalable.

4.4.1 AMI Physical Components

Smart Meter: A group of smart meters with similar properties is represented by a
meter class using the predicate `meterProfile`. Each meter class is identified
by a unique *ID*. The meter type (especially the vendor type) is represented by
type. *Reporting-mode* denotes the reporting mode of the meter, which can be either
passive (pull) or *active* (push). The *transmission-rate* represents the maximum
rate of traffic (in Mbps) in which a meter can transmit. The parameter *sampling-
rate* consists of two components: *sample-size* (in KB) and *sampling-interval* (in
seconds). Though there can be a list of patches installed in a meter, we simplify
by modeling the patch-information as boolean (*patch-status*) denoting whether the
meter is correctly patched or not. An example of a meter class *m*001 is shown in
Table 4.1.

Intelligent Data Collector: A class of data collectors is represented by *collectorProfile* (as shown in Table 4.1), which consists of *ID*, *type*, *patch-status*,
reporting-mode, *transmission-rate*, *connected-meters* and *link-to-meter*. *Connected-
meters* represents the IDs of the meter classes connected to the collector along
with their counts. *Link-to-meter* denotes the type of the communication link to a
meter. For a particular collector, the links to the meters are assumed to be of the

Table 4.1 Modeling of AMI

Meter Profile:
```
meterProfile(m00003,ge,yes,[18,40],
  active,nil,[lontalk]).
```

Collector Profile:
```
collectorProfile(c0003,rev03,yes,
  passive,[[m00003,5],[m00123,4]],
  powerline1,[22,53,161,222],
  [lontalk,ip]).
bufferConfig(c0003,[[data,9000,1]],
  nil).
```

Headend Profile:
```
headendProfile(hs001,nil,
  'win2010',yes,[22,53,161],[ip]).
```

Zone:
```
zone(zc101,[[150,24,1,0],24],
  [[c0003,200],[c0005,220]],v1]).
collectorHeadendPair(zc101,zh101]).
```

Data Reporting Schedule:
```
reportSchedule(m00003,15,40).
```

Data Requesting Schedule:
```
reportRequestSchedule(hs001,180,2880).
```

Authentication Profile:
```
authProfile(auth1,sha1,96).
authProfile(auth2,sha1,160).
```

Authentication Property:
```
authProperty(m00123,m00123,_,auth0).
authProperty(c0003,c0003,m00123,auth1).
```

---

same type. A collector has buffers for storing the data from the meters. The predicate `bufferConfig` represents the buffer configuration for a collector. It consists of two arguments, namely, *buffer-info* and *flow-schedule*. *Buffer-info* includes the *buffer-ID*, *buffer-size* and a *weight*. Here, *weight* associated with a specific buffer indicates the fraction of the transmitted traffic that will be scheduled from this buffer. This actually represents the priority among the buffers, if there are more than one. *Flow-schedule* is a list showing the assignments of different flows to output buffers. If only one buffer exists in a collector, then this is not required.

Headend System: A headend system class profile is represented by headendProfile consisting of *ID*, *type*, *OS*, *patch-status* and *transmission-rate*. *OS* is the operating system of the headend system, which helps to know possible vulnerabilities (which are common to that OS) and necessary patches.

Hosts: AMI smart grid network contains different kinds of hosts: (1) enterprise internal hosts, (2) enterprise application servers (backend systems), (3) hosts from HAN (enterprise clients), and (4) external hosts from Internet. These hosts are modeled similar to the headend system.

Routing and Security Devices: We model router, firewall, and IPSec device and their policies similar to the work [6]. In the case of firewall, we only add traffic limit in firewall rule assuming that firewall can act as a traffic limiter for controlling specific traffic flows.

4.4.2 AMI Network Topology

We adopt the concept of network zones in order to model the large number of AMI devices. While this concept is considered mainly for meters and collectors, we apply the same for all AMI devices, so that we can have identical models for them. We also model links and domains to represent AMI topology.

Zone: We define *zone* (refer to Table 4.1) as a collection of similar terminal devices. The predicate zone comprises of *ID*, *IP-address*, *connected-devices*, and *gateway*. A zone *IP-address* (usually a subnet IP) covers all the devices within the zone. Argument *connected-devices* identifies the classes of the devices residing in the zone along with their numbers. A zone can have a single device only, which might be useful for granular level of analysis. The argument *gateway* represents the gateway router connected to the devices of the zone. We also define a predicate collectorHeadendPair, particularly for the zones of collectors, to denote the report-delivery relation between a collector class and a headend system class. This takes two arguments: *collector-zone* and *headend-zone*.

Link: Each link is represented by a *node-pair*, *link-status* (i.e., up or down) and *link-type* using the predicate link. The *link-type* basically binds the specified link to a predicate linkProperty. The linkProperty defines the *media-type*, *shared-status*, *channel-mode*, *bandwidth* (in Mbps), and *miscellaneous*. Argument *shared-status* denotes whether the link is shared media or not. The argument *miscellaneous* is a list consisting of special properties based on media type. For example, in the case of *wireless* media type, it consists of *license-status*, *signal-range*.

Domain: A domain defines a logical collection of network devices. For example, all of the meters in the AMI network are considered as a single domain. We define a rule domain that takes *domain-name* and a *device-class* as arguments and results whether the device-class falls in that domain. We also define predicates attackDomain and targetDomain to denotes the expected attack sources and victims respectively. These predicates guide the threat analysis showing the possible targets and sources of attacks.

4.4.3 AMI Data Delivery Modes

AMI devices usually follow one of the data delivery modes: *pull-driven* and *push-driven* modes. In the case of *push-driven* mode, a device reports based on its own time schedule. This property has been modeled using the fact, reportSchedule with *reporting-node, base-time* and *interval* arguments. This predicate indicates that the reporting device will report periodically starting from the base time. In the case of *pull-driven* mode, a meter or collector is requested for data, which is accordingly delivered to the requesting node. Here, the requesting device usually generates request following a time schedule. This has been modeled using the predicate reportRequestSchedule, which takes *requesting-node, base-time* and *interval*. The node to which a device will report or request for report depends on the argument *connected-meters* in collectorProfile (in the case of reporting from meters to collectors) or collectorHeadendPair (in the case of reporting from collectors to headend systems).

4.4.4 Miscellaneous Modeling

The communication to or from AMI devices usually follow different authentication and encryption properties to achieve end-to-end security in the network. We model different authentication protocols (refer to Table 4.1) using authProfile predicate that consists of *auth-ID, auth-algorithm* and *key-length*. The authentication property of a node have been represented using authProperty predicate. It consists *device-ID, source-ID, destination-ID* and *auth-ID*. To achieve authenticated communication, the communicating devices must agree with their authentication property. Similar to authentication, encryptProfile and encryptProperty predicates are defined to model encrypted communication.

We model the flow policy of the enterprise smart grid network to establish appropriate resource allocation (i.e., priority) for different flows. This policy is modeled using the predicate, smartGridFlowPolicy consisting of *destination, destnation-port, protocol, flow-name* and *flow-priority*).

4.5 AMI Threat Analysis

The analysis of potential threats in AMI is classified into two categories: (i) AMI configuration analysis, and (ii) security control analysis.

4.5.1 AMI Configuration Analysis

In this section we model the assured data delivery operation along with some potential threats due to misconfiguration.

4.5.1.1 Reachability Analysis

Reachability must hold between a pair of devices, if data is required to transmit between them. This analysis is the core for determining various threats. It verifies different possible misconfigurations: (i) topological, (ii) cryptographic protocol mismatch; and (iii) access control violation. For example, although there are 4 m of $m000123$ class connected with $c0003$ collector (in Fig. 4.2), they will fail to report to the collector as authentication fails due to protocol mismatch ($auth0$ and $auth1$, refer to Table 4.1). The traffic reachability is evaluated between a source-destination pair considering various security device policy configurations as well as authentication and encryption profiles. Thus, a traffic Tr is reachable from source node S to destination node D, iff (i) there exists a path from S to D; (ii) S and D follow appropriate authentication/encryption profile; and (iii) Tr is allowed along the path through security devices (say, firewall).

4.5.1.2 Data Delivery Analysis

We evaluate data reporting between different devices based on traffic reachability and data delivery modes. A particular reporting time *reportTime* is computed by getTimeToReport from *time-bound*. The parameter *time-bound* indicates that within this time bound (typically in seconds) the latest reporting is occurred at *report-time*. The definition of getTimeToReport is shown in Table 4.2. The predicate isActive checks whether S follows push-driven delivery. The predicate timeToReport utilizes the reportSchedule predicate (refer to Sect. 4.4.3) to calculate the *reporting-time* T closest to the *time-bound* TT. This has been calculated by checking the *basetime*, *interval* specified in reportSchedule. The predicate isPassive checks whether S follows pull-driven delivery or not. In this case, the predicate timeToRequestReport is invoked, which uses reportRequestSchedule predicate to compute the reporting time. The predicate canReport defines that S reports to D successfully at T (closest to TT). It invokes getTimeToReport to get T and canReach to check if *traffic* is reachable from S to D.

We also evaluate the successful delivery of reports from a smart meter to a headend system through a collector. We model this functionality using the predicate isReportDelivered presented in Table 4.2. We consider that a meter report

Table 4.2 Modeling of threats based on AMI configuration

Reporting Time:
```
getTimeToReport(S,D,TT,T):-
  isReportTo(S,D),
  (isActive(S),timeToReport(S,TT,T));
   (isPassive(S),timeToRequestReport(D,S,TT,T)).
```

Report Delivery:
```
canReport(S,D,TT,T):-
  Traffic=[S,SP,D,DP,P],
  getFlowByType(Traffic,report),
  getTimeToReport(S,D,TT,T),canReach(Traffic,_,_).
```

Report Delivery from a Meter to a Headend:
```
isReportDelivered(M,H,TT,T1,T):-
  isMeter(M),isHeadend(H),isIC(C),
  canReport(C,H,TT,T),canReport(M,C,T,T1).
```

Potential Data Overwriting in Collector Buffer:
```
isDataOverwritten(N):-
  isIC(N),getReportInterval(N,Interval),
  getAggMeterReportSize(N,Interval,B1),
  getReportBufferSize(N,B2),B1>B2.
```

Report Delivery that does not Face Overwriting:
```
isReportDeliveredSafely(M,H,T1,T):-
  isMeter(M),isHeadend(H),isIC(C),
  canReport(C,H,T,T),canReport(M,C,T1,T1),
  T1<T,Interval is T-T1,
  getAggMeterReportSize(C,Interval,B1),
  getReportBufferSize(C,B2),B1<B2.
```

Potential Data Loss due to Collector Transmission Rate Limitation:
```
isTxRateOverflow(N):-
  isIC(N),getReportInterval(N,Interval),
  getAggMeterReportRate(N,Interval,TxR1),
  getTxRate(N,TxR2),TxR1>TxR2.
```

will be successfully delivered to a headend if the following sequences occur: (i) Meter successfully reports to the collector at time T following its report schedule; and (ii) collector successfully reports to the headend at time $T1$ following the collector's report schedule; and (iii) $T \leq T1 \leq TT$ and this relation is the closest to time-bound TT.

4.5.1.3 Schedule Misconfiguration Analysis

Data may be lost in AMI devices, especially in a collector due to asynchronous report schedules. For example, in Fig. 4.2, $c0005$ collector receives reports from 5 m of $m00129$ class (sampling rate: 20 KB/30 s) and 5 of $m0003$ class (sampling rate: 18 KB/40 s). Therefore, $c0005$ will receive 335 KB (average) data in every 60 s, which is to be stored in its buffer. Now, based on the report schedule, collector pushes the data to headend in every 1,440 s. Thus, in this period, in an aggregate 8,040 KB data will be sent to the collector by these meters. This amount of data will flood the collector buffer (size 80,000 KB), which will in turn cause data loss (i.e., initial 40 KB report data will be overwritten). This is modeled using the predicate isDataOverwrite, which is shown in Table 4.2. Here, getReportInterval predicate finds the request/report interval for the node N. The getAggregateReportSize predicate calculates the aggregate report size of all reporting nodes (specified in a list HList) to node N during this Interval. Finally, the isDataoverwrite predicate checks whether the transmitted data is greater than the buffer size of N.

    Similarly, we define the predicate isTxRateOverflow to model the data loss that may happen due to excessive incoming data to a collector from the meters associated to the collector. If the maximum possible transmission rate (towards the headend) of the collector is lower than the incoming data rate, then part of the data will be dropped in the collector.

4.5.2 AMI Security Control Analysis

The *AMISecChecker* models and evaluates different security controls based on NISTIR [12] guidelines. In this subsection, we mainly discuss two important threat types: DoS attacks and violations of boundary protection.

4.5.2.1 Analyzing DoS Attacks

Internal/External hosts can launch denial of service attacks to different AMI components (i.e., IC, HS, etc.) by sending large amount of traffic to the target end-point devices. DoS attacks in AMI can be classified into two categories: *Cyber DoS*, and *Self DoS*. First kind is the common DoS attacks found in the traditional networks. Self-DoS may happen between AMI devices (especially between collectors and headend) due to misconfiguration in report scheduling. This problem is similar to endpoint DoS or link DoS except for the fact that here the attack sources are legitimate AMI nodes. In Table 4.3, we present a modeling of self DoS attack on link. Since reporting usually follows TCP protocol, we here intend to find potential congestions. In this case, data delivery faces unexpected delay, which may end up with data loss at the end-points. We model this control using the predicate

Table 4.3 Modeling of threats based on AMI security controls

```
Self (TCP-based) DoS on Link:
findSelfLinkDoS(_,[],_,_):- fail.
findSelfLinkDoS(N,[S|HList],PPath,PRTx):-
  Tr=[S,SP,N,NP,tcp],getFlowByType(Tr,report),
  canReach(Tr,Path,_,_),
  getMinReportRate(N,RTx),
  getSharedPath(PPath,Path,SPath),
  getAggRTx(PRTx,RTx,AggRTx),
  (isLinkOverflow(SPath,AggRTx)-> true;
    (findSelfLinkDoS(N,HList,nil,0);
      (isNotEmpty(SPath),
        findSelfLinkDoS(N,HList,SPath,AggRTx)))).
isSelfLinkDoS(N):-
  isHeadend(N),isTime(TT),
  findall(H,(isIC(H),
    getTimeToReport(H,N,TT,T)),HList),
  findSelfLinkDoS(N,HList,nil,0).
```

```
Boundary Protection Violation:
isBoundarySecurityViolation(Dm,Dm1):-
  domainMember(N,Dm), domainMember(N1,Dm1),
  Tr=[N,_,N1,_,_],canReach(Tr,Path,_,_),
  isSecurityDeviceNotExist(Path).

Boundary Encryption Protection Violation:
isBoundaryAuthenticationViolation(Dm,Dm1):-
  domainMember(N,Dm), domainMember(N1,Dm1),
  Tr=[N,_,N1,_,_],canReach(Tr,_,SecPath,_),
  isAuthenticationNotExist(SecPath).
```

isSelfLinkDoS. In this case, the aggregate report rate from a collection of collectors, who have the same reporting time, exceeds a link bandwidth along the shared path to the end node. We model this threat considering a minimum acceptable report rate (i.e., the maximum acceptable reporting delay) from the collectors to the headend. The predicate getMinReportRate is invoked for this purpose.

4.5.2.2 Analyzing Violation of Boundary Protection

In this control, we check whether communication between different boundaries in AMI network are protected with security devices (i.e., Firewalls, IDS, IPSec etc.) and appropriate authentication and data encryption methods. The predicate isBoundarySecurityViolation checks for security devices between two boundaries and returns true if no security device exists in any path between these boundaries. It invokes `isSecurityDeviceNotExist` to checks if there is no security device in the path (between the given pair of nodes) by searching security devices along the path (achieved from `canReach`). Similarly, we check whether their exists authentication and encryption between a boundary pair. Modeling of these predicates are shown in Table 4.3.

4.5.2.3 Miscellaneous Threat Analysis

We also model several other security controls. One of these controls is the *verification of the buffer priority configuration*, especially, of a collector. It checks if multiple buffers with correct priority settings do exist in the collector. The predicate `bufferConfig` and `smartGridFlowPolicy` are utilized for this verification. Another one of the controls that we model is the identification of potential *link (wireless) jamming*. In this modeling, we utilize the topology (i.e., `link` predicate) and link properties (i.e., `linkProperty`). Here we checks whether there exists any license-free and high-bandwidth wireless link along the path towards a target node (especially the path from meters to a collector or collectors to a headend). This scenario can potentially launch Jamming attack to the wireless link.

4.6 Implementation and Evaluation

The proposed *AMIAnalzer* tool has been implemented using SWI Prolog. A parser has been developed for parsing the smart grid network configuration templates. It reads the configuration data from an Excel file (CSV format) as shown in Fig. 4.2 and generates corresponding Prolog facts. *AMISecChecker* takes this facts as inputs, and produces a threat report based on the verification results. We have evaluated our *AMISecChecker* tool in terms of *efficacy* and *scalability*.

4.6.1 Efficacy

We evaluate our tool with the ground truth scenarios deploying it in a small AMI testbed created in our university [2]. The testbed setup represents a small subset of the network shown in Fig. 4.1. We analyze data overwrite and DoS threats. The results of our tool are cross-validated with the real scenario. For the purpose of analysis we slide different configuration parameters, such as taking very low bandwidth links or changing pull schedule interval of headend system very high, and find data loss and DoS attacks. In addition, we inject high amount of data by simulation (i.e., adding multiple simulated collectors in the testbed) to observe its effect on link bandwidth. After observing the constraint violations, we reconfigure the setup based on the reasoning shown by the reports, and reevaluate the constraint to see the effect. For example, in the case of link flooding, we add traffic limit in firewall rules and observe resolving of the attack. These real tests significantly help us in verifying the accuracy of the tool. The efficacy of the tool is also evaluated by deploying it in an enterprise smart grid network and running different configurations by extensively varying the number of nodes and configuration parameters.

4.6.2   Scalability

The scalability of the *AMISecChecker* tool has been evaluated by analyzing the security controls with varying AMI network sizes. We consider the network size as the total number of smart meters since the number of data collectors is proportional to that of meters. We vary the number of collector zones, which varies the number of meters (one to five millions). We assume 5 m classes and 5 collector classes while 1 headend class. Each collector zone consists of 500 collectors and each collector is associated with 10 m on average. In a zone, we take a random number of collector classes.

Impact of network size on analysis time: Figure 4.4a shows the analysis times for the security control compliance checking for DoS attacks and boundary protection. The analysis time increases almost quadratically with the increase of network size. This is because of the fact that we analyze these threats for all possible AMI target nodes. If the number of zones increases, the number of potential target nodes increases. Remember that we denote a target/source using a class name and a zone. Overall, for 2,500,000 m, the analysis time lies within 30 s, which is reasonably good for large-scale enterprise smart grid. We also show the analysis time of a single execution of each of these queries in Fig. 4.4b. It also shows that the analysis time increases with the network size, but here the increase is sublinear. The number of predicates, a query requires to cover for a particular evaluation, merely increases with the increase of network size. However, the time still increases because of the increase of total number of predicates, which in turn increases execution time. In all of the cases, the query for boundary protection violation takes smaller time than other two. Because, there is a small number of domains and the query satisfies if security violation is found between any two nodes of the domains.

Impact of zone size on analysis time: Figure 4.4c shows that the analysis time reduces exponentially if we increase the number of members (here collectors) in the zone. Because, if the size of a zone increases, the number of zones decreases and so does the number of potential targets for evaluation.

Impact of number of classes on analysis time: We have evaluated the security controls by changing the similarities between different devices, that is, by changing the number of device classes without changing the total number of nodes in the system. The evaluation result (Fig. 4.4d) shows that the analysis time significantly increases as the number of classes increases (i.e., similarity reduces).

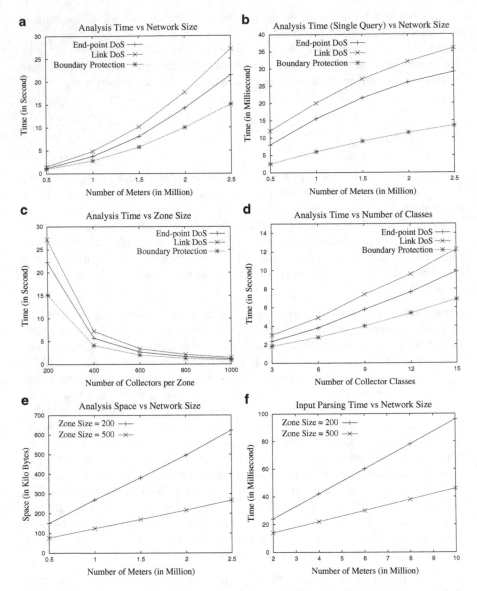

Fig. 4.4 (**a**) Impact of network size on total analysis time, (**b**) impact of network size on analysis time (single query), (**c**) impact of zone size on analysis time, (**d**) impact of number of classes on analysis time, (**e**) space requirement w.r.t. network size, and (**f**) parsing time w.r.t. network size

Space requirement for modeling: The space requirement (mainly memory used for predicate database) in Prolog is evaluated by changing the network size (i.e., the number of zones). Such analysis results are shown in Fig. 4.4e. We observe that the space requirement increases linearly with the network size. As the number of zones increases, the number of predicates increases and so does the space. However, compared to the number of meters, the increase in the number of zones are significantly low. That's why for a big network, our tool does not cost high memory space. In the figure, the space requirement is shown for two different zone sizes. We find that network with smaller zone size requires larger memory space than that of with higher zone size. The reason obviously is that the number of zones in the latter case is two times less than that in the former case.

Parsing time: We have evaluated the time required for parsing an input configuration (given in CSV format) with respect to the total number of nodes in the system. The evaluation result (Fig. 4.4f) shows that the analysis time increases linearly with the number of classes. The reason is similar to that of the space requirement.

4.7 Related Work

Throughout the last decade, significant amount of works [3, 12] have been initiated on describing the interoperability among heterogeneous smart grid components including security issues based on different attack scenarios. These works also describe the operational functionalities of AMI components and energy providers internal system with guidelines for secured communication between them.

McDaniel and Smith [9] and McLaughlin et al. [10] present the security and privacy challenges in smart grid networks. This work reports that energy usage information stored at the meter and distributed thereafter acts as an information-rich side channel, exposing customer behaviors. Thus, appropriate security policies need to be enforced for communication between the home users and energy providers' internal system. Wang et al. [14] presents an artificial intelligent based approach for analyzing risks in smart grid networks. Anwar et al. present couple of frameworks [4,5] for modeling a power grid and its control elements using first order logic. These frameworks are capable of evaluating energy flows and overloading problems in smart grid networks. Liu et al. [8] presents a study on false data injection attacks in power grid. McLaughlin et al. [11] present an approach for penetration testing on AMI systems. They develop concrete attack trees for energy fraud, denial of service, and targeted disconnect attacks. However, these works do not analyze various misconfiguration problems and security controls (such as report-schedule misconfiguration, authentication, and integrity violation, DoS, self-DoS, etc.) on power grid networks.

Researchers have proposed different network security analysis tools [1, 13] using formal methods and logic programming. These tools concentrate on misconfiguration problems in traditional networks. However, this work is for general purpose networks and thus do not model heterogeneous configurations and different security controls in smart grid. In [7], we presented a security analysis of AMI Smart Grid based on propositional logic. Though the work addressed the threats in AMI as a constraint violations, the model was built using SMT based propositional logic, where we required to consider many assumptions (bounds or normalizations) on the properties values. In this paper, we present declarative approach to model AMI configuration and associated threats in declarative logic (i.e., Prolog). Declarative logic is easy to understand and popular for its extensibility. To the best of our knowledge, this is the first work on declaratively analyzing AMI security.

4.8 Conclusion

Due to the heterogeneity in AMI device configurations and emerging security threats on it, automated analysis of AMI configuration is a challenging problem. In this work, we propose a model and develop a tool, called *AMISecChecker*, based on declarative logic for non-invasive analysis of security threats in AMI smart grid. It allows users to specify the network configurations and then analyze various type of security threats. If an attack is found, the tool generates a report describing the attack sources and targets, and the reasoning behind the attack. The efficacy and scalability of the tool have been evaluated in different test networks. We use property level abstraction in the model to achieve the scalability in the analysis. *AMISecChecker* has been tested by deploying it in an enterprise AMI network. In future, we plan to explore the modeling of more security controls as well as AMI interactions with other smart grid components, such as distribution automation systems.

Acknowledgements It is a pleasure to thank the Engineers of Duke Energy Corp. for their feedback and support in design and evaluation of our tool. We would also like to thank Mohammad Mazumdar, MphasiS Corp., Texas, for his precious editorial help.

References

1. Al-Shaer, E., Marrero, W., El-Atawy, A., Elbadawi, K.: Network configuration in a box: towards end-to-end verification of network reachability and security. In: IEEE International Conference on Network Protocols, Princeton (2009)
2. Ami smart grid testbed at UNC Charlotte: http://www.cyberdna.uncc.edu/events.php
3. Ami system security requirements: volume 1.01: AMI-SEC Task Force, pp. 84–89 (1991). Available in http://osgug.ucaiug.org/utilisec/amisec/
4. Anwar, Z., Campbell, R.: Automated assessment of critical infrastructures for compliance to (cip) best practice. In: The 2nd IFIP WG 11.10 International Conference on Critical Infrastructure Protection, Arlington (2008)
5. Anwar, Z., Shankesi, R., Campbell, R.: Automatic security assessment of critical cyber-infrastructures. In: IEEE/IFIP International Conference on Dependable Systems and Networks, Anchorage (2008)
6. Ashiqur Rahman, M., Al-Shaer, E.: A declarative approach for global network security configuration verification and evaluation. In: IM Miniconference (2011)
7. Ashiqur Rahman, M., Al-Shaer, E., Bera, P.: Smartanalyzer: a noninvasive security threat analyzer for ami smart grid. In: The 31st IEEE International Conference on Computer Communications, Orlando (2012)
8. Liu, Y., Ning, P., Reiter, M.K.: False data injection attacks against state estimation in electrical power grids. In: ACM Conference on Computer and Communications Security, Chicago (2009)

9. McDaniel, P., Smith, S.W.: Security and privacy challenges in smart grid. In: IEEE Security and Privacy (2009)
10. McLaughlin, S., Podkuiko, D., McDaniel, P.: Energy theft in the advanced metering infrastructure. In: The 4th International Workshop on Critical Information Infrastructure Security, Bonn (2009)
11. McLaughlin, S., Podkuiko, D., Miadzvezhanka, S., Delozier, A., McDaniel, P.: Multi-vendor penetration testing in the advanced metering infrastructure. In: International Conference ACSAC, Austin (2010)
12. Nistir 7628: Guidelines for smart grid cyber security. Smart Grid Interoperability Panel – Cyber Security Working Group (2010)
13. Ou, X., Govindavajhala, S., Appel, A.: Mulval: a logic-based network security analyzer. In: The 14th USENIX Security Symposium, Baltimore (2005)
14. Wang, Y., Ruan, D., Xu, J., Wen, M., Deng, L.: Computational intelligence algorithms analysis for smart grid cyber security. Lect. Notes Comput. Sci. **6146**, 77–84 (1993)

Chapter 5
Risk Based Access Control Using Classification

Nazia Badar, Jaideep Vaidya, Vijayalakshmi Atluri, and Basit Shafiq

Abstract Traditional access control operates under the principle that a user's request to a specific resource is denied if there does not exist an explicit specification of the permission in the system. In many emergency and disaster management situations, access to critical information is expected because of the 'need to share', and in some cases, because of the 'responsibility to provide' information. Therefore, the importance of situational semantics cannot be underestimated when access control decisions are made. There is a need for providing access based on the (unforeseen) situation, where simply denying an access may have more deleterious effects than granting access, if the underlying risk is small. These requirements have significantly increased the demand for new access control solutions that provide flexible, yet secure access. In this paper, we quantify the risk associated with granting an access based on the technique of classification. We propose two approaches for risk-based access control. The first approach, considers only the simple access control matrix model, and evaluates the risk of granting a permission based on the existing user-permission assignments. The second assumes role-based access control, and determines the best situational role that has least risk and allows maximum permissiveness when assigned under uncertainty. We experimentally evaluate both approaches with real and synthetic datasets.

N. Badar (✉) • J. Vaidya • V. Atluri
Rutgers University, New Brunswick, NJ, USA
e-mail: nbadar@cimic.rutgers.edu; jsvaidya@cimic.rutgers.edu; atluri@cimic.rutgers.edu

B. Shafiq
Lahore University of Management Sciences, Lahore, Pakistan
e-mail: basit@lums.edu.pk

E. Al-Shaer et al. (eds.), *Automated Security Management*,
DOI 10.1007/978-3-319-01433-3_5, © Springer International Publishing Switzerland 2013

5.1 Introduction

Traditional access control operates under the principle that a user's request to a specific resource is honored if there exists an explicit policy specifying that the user is allowed to access that resource. However, there exist a number of situations in which specific user permission assignments based on the security policy cannot be a priori decidable. These may include emergency and disaster management situations where access to critical information is expected because of the 'need to share', and in some cases, because of the 'responsibility to provide' information. Therefore, there are a number of situations where there is a need to permit users to access certain needed resources, who otherwise should not have been allowed. Simply denying an access may have more deleterious effects than granting access, if the underlying risk is small. It is not an easy task – if not impossible – to envision all possible situations beforehand at the time of security policy specification, especially when complex processes are involved.

As an example, consider an access control policy pertaining to the operations of a distillation column in an Industrial system. Under normal operation, the access control policy requires that only the on duty supervisor from a local terminal of the distillation column or from a remote terminal with IP address 165.230.154.45 is authorized to close the steam valve. However, in an emergency or if there is a safety concern, other operators may need to be allowed to close the steam valve even though it is not permitted under the specified security policy. As it can be seen from the above example, the hard coded policy fails to cater to the dynamics of unexpected situations that arise.

Recently, several break glass approaches [3, 8, 14] have been proposed, that allow overriding of the existing policies in case of emergency. While traditional access control is too restrictive since it does not permit any access that has not been pre-specified in the system, the break glass approaches are too permissive in that they allow all requested accesses based on the situation at hand. Since both these are at two extremes, a fine balance between permissiveness and restrictiveness is desirable.

To accomplish this, in this paper, we present approaches to quantify the risk associated with granting an access based on the technique of classification. We propose two approaches for risk-based access control that determine whether or not to honor requests by computing the associated risk. The first approach, considers only the simple access control matrix model, and evaluates the risk of granting a permission based on the existing user-permission assignments (UPA). Essentially, a classification model is built for every permission in UPA that gives the probability of whether that permission is assigned to a user or not. When a user requests a permission which is not included in the UPA, the classification model comprising of the probabilities of the requested permission is used to compute the risk. The second approach assumes role-based access control, and determines the best situational role that has least risk and allows maximum permissiveness when assigned under uncertainty. This will also employ the classification model for risk computation. When the evaluated risk for granting a (non-existing) permission is lower than a given threshold value, the requested access is allowed. The threshold value may also vary from one situation to another. We experimentally evaluate both approaches with synthetic as well as real datasets. The effect of noise is also studied.

The remainder of the paper is organized as follows. In Sect. 5.2, we review the preliminaries needed to present our approaches. In Sect. 5.3, we present our proposed approaches to facilitate Risk Based Access Control. In Sect. 5.4 we present the experimental evaluation. In Sect. 5.5, we discuss the related work in this area. Finally, in Sect. 5.6 we provide conclusions and discuss some future directions to this line of work.

5.2 Preliminaries

In this section, we review some preliminaries that are used in the rest of the paper. Specifically, we review the Role Based Access Control (RBAC), and the Classification approach (one of the data mining techniques).

5.2.1 RBAC

Formal definition of Role Based Access Control (RBAC) that we adopted in this paper was given in [7], where RBAC is defined as follows:

- U, R, OPS and O are sets of users, roles, operations and objects respectively.
- $UA \subseteq U \times R$ is a many to many user to role assignment relation.
- P (the set of permissions) $\subseteq \{(op, o)|op \in OPS \wedge o \in O\}$
- $PA \subseteq P \times R$ is a many to many permission to role assignment relation.
- $assigned\_users(R_i) = \{U_j \in U|(U_j, R_i) \in UA\}$, the mapping of role R_i onto a set of users.
- $assigned\_permissions(R_i) = \{R_i \in R|(U_j, R_i) \in UA\}$, the mapping of role R_i onto a set of permissions.

For our presented approaches, we assume that an organization maintains its PA and UA in a form of binary matrix. UPA can be derived from existing PA and UA. We use a simple example with 10 users, 5 permissions, and 5 roles, with UPA, UA and PA as shown in Fig. 5.1a–c to explain our approaches.

5.2.2 Classification

Classification is one of the most important data mining problems, applicable in many diverse domains. Classification refers to the problem of categorizing observations into classes. Predictive modeling uses samples of data for which the

a

	P1	P2	P3	P4	P5
U1	1	1	1	0	1
U2	1	1	1	0	1
U3	0	1	1	0	1
U4	0	1	1	0	1
U5	1	1	1	0	0
U6	1	0	1	0	0
U7	1	0	0	1	1
U8	1	1	1	0	1
U9	1	1	1	0	0
U10	1	0	1	1	1

b

	R1	R2	R3	R4	R5
U1	1	1	0	0	0
U2	1	0	1	0	0
U3	0	0	1	0	0
U4	0	0	1	0	0
U5	1	0	0	0	1
U6	0	0	0	0	1
U7	0	1	0	1	0
U8	1	1	0	0	1
U9	1	0	0	0	0
U10	0	0	0	1	1

c

	P1	P2	P3	P4	P5
R1	1	1	1	0	0
R2	1	0	0	0	1
R3	0	1	1	0	1
R4	0	0	0	1	1
R5	1	0	1	0	0

Fig. 5.1 Example of UPA, UA and PA matrices. (**a**) User permission assignment (UPA). (**b**) User assignment (UA). (**c**) Permission assignment (PA)

class is known to generate a model for classifying new observations. Thus, the goal of classification is to build a model which can predict the value of one variable, based on the values of the other variables. For example, based on financial, criminal and travel data, one may want to classify passengers associated with high security risks. In the financial sector, categorizing the credit risk of customers, as well as detecting fraudulent transactions are both classification problems.

Several classification models have been proposed including: decision trees [19], PRISM [4], Naive Bayes [9, 24], Nearest Neighbor [6], Neural nets [24] and Rule based classification [1, 11]. There may be different algorithmic implementations for each classification model, for example ID3 and random trees for classification using the decision tree model. In this paper, we use classification to quantify the risk associated with an access request. We experimented with using several different classification techniques including J48 [20], RandomForest [2], and Naïve Bayes classification. We finally used the RandomForest technique with ten trees, since it is quite robust to noise. However, the proposed risk-based access control approach is agnostic to the classification model.

5.3   Risk Based Access Control

We propose two approaches for risk-based access control. The first approach, *risk based permission authorization*, considers a simple access control matrix for policy specification (only the user permission assignment is given). The second approach *risk based role authorization* assumes that role-based access control is deployed. In both these approaches, we first quantify the risk associated with the requested access, and permit access if it is less than a prespecified threshold value. Depending on the access control model being considered, the access request and authorization semantics of these approaches are different as formally stated below:

1. **Risk based permission authorization**
   Given an access request $(U_i, P_j, \{P_{i_1}, \ldots, P_{i_m}\})$, where:

   - U_i is the user making the access request;
   - P_j is the requested permission; and
   - $\{P_{i_1}, \ldots, P_{i_m}\}$ is the set of permissions for which U_i currently has the authorization.

   The access request is granted if the computed risk is lower than the threshold value specified by the system for the requested permission.
   In case of role-based access control, the access request may be either for a specific role or a permission. If the request is for a role the risk of the role being assigned needs to be computed. Otherwise the risk of all roles having the requested permission needs to be computed and the role with the lowest risk assigned. This is formally specified as below:

2a. **Risk based role authorization**
   Given an access request $(U_i, R_x, \{R_{i_1}, \ldots, R_{i_m}\})$, where R_X is the requested role and $\{R_{i_1}, \ldots, R_{i_m}\}$ is the set of roles for which U_i has the authorization. The access request is granted by assigning U_i to role R_x if the risk associated with the (U_i, R_x) assignment is lower than the threshold value specified by the system for the requested role.

2b. **Risk based role authorization**
   Given an access request $(U_i, P_j, \{R_{i_1}, \ldots, R_{i_m}\})$, where $\{R_{i_1}, \ldots, R_{i_m}\}$ is the set of roles for which U_i has the authorization. The access request is granted by assigning U_i to role R_x such that:

   - $(P_j, R_x) \in PA$;
   - Risk associated with the (U_i, R_x) assignment is the minimum over assignment to any other role R_y for which $(P_j, R_y) \in PA$; and
   - Risk associated with the (U_i, R_x) assignment is lower than the threshold value specified by the system for the requested permission.

The specific approach for each case is discussed below. To illustrate the procedure, we will use the user permission assignment (UPA) matrix depicted in Fig. 5.1a. When role based access control is assumed to be deployed, we will use the user assignment (UA) matrix and permission assignment (PA) matrix depicted in Fig. 5.1b, c, respectively.

5.3.1   Risk Based Permission Authorization

Given the UPA matrix, in this approach, we first build the *classification model* (CM) for each permission. This process, of building the classification models, is typically carried out at the start, though the models may be refined (either incrementally or completely recomputed) if the system state changes significantly. Once models are built for all permissions, these models are then stored and utilized for future risk assessment. Suppose that user U_6 (depicted in Fig. 5.1a) requests permission P_2. From Fig. 5.1a, it can be seen that U_6 has been assigned permissions P_1 and P_3. Since all the users who have been assigned permission P_2 in the UPA matrix of Fig. 5.1a have been assigned either permission P_1 or permission P_3, the risk for granting this access request is relatively low and it may be secure to assign permission P_2 to U_6. We now show how this risk can be quantified.

Essentially, we can treat the permission request as a new instance to be classified for the appropriate model. Thus, if user U_i requests permission P_j, then the classifier model for P_j needs to be used. This classification model makes a decision based on the existing permission set of U_i. Thus, the permissions of U_i form the new instance which is classified by the model, and the classifier returns the probability of that instance belonging to the class of permission P_j or not. Thus, the output of this classification corresponds to the *AssessedRisk* value. If this value is lower than the threshold, then permission can be granted to the requesting user; otherwise the request is denied.

The procedure consists of the following two steps:

Step 1:   *Model building for each-permission* In this step, a classification model is built for each permission within an organization. This step uses the *UPA* matrix which represents the user-to-permission assignments within an organization. For each permission, there is one column in *UPA*. A cell value of '0' represents the absence of the permission, while '1' represents presence of that permission in the corresponding user's permission set. Essentially, if there are n permissions, n classification models are built – one for each permission. When creating the classification model for each permission, the column for that permission is denoted as the class, while the remaining data are used to train the classifier model. The models built for each permission are then stored for later use. Algorithm 5.1 gives the formal specifications for this step.

Step 2:   *Classification of request* User may want to have a permission which was not assigned to him before. For determining whether a user should be given that

---

Input: User-Permission assignment, UPA ;
Input: Classification Algorithm, CA ;
Output: CMlist;
1 $CMlist \leftarrow \phi$;
2 **for** *each perm P_j* ;
3 **do**
4 | Denote the column for P_j in UPA as the class attribute ;
5 | $CM \leftarrow BuildClassifier(CA, UPA)$;
6 | STATE $CMlist \leftarrow CMlist \cup CM$;
7 **end**
8 **return** $CMlist$

Algorithm 5.1: *BuildPermissionClassificationModel()*

permission or not, a request is classified on the basis of existing permission set of a user. This is done by first retrieving a classification model for a requested permission and then classifying the request. The output of this classification is the probability that the new instance belongs to the class (probability that the access request should be granted). Thus, the inverse gives the *AssessedRisk* value.

Algorithm 5.2 gives the formal specifications for access request classification step.

Input: $Perms(U_i)$ represents existing permission set of user U_i;
Input: Classification Algorithm, CA ;
Input: δ, the threshold for classification ;
Input: $CMlist$, the list of classification models built from Algorithm 5.1 ;
Output: $AssessedRisk$
1 $CM \leftarrow$ Retrieve the classifier model for permission P_j from $CMlist$;
2 $AssessedRisk \leftarrow CA(CM, Perms(U_i), P_j)$;
3 **return** $AssessedRisk$

Algorithm 5.2: PermissionRisk(U_i, P_j)

Figure 5.2 shows the risk values for the UPA matrix of Fig. 5.1a. The risk values are computed for those permissions that have not been assigned to users in the original policy. For example, the risk value for assigning permission P_2 to user U_6 is 0.24. This low risk value is due to the fact that all the users who have permission P_2 have been assigned either permission P_1, or permission P_3 and U_6 has authorization for both of these permissions. On the other hand, the risk value of permission P_5 for U_6 is 0.8. Intuitively, the reason for this high risk value is that in 5 out of 7 instances of P_5 in Fig. 5.1a, P_5 occurs together with P_2. The risk values in Fig. 5.2 are computed using the Random Forest classification model.

Fig. 5.2 Assessed risk values
for permission authorizations
considering the UPA matrix
of Fig. 5.1a

	P1	P2	P3	P4	P5
U1				1.0	
U2				1.0	
U3	0.323			1.0	
U4	0.323			1.0	
U5				1.0	0.469
U6		0.24		0.8	0.8
U7		1.0	0.308		
U8				1.0	
U9				1.0	0.469
U10		1.0			

5.3.2 Risk Based Authorization of Roles

We now discuss the case where role based access control is used. As discussed above, in this case the user may request a specific role or a specific permission (if so, the user is requesting any role that allows him to access the requested permission). We again use the *UA*, *PA* and *UPA* depicted in Fig. 5.1a to illustrate the approach.

Note that in either approach, classification models have to be built for each permission. This classification model building follows the same procedure given in Algorithm 5.1, except that the *UPA* matrix used needs to first be constructed from the *UA* and *PA* matrices. Therefore, we assume that the classification models have already been built.

We now examine the case where a specific role is requested. In this case, the risk of the role is computed on the permissions that are present in the role. For a permission that is already owned by the user, the risk is 0 (clearly, there is no risk). For the remaining permissions, we can use the $PermissionRisk$ procedure (Algorithm 5.2) to determine the risk of assigning that permission to the requesting user. Now, we simply need to compute the aggregated role risk from individual permission risks. This can be done as follows:

Assume role R_x consists of permissions $P_1, \ldots, P_k$. Further assume that the risk of permission P_i for the requesting user is denoted by $risk_{P_i}$ and the risk for role R_x is denoted by $risk_{R_x}$:

$$
\begin{aligned}
risk_{R_x} &= 1- \text{Risk of not assigning } R_x \\
&= 1 - \text{Risk of not assigning } (P_1, \ldots, P_k) \\
&= 1 - \prod_{\forall s}(1 - risk_{P_s})
\end{aligned}
\tag{5.1}
$$

This procedure is formally specified in Algorithm 5.3.

Figure 5.3 shows the risk values for role authorizations considering the UA and PA matrices of Fig. 5.1. Similar to Fig. 5.2, the risk values for roles are reported for those roles only that have not been assigned to the user.

Fig. 5.3 Assessed risk values for role authorizations considering the UA and PA matrices of Fig. 5.1b, c

	R1	R2	R3	R4	R5
U1			0.0	1.0	0.0
U2		0.0		1.0	0.0
U3	0.323	0.323		1.0	0.323
U4	0.323	0.323		1.0	0.323
U5		0.469	0.469	1.0	
U6	0.24	0.8	0.848	0.96	
U7	1.0		1.0		0.308
U8			0.0	1.0	
U9		0.469	0.469	1.0	0.0
U10	1.0	0.0	1.0		

In the case when a specific permission is requested, we first determine the roles having that permission. Next we compute the risk of each of these roles using the $RoleRisk$ procedure (Algorithm 5.3). Finally, we select the role with the lowest risk value. This is formally specified in Algorithm 5.4.

Input: User-Permission assignment, UPA ;
Input: Permission to role assignment, PA ;
Input: Classification Algorithm, CA ;
Input: $Perms(U_i)$ represents existing permission set of user U_i ;
Input: R_j represents requested role;
Input: $CMlist$, the list of classification models built from Algorithm 5.1;
Output: $risk_{R_j}$;
1 **for** *each permission* $P_k \in R_j$;
2 **do**
3   **if** $P_k \notin Perms(U_i)$;
4   **then**
5       $risk_{P_k} \leftarrow PermissionRisk(U_i, P_k)$ (Algorithm 5.2);
6   **else**
7       $risk_{P_k} \leftarrow 0$;
8   **end**
9 **end**
10 $risk_{R_j} \leftarrow 1 - \prod_{\forall P_k \in R_j}(1 - risk_{P_k})$;
11 **return** $risk_{R_j}$

Algorithm 5.3: RoleRisk(U_i, R_j)

Figure 5.4 shows the risk values for user permission assignments assuming the RBAC policy with UA and PA matrices depicted in Fig. 5.1. As can be seen in Fig. 5.1c, a given permission can be accessed through multiple roles. The risk value in Fig. 5.4 is computed for all the roles by which the requested permission can be accessed and the role with the lowest risk value is assigned to the user. For example, U_6 can gain permission P_2 through role R_1 with risk value 0.24 or through role R_3 with risk value 0.848. Since role R_1 has the lowest risk value, it is assigned to U_1 for granting permission P_2.

Input: User-Permission assignment, UPA;
Input: Permission to role assignment, PA;
Input: Classification Algorithm, CA;
Input: $Perms(U_i)$ represents existing permission set of user U_i;
Input: P_j represents requested permission;
1 $crlslist \leftarrow$ each role R_k in PA having P_j;
2 **for** *each role R_k in $crlslist$* ;
3 **do**
4 $\quad\mid\quad rlRisk_k \leftarrow RoleRisk(U_i, R_k)$ (Algorithm 5.3) ;
5 **end**
6 **return** *(*$\min_k rlRisk_k, R_k$*)*;
7 Return the Role with the lowest risk

Algorithm 5.4: RBACPermissionRisk(U_i, P_j)

	P1	P2	P3	P4	P5
U1				Risk of R4 (1.0)	
U2				Risk of R4 (1.0)	
U3	Risk of R1 **(0.323)** Risk of R2 **(0.323)** Risk of R5 **(0.323)**			Risk of R4 (1.0)	
U4	Risk of R1 **(0.323)** Risk of R2 **(0.323)** Risk of R5 **(0.323)**			Risk of R4 (1.0)	
U5				Risk of R4 (1.0)	Risk of R2 **(0.469)** Risk of R3 (0.469) Risk of R4 (1.0)
U6		Risk of R1 **(0.24)** Risk of R3 (0.848)		Risk of R4 (0.96)	Risk of R2 **(0.8)** Risk of R3 (0.848) Risk of R4 (0.96)
U7		Risk of R1 (1.0) Risk of R3 (1.0)	Risk of R1 (1.0) Risk of R3 (1.0) Risk of R5 **(0.308)**		
U8				Risk of R4 (1.0)	
U9				Risk of R4 (1.0)	Risk of R2 **(0.469)** Risk of R3 (0.469) Risk of R4 (1.0)
U10		Risk of R1 (1.0) Risk of R3 (1.0)			

Fig. 5.4 Assessed risk values for user permission assignments assuming the RBAC policy of Fig. 5.1b, c

5.4 Experimental Evaluation

We now present the details of our implementation of the risk-based permission and role authorization approach. The experimental implementation uses Weka [22] to build the classification model and compute the risk for each of the permissions. The risk for a role is computed as per Eq. 5.1. Weka, developed at the University of Waikato in New Zealand, is a collection of machine learning algorithms for data mining tasks implemented in Java. Apart from providing algorithms, it is a general implementation framework, along with support classes and documentation. It is extensible and convenient for prototyping purposes. We have used the Random Forest algorithm for building the UPA classification model. We have evaluated the risk based permission authorization approach with both real and synthetic datasets. The real datasets used are described below [15]:

- *Healthcare dataset*: This dataset comprises of 46 users and 46 permissions. Overall, there are 1,486 user permission assignments and the density of the UPA matrix is 0.702.
- *Domino*: This dataset comprises of 79 users and 231 permissions. Overall, there are 730 user permission assignments and the density of the UPA matrix is 0.04.
- *Firewall 1*: This dataset comprises of 365 users and 709 permissions. Overall, there are 31,951 user permission assignments and the density of the UPA matrix is 0.123.
- *Firewall 2*: This dataset comprises of 325 users and 590 permissions. Overall, there are 36,428 user permission assignments and the density of the UPA matrix is 0.19.
- *APJ*: This dataset comprises of 2,044 users and 1,146 permissions. Overall, there are 6,841 user permission assignments and the density of the UPA matrix is 0.003.
- *EMEA*: This dataset comprises of 35 users and 3,046 permissions. Overall, there are 7,220 user permission assignments and the density of the UPA matrix is 0.068.
- *Customer*: This dataset comprises of 10,961 users and 284 permissions. Overall, there are 45,428 user permission assignments and the density of the UPA matrix is 0.015.
- *Americas-small*: This dataset comprises of 3,477 users and 1,587 permissions. Overall, there are 105,206 user permission assignments and the density of the UPA matrix is 0.019.
- *Americas-large*: This dataset comprises of 3,485 users and 10,127 permissions. Overall, there are 185,295 user permission assignments and the density of the UPA matrix is 0.005.

The synthetic datasets were created using the test data generator from Vaidya et al. [21]. The test data generator performs as follows: First a set of roles are created. For each role, a random number of permissions up to a certain maximum are chosen to form the role. The maximum number of permissions to be associated with a role is set as a parameter of the algorithm. Next, the users are created. For each user, a random number of roles are chosen. Again, the maximum number of concurrent roles a user can have is set as a parameter of the algorithm. Finally, the user permissions are set according to the roles to which the user has been assigned. Table 5.1 gives the characteristics of the datasets created. Since the effect of large number of users, permissions, and varying densities has already been studied with the real datasets, the synthetic datasets were created with a limited size to enable focused testing of the effect of noise, and of the role risk. As the test data creator

Table 5.1 Synthetic data sets

	NRoles	NUsers	NPerms	MRolesUsr	MPermsRole
data1	20	100	200	5	10
data2	20	200	200	5	10
data3	20	300	200	5	10
data4	20	500	200	5	10

Table 5.2 Average permission risk for real datasets

Dataset	A0–P0	A0–P1
Healthcare	0.96995 (28.1191 %)	0.102286 (1.65406 %)
Domino	0.990807 (95.8737 %)	0.232318 (0.120555 %)
Firewall1	0.999191 (87.6113 %)	0.235806 (0.0417335 %)
Firewall2	0.999905 (80.9961 %)	0.283333 (0.00625815 %)
APJ	0.998631 (99.1011 %)	0.164787 (0.563963 %)
EMEA	0.983113 (92.9369 %)	0.269579 (0.289841 %)
Customer	0.994464 (98.2509 %)	0.290119 (0.289728 %)
Americas-small	0.999787 (98.0862 %)	0.273659 (0.00723088 %)
Americas-large	0.999643 (99.4671 %)	0.297221 (0.00785151 %)

Table 5.3 Average permission risk for real datasets

Dataset	A1–P0	A1–P1
Healthcare	0.745429 (1.32325 %)	0.00772222 (68.9036 %)
Domino	0.889158 (1.21651 %)	0.0333792 (2.78919 %)
Firewall1	0.925063 (0.233012 %)	0.00321427 (12.1139 %)
Firewall2	0.66037 (0.0140808 %)	0.00019505 (18.9836 %)
APJ	0.860487 (0.0511018 %)	0.0269798 (0.283824 %)
EMEA	0.871483 (3.67414 %)	0.150757 (3.09915 %)
Customer	0.813936 (0.795715 %)	0.184826 (0.66362 %)
Americas-small	0.743298 (0.0280355 %)	0.00734629 (1.87856 %)
Americas-large	0.756415 (0.042754 %)	0.0364984 (0.482271 %)

algorithm is randomized, three datasets for each combination of parameters are created, and the results are averaged.

5.4.1 Risk-Based Permission Authorization

Tables 5.2 and 5.3 gives the average risk that was computed for each of the real datasets. In each case, we give the average risk for four discrete cases, as well as the percentage of occurrence for each case:

- Risk for permissions that were actually unassigned to a user, and were correctly predicted by the classifier as not to be assigned (A0–P0).

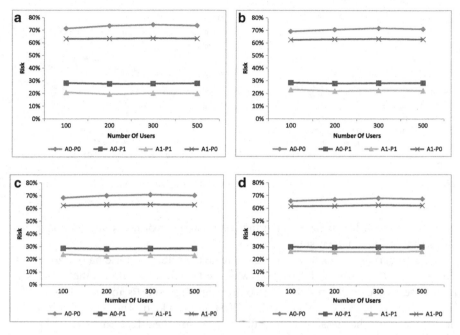

Fig. 5.5 Average permission risk for synthetic datasets. (**a**) With 0 % noise. (**b**) With 7 % noise. (**c**) With 10 % noise. (**d**) With 20 % noise

- Risk for permissions that were actually unassigned to a user, and were incorrectly predicted by the classifier as to be assigned (A0–P1). This case corresponds to incorrect over privilege.
- Risk for permissions that were actually assigned to a user, and were incorrectly predicted by the classifier as not to be assigned (A1–P0). This case correspond to incorrect under privilege.
- Risk for permissions that were actually assigned to a user, and were correctly predicted by the classifier as to be assigned (A1–P1).

It is clear that for all of the real datasets, the average risk for the A0–P0 permissions is very high (ranging from 0.96 to 0.99), while the average risk for the A1–P1 permissions is very low (ranging from 0.0001 to 0.18). The risk for A0–P1 is incorrectly low while the risk for the A1–P0 permissions is incorrectly high. However, the combined percentage of such cases is quite low (less than 4 % in all cases). Thus, the results are quite good.

Figure 5.5 gives the average risk for the synthetic datasets. The x-axis shows the varying number of users in the four datasets (since the other parameters are the same), while the y-axis shows the average risk. As expected, the risk for the permissions that are actually 0 and are correctly predicted to be 0 is quite high, while the risk for the permissions that are actually 1 and are correctly predicted to

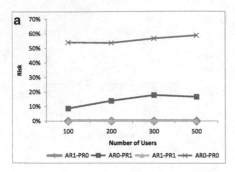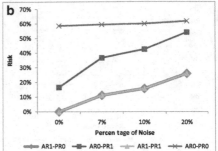

Fig. 5.6 Average role risk in synthetic datasets. (**a**) Without noise. (**b**) With noise

be 1 is quite low. It is clear that the increasing number of users does not have any deleterious effect on the results.

We also carried out experiments to evaluate the effect of noise on our approach. To do this, the noise model of [21] was used, and all of the synthetic datasets had noise added to them using randomly (flipping both 0s to 1s and 1s to 0s). Figure 5.5b–d gives the results with 7–20 % noise added. The main result of the noise is to make the classification results imprecise. The effect can be seen through the lowering risk for the permissions predicted to be 0 and the increasing risk for the permissions predicted to be 1.

5.4.2 Risk-Based Role Authorization

To evaluate the risk-based role authorization, we used the same synthetic datasets described in Table 5.1. For each user and each role, the risk was calculated as per Eq. 5.1. The risk was then averaged over all of the users and all of the roles. We carried this process out both without noise and after the introduction of noise, as described earlier. The results are depicted in Fig. 5.6. Figure 5.6a shows that the risk of getting an already authorized role is always 0 regardless of whether the role is predicted to be 0 or 1 (AR1–PR0 or AR1–PR1), since all of the permissions associated with that role are already held by the user. However, when the role is not authorized, the risk is quite high if it is predicted to be unauthorized (AR0–PR0) and fairly low if it is predicted to be authorized (AR0–PR1). The results do not vary much based on the number of users. Figure 5.6b shows the results when noise is introduced. In the interest of space, we only depict the results in the case of data4 (500 users), though they are the same for all of the other datasets too. It is clear that with the introduction of noise, the risk in all four cases increases proportionally to the level of noise. The risk increase is marginal for AR0–PR0 (where it is already high), while being significant in all of the other three cases.

5.5 Related Work

Several risk based access control models have been proposed in recent years. The Benefit And Risk Access Control (BARAC) [25] is based on assessing the benefits of information sharing and the risks of information disclosure. It uses allowed transactions (AT graph) and flow paths, and a BARAC accessibility graph (AC graph) that describes the objects accessible by subjects, both with allocated budgets, to determine whether or not to allow access. Access is allowed only if the benefits outweigh the risks. In [17], different permissions are associated with different levels of risks, and the role hierarchy relations are used for selecting a role for delegation of tasks that would yield least risks. The approach in [5] is a risk-adaptive access control model where the estimated quantified risk is based on the probability of damage times value of damage. The approach in [16] employs Fuzzy logic control to estimate the risk vs. benefits tradeoffs. The adaptive risk based access control model in [13] is based on probability computation to ascertain future risk where the estimated quantified risk is based on the probability of damage multiplied by the value of the damage. All these approaches are based on risk-benefit estimates, which are used to determine access; if the benefit of sharing information outweighs risk, then access is granted, but if the risk involved in sharing is above tolerable limit and benefit involved in sharing is not significant then access to such information is denied. However, these approaches either do not discuss how risk or benefit can actually be computed, or compute the risk based on the extraneous attributes. In this paper, we compute the risk based on the existing access control permissions.

Other line of work to providing flexible access are break-glass approaches [3, 14] that are based on the idea of overriding access control policies if the situation warrants. The earlier break-glass solutions were implemented by issuing temporary accounts in case of emergency mode. Recent break-glass approaches supplement the deployed access control model through an additional layer that handles access requests in case of emergency.

5.6 Conclusions

Decision outcomes of traditional access control systems are based on hard coded access control policies. In reality, it is not possible to hard code all situations. When any unforeseen situation occurs, traditional access control models lack the ability to handle them. Moreover, traditional access control systems do not incorporate dynamics associated with situation, in decision making process. In this paper we presented two approaches for facilitating Risk Based Access Control. Our first approach addresses the problem of quantifying risk that is based on dynamics of a situation. Our second approach is based on identifying situational role for a user under uncertain circumstances. Our approaches are based on allowing maximum permissiveness and least restrictiveness in a secure manner. Our experimental evaluation validates the effectiveness of the approach. There are several possible future directions of this work such as: analyzing how well these approaches can work in collaborative environments where requesting users may belong to an inter domain organization. For now, we plan to extend these approaches to address the problem of misconfiguration in access control.

Acknowledgements This work is partially supported by the National Science Foundation under grant numbers CNS-0746943 and CNS-1018414.

References

1. Agrawal, R., Srikant, R.: Fast algorithms for mining association rules. In: Proceedings of the 20th International Conference Very Large Data Bases, VLDB, Santiago (1994)
2. Breiman, L.: Random forests. Mach. Learn. **45**, 5–32 (2001)
3. Brucker, A.D., Petritsch, H.: Extending access control models with break-glass. In: SACMAT, Stresa (2009)
4. Cendowska, J.: Prism: an algorithm for inducing modular rules. Int. J. Man Mach. Stud. **27**, 349–370 (1987)
5. Cheng, P., Rohatgi, P., Keser, C., Karger, P.A., Wagner, G.M., Reninger, A.S.: Fuzzy multi-level security: an experiment on quantified risk-adaptive access control. In: IEEE Symposium on Security and Privacy, Berkeley, pp. 222–230 (2007)
6. Cover, T., Hart, P.: Nearest neighbor pattern classification. IEEE Trans. Inf. Theory **13**, 21–27 (1967)
7. Ferraiolo, D., Sandhu, R., Gavrila, S., Kuhn, D., Chandramouli, R.: Proposed nist standard for role-based access control. TISSEC **4**, 224–274 (2001)
8. Ferrira, A., Chadwick, D., Farinha, P., Correia, R., Zao, G., Chilro, R.: How to securely break into rbac: the btg-rbac model. In: Annual Computer Security Application Conference, Honolulu (2009)
9. Geiger, D., Friedman, N., Goldszmidt, M.: Bayesian network classifiers. Mach. Learn. **29**, 131 (1997)
10. Hsu, W., Liu, B., Ma, Y.: Integrating classification and association rule mining. In: Knowledge Discovery and Data Mining Integrating, New York City (1998)
11. Imirlinksi, T., Agrawal, R., Swami, A.: Mining association rules between sets of items in large databases. In: Proceedings of the 1993 ACM SIGMOD International Conference on Management of Data, Washington, DC (1993)
12. Ishibuchi, H., Nozaki, K., Tanaka, H.: Adaptive fuzzy rule-based classification systems. Fuzzy Syst. IEEE **4**, 238–250 (1996)
13. Kandala, S., Sandhu, R., Bhamidipati, V.: An attribute based framework for risk-adaptive access control models. In: Availability, Reliability and Security (ARES), Vienna (2011)
14. Marinovic, S., Craven, R., Ma, J., Dulay, N.: Rumpole: a flexible break glass access control model. In: SACMAT, Innsbruck (2011)
15. Molloy, I., Li, N., Li, T., Mao, Z., Wang, Q., Lobo, J.: Evaluating role mining algorithms. In: Carminati, B., Joshi, J. (eds.) SACMAT, Stresa, pp. 95–104. ACM (2009)
16. Ni, Q., Bertino, E., Lobo, J.: Risk based access control systems built on fuzzy inferences. In: ASIAACCS, Beijing (2010)
17. Nissanke, N., Khayat, E.J.: Risk based security analysis of permissions in rbac. In: International Workshop on Security in Information Systems, Porto (2004)
18. Prabhakar, S., Qin, B., Xia, Y., Tu, Y.: A rule-based classification algorithm for uncertain data. In: IEEE International Conference on Data Engineering, Shanghai (2009)

19. Quinlan, J.R.: Induction of decision trees. Mach. Learn. **1**, 81–106 (1986)
20. Quinlan, J.R.: C4.5 Programs for Machine Learning. Morgan Kaufmann, San Mateo (1993)
21. Vaidya, J., Atluri, V., Warner, J., Guo, Q.: Role engineering via prioritized subset enumeration. IEEE Trans. Dependable Secur. Comput. **7**, 300–314 (2010)
22. Witten, I.H., Frank, E.: Data Mining: Practical Machine Learning Tools and Techniques with Java Implementations. Morgan Kaufmann, San Francisco (1999)
23. Yuan, Y., Shaw, M.J.: Induction of fuzzy decision trees. Fuzzy Sets Syst. **69**, 125–139 (1995)
24. Zhang, G.: Neural networks for classification: a survey. IEEE Trans. Syst. Man Cybern. C **30**, 451–462 (2000)
25. Zhang, L., Brodsky, A., Jajodia, S.: Towards information sharing: benefit and risk access control (barac). In: IEEE, International Workshop on Policies for Distributed Systems and Networks, London (2006)

Part III
Configuration Analytics

Chapter 6
GCNav: Generic Configuration Navigation System

Shankaranarayanan Puzhavakath Narayanan, Seungjoon Lee, and Subhabrata Sen

Abstract Configuration navigation and change-auditing is one of the most complex yet common tasks performed by network operators on a regular basis. Change-auditing router configuration files accurately is a challenging task due to presence of structure and hierarchy in the config content. Generic diff tools do not have the notion of context or syntactic structure while comparing files and produce diff reports (using minimum edit distance) that often do not match operator expectations. Moreover, these tools perform redundant (and expensive) comparison operations across contextually unrelated sections of the config file which makes them scale poorly even for config files of moderate size. On the other hand, vendor specific and customized diff solutions are not generic enough to be applied uniformly across a heterogeneous network. Also, modeling the configuration semantics for different vendors is a non-trivial and expensive process.

In this paper, we introduce *GCNav*, a system that helps network operators perform general or customized change-auditing at varying levels of granularity on the network. Unlike existing solutions, *GCNav* makes use of the inherent syntactic structure common to all config files and thereby remains generic without compromising on the accuracy of results. Our experience with the deployment of *GCNav* on a large operational customer-facing IP network shows that it is able to provide a generic, accurate and scalable solution for change-auditing router config files. Our results show that *GCNav*'s diff results matches operator expectation while generic diff tools reported at least some misleading diff in 95 % of the files analyzed. We also find that *GCNav* performs seven times faster than customized auditing tools making it a feasible solution for online and interactive config auditing.

S.P. Narayanan (✉)
Purdue University, West Lafayette, IN, USA
e-mail: spuzhava@purdue.edu

S. Lee • S. Sen
AT&T Research, Florham Park, NJ, USA
e-mail: slee@research.att.com; sen@research.att.com

E. Al-Shaer et al. (eds.), *Automated Security Management*,
DOI 10.1007/978-3-319-01433-3_6, © Springer International Publishing Switzerland 2013

6.1 Introduction

Operators who manage large networks are required to perform a wide range of evolutionary, operational and maintenance activities which are often realized through modifications to the router config files. These activities usually cause a flurry of changes to a number of router config files consisting of tens of thousands of lines of arcane, complex, low level vendor-specific code that require a high degree of domain knowledge about the structure and vendor-specific details to understand and modify. Any errors in such operational activities can have serious adverse implications for the operation of the network ranging from immediate network outages and SLA violations to "hidden time bomb" latent misconfiguration [9, 16, 17].

Operators usually perform static analysis of their network device config files (called config auditing) to minimize and troubleshoot misconfiguration-induced outages. In this paper, we focus on one of the basic static analysis aspects: finding the differences between two configs. This is a key task that network operators perform in outage scenarios (e.g., identify config changes that occurred prior to the outage). Also, operators apply this capability to *template auditing* [3] to ensure router configs have all the intended configuration policies (captured in a *template*).

While conceptually simple, computing the *diff* of config files is challenging due to structure and hierarchy of content in these files, as well as the need to accurately identify the context of a change. Operators need to understand precisely where in the hierarchy the changes have occurred (e.g., for rapid understanding of the context of a change, or because changes high up in the config hierarchy might have a larger impact on the configuration). Today operators typically resort to a laborious, manual-intensive and error-prone approach involving a combination of "stare and compare" and the use of UNIX *diff* tools (like *GNUDiff* [10]) for comparing two config files. However generic tools like *GNUDiff* are poorly suited to the task as they compute the minimum edit distance between the two config files and do not have any notion of structure or hierarchy. As a result these tools often produce misleading diff results (see Sect. 6.5.2.2). Similar issues are also observed with the generic *diff* tools that operate on structured documents (like XML [7, 23]). While XML helps capture the syntactic structure of config files, existing XML diff tools compute minimal edit distance which is inaccurate for our purpose as we shall see in Sect. 6.5.2.1. Also, these generic tools perform certain computationally expensive content-match operations (that are redundant when comparing config files) making them scale poorly for even small config files as we observe in Sect. 6.5.3.

There are two broad approaches for a more tailored static analysis of config files. The first involves using vendor-specific solutions like [4]. However, these solutions face several challenges like high development cost, lack of flexibility and availability for devices from multiple vendors and different config languages. The second approach is to convert the various config languages to a common model and compare them. However, such extensive modeling of device configs is an extremely expensive process. It is also non-trivial to design a generic model that captures enough details for subtle differences in different config languages, especially when vendors constantly come up with different languages (i.e., OS upgrades) and new features for enhanced services (e.g., new policy statements).

In this paper, we present *GCNav*, a flexible config auditing system that is accurate yet generic enough to be applicable to a wide range of config languages and vendor types. Unlike existing solutions, *GCNav* makes use of the inherent syntactic structure in the config files that is not only common to a majority of routers (and vendor types) but also independent of the functionality that is associated with the specific configuration logic. We designed *GCNav* to work with XML config files based on the following key observations. (i) XML has rapidly become the de-facto standard for representing any hierarchical information that has consistent structure. (ii) All major vendors in the networking industry have adopted XML config files [5, 11]. (iii) Large ISPs have already built parsers (e.g. [2]) to convert the CLI config files to XML config files.

To summarize, our contribution in this paper is *GCNav*, a configuration navigation system that provides accurate and contextual change-audit reports for router config files. We design *GCNav* with the goal of achieving the following key design goals:

- Developing a generic and scalable structured-*diff* methodology based on the syntactic and structural properties of config files that is independent of the semantics of the config language.
- Building on the existing XML *diff* techniques and adapt them to leverage the key structural properties exhibited by config files.

Our evaluation of *GCNav* on a large operational customer-facing enterprise IP network (anonymized as *IPNet*) show that it provides accurate *diff* reports. In comparison, more than 20 % of the diff reported by *GNUDiff* was misleading in more than half the config files in the network that had reported some change. Our evaluation also shows that *GCNav* is seven times faster than GSAT [3] (a domain specific tool developed for template auditing) while performing the same audit task.

6.2 Background and Problem Motivation

In this section, we discuss the nature of router config files and the structural properties exhibited by them. We then discuss the limited utility of existing *diff* tools for generating accurate *diff* on hierarchical content.

6.2.1 Nature of Config Files

We first illustrate some key properties of router config files, as noted in a previous work [19]. Figure 6.1a shows a section of the anonymized CLI (Command Line Interface e.g., [20]) code from the config files of an Alcatel router deployed in

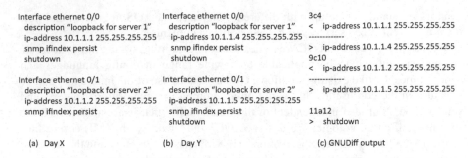

```
Interface ethernet 0/0              Interface ethernet 0/0              3c4
  description "loopback for server 1"   description "loopback for server 1"   <   ip-address 10.1.1.1 255.255.255.255      •
  ip-address 10.1.1.1 255.255.255.255   ip-address 10.1.1.4 255.255.255.255   -------------
  snmp ifindex persist                snmp ifindex persist                >   ip-address 10.1.1.4 255.255.255.255
  shutdown                            shutdown                            9c10
                                                                          <   ip-address 10.1.1.2 255.255.255.255
Interface ethernet 0/1              Interface ethernet 0/1              -------------
  description "loopback for server 2"   description "loopback for server 2"   >   ip-address 10.1.1.5 255.255.255.255
  ip-address 10.1.1.2 255.255.255.255   ip-address 10.1.1.5 255.255.255.255
  snmp ifindex persist                snmp ifindex persist                11a12
                                      shutdown                            >   shutdown

      (a)  Day X                          (b)  Day Y                          (c) GNUDiff output
```

Fig. 6.1 *GNUDiff* does not provide sufficient context when a router config changes

the *IPNet* network. This CLI code configures two ethernet interfaces on the router along with its properties like description, IP address and mask, an option for SNMP (Simple Network Management Protocol), and interface status (i.e., enabled or not). We make the following important observations from the example.

Low-level complex code: Router config files consist of thousands of lines of complex low-level commands. While we present a straightforward example here for simplicity, in reality, it is highly challenging to comprehend the intent and impact of these config code without sufficient domain knowledge and context information.

Structure and hierarchy: Router config files have some inherent syntactic structure and hierarchy enforced by the configuration logic. For example, in Fig. 6.1, the CLI code can be grouped into logical blocks and sub-blocks such as $interface$, $ip - address$ or $description$. Also the $interface$ block encloses the $ip - address$ and $description$ blocks. This structural nature of config files is common to all devices, vendor types and is completely independent of the semantics of the config logic. *GCNav* takes advantage of these properties to gain accuracy and provide contextual information when comparing two config files.

Modeling configs as trees: A key abstraction that we use in *GCNav* is to utilize syntactic structure of config files and view them as trees [3]. Figure 6.2 shows an example of two simple config snippets modeled as trees where each config tree has four interfaces and for simplicity, we show only two properties (i.e., description and IP nodes) for each interface node. While modeling config files as trees help capture the structure without having to understand semantics, the next section explains why computing config *diff* is still a challenging task with existing *diff* tools.

6.2.2   Limited Utility of Existing Diff Tools

In this section we discuss the existing generic *diff* tools that broadly fall into two categories, text and XML *diff* tools.

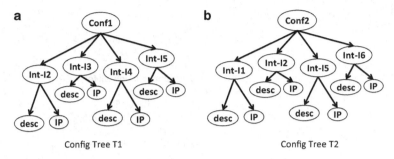

Fig. 6.2   Comparing config trees

6.2.2.1   Text Diff Tools

We first focus on *GNUDiff* [10] which we shall use extensively for comparison in the rest of this paper. Though *GNUDiff* is very different to *GCNav* in its design and operation, we find that it was the most frequently used diff solution by the network operators due to familiarity and simplicity of the tool. *GNUDiff* is widely available and can be used to *diff* any two text files making it the de-facto *diff* tool of choice. We use the comparison between *GCNav* and *GNUDiff* to highlight the lack of accuracy with generic *diff* tools and emphasize the need for a novel approach.

Consider the *GNUDiff* output for the config snapshots shown in Fig. 6.1. Here, *GNUDiff* identifies the changes between the two configs (i.e., IP address change in both interfaces and status change in the second interface), but does not associate the change with the corresponding *interface*. This is because *GNUDiff* has no notion of the syntactic structure of the router config and is therefore unable to provide sufficient context to detected changes. While making this association is simple in our small example, as config files become longer (e.g., thousands of lines), this information becomes critical for network operators to understand the implications of the change. Also, *GNUDiff* reports are often misleading since computing the minimal edit distance can potentially match equivalent but contextually unrelated blocks (see Sect. 6.5.2.1).

6.2.2.2   XML Diff Tools

We shall now see why the generic XML *diff* tools are not suitable for the static analysis of XML config files. Figure 6.3 shows the XML config snippet corresponding to Interface 0/0 in CLI sample from Fig. 6.1a. While XML helps capture the syntactic structure of config files, the problem of identifying the *diff* presents many challenges. Existing XML and structured diff tools (e.g., [7, 23]) compute minimal edit distance which is inaccurate for our purpose. Moreover, these tools try to perform expensive operations like matching sub-blocks of config code in an entire config file which does not scale even for small config files (see Sect. 6.5.3).

Fig. 6.3 XML config
corresponding to interface 0/0
from Fig. 6.1a

```
<Interface >
    <Naming>
        <Type> ethernet </Type>
        <ID>0/0 </ID>
    </Naming>
    <description> loopback for server 1 </description>
    <ip-address >
        <ip>10.1.1.1 </ip>
        <msk>255.255.255.255 </msk>
    </ip-address>
    <snmp>ifindex persist</snmp>
    <shutdown/>
</Interface>
```

Therefore, we design *GCNav*'s algorithms based on our insights on the syntactic and structural characteristics of config files to generate accurate reports in an efficient manner.

6.3 *GCNav* Architecture

Our design of *GCNav* takes advantage of the following properties exhibited by config files.

1. Blocks (nodes in config tree) of config code do not move to arbitrary sections of the config file. Consider the config trees in Fig. 6.2. The *ip* nodes would be a child of some *interface* node but would not be the child of any other arbitrary node such as *desc* or *conf*, as certain config commands are allowed only in relevant contexts.
2. Two nodes that look similar but have a different *signature* (path to the root) can represent contextually different parts of the config code. For example, an *ip* node attached to *Int-I2* is contextually different from the *ip* node that is attached to *Int-I3*, even if the two *ip* blocks have the same content. This is because they configure two different interfaces and comparing them would result in a *diff* that misleads the network operators.

We derive these key insights from configuration logic and syntax of config files that are common to all routers and vendor types. Since potential matches occur only at nodes that have similar *signatures*, *GCNav* only compares the nodes at the same depth in the config tree. Conventional tree *diff* algorithms [6] typically tend to match the above mentioned cases, which is both incorrect and expensive. On the other hand, *GCNav* benefits from these insights by pruning parts of the tree and improving the scalability of the system.

Figure 6.4 shows the block diagram of the architecture of *GCNav*. We first present the two core phases that are performed on the XML config files in the following sequence to obtain the *diff*: (1) Characterization of the XML files and (2) Comparing the XML files.

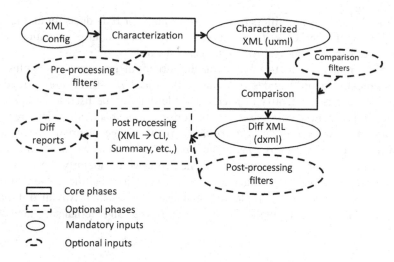

Fig. 6.4 Architecture of *GCNav*

6.3.1   Characterization

In order to accurately compare any two config files (trees) $T1$ and $T2$, we need to efficiently (1) identify whether for each node $T1$, there exists a corresponding node in $T2$ to compare against and (2) determine if the two corresponding nodes are identical or different. For this purpose, we annotate every node of the XML config file with two special attributes (internal to *GCNav*) in the *Characterization* phase. The annotated XML config file produced by this step (called a *characterized* XML file) is used as input to the comparison phase. We further elaborate on the above two points in this section.

6.3.1.1   Identifying Corresponding Nodes

Suppose we want to compare two config trees $T1$ and $T2$ shown in Fig. 6.2. The *diff* process should be able to associate the node *Int-I2* from $T1$ with its corresponding node *Int-I2* in $T2$. Brute-force approaches like pair-wise comparison (e.g. every child of *Conf1* in $T1$ with every child of *Conf2* in $T2$) can considerably slow down the *diff* process. Therefore, we introduce a new attribute called *UID* (Unique Identifier) to every node in a config tree which is used to identify the corresponding nodes in the comparison phase. For the ease of exposition, we show a simple *UID* (e.g., *I2*) for each interface node in Fig. 6.2, while we use a MD5 hash in practice.

Computing the *UID*:   If a node in a config file has identifying attributes such as *ID* or *NAME*, then a simple solution for computing the *UID* is to use those attributes. However, node attributes are not always mandatory. The content of child nodes can sometimes be used as identifiers (e.g., interface name or IP address for an interface node). This approach necessitates detailed knowledge of config semantics, which should be avoided to make *GCNav* generic and flexible.

GCNav employs heuristics based on the structural properties of config files to automatically identify nodes that can be used as *UID*. To ensure correctness, the heuristic needs to identify at least one node that can be used to compute the *UID*. A simple heuristic is based on the observation that leaf nodes are often good candidates for *UID* (e.g., *description*, *ip*). A stronger heuristic that worked very well for our network is to use the *HashValue* of non-repeating children to compute the *UID* for a given node. This heuristic would identify the nodes like *Naming* and *description* (in Fig. 6.3) that are used as identifiers even in their semantic model. Apart from implementing these heuristics, *GCNav* also provides the operators the option to explicitly suggest an *UID* as an external specification to the system.

6.3.1.2   Summary Information for Node Content

Once the corresponding nodes from given two trees are identified, we need to determine whether the two nodes are equivalent in its content (sub-tree) and value (attributes). A simple but expensive solution is to traverse the two subtrees recursively and check the equivalence at every level in the tree. To avoid the expensive tree traversals during the comparison phase, we calculate a simple MD5 hash on an entire subtree and annotate the root of the subtree with the hash value. Thus, the equality of content can be quickly determined for the given two nodes by comparing the hash values. The *HashValue* can be efficiently computed by performing a bottom-up traversal of the config tree and propagating the *HashValue* of a node to its immediate parent node. Computing the *UID* and *HashValue* attributes is independent of the *diff* process and needs to be done exactly once for each config file. Therefore, *GCNav* performs the characterization as a part of the pre-processing phase that can be delegated as an offline process.

Putting it together: At a high level, the characterization algorithm computes and adds the *HashValue* and *UID* (*computeHash()* and *computeUID()*) for every node in the config tree using the standard bottom up tree traversal. The annotated XML file produced by the characterization phase is called the *uxml* file.

6.3.2   Comparison

The *comparison* phase is undoubtedly the most important component of *GCNav*'s architecture which performs the actual *diff* between the two config files that need to be audited. The *comparison* phase takes the *characterized* files as its input and executes the diff algorithm to produce the *diff* result as a set of modifications, additions and deletions. It is important to note that the *comparison* phase is generic and totally independent of the type or vendor of the config files. The output of the *comparison* phase is an annotated XML file (*dxml* file) with attributes added to each node indicating the *added, deleted, modified* or *unchanged* status of the node.

At a high level, the comparison algorithm performs a BFS (Breadth First Search) tree traversal on both the config trees simultaneously. Based on our observations described earlier in this section, the algorithm looks for a potential match only between nodes that have a consistent *signature* (path from the root). Among those nodes with the same signature and depth, the algorithm identifies the corresponding node pairs using *UID* and determines the equivalence using *HashValue*.

The following are the possible cases after a comparison:

1. Nodes have equivalent *UID* and *HashValue* and do not have a *diff*. Our construction of the *HashValue* ensures that the entire subtrees are the same and therefore further traversal down the subtrees are redundant.
2. There exist corresponding node pairs with the same signature, depth, and *UID*, but they have different *HashValue* values. This indicates a *modification* (*mod*) in the subtree and we further process the subtrees according to the BFS traversal order.
3. A node that has no corresponding node with a matching signature, depth, or *UID*. This indicates an *addition* or *deletion* of the node based on the config tree where the node is located.

Algorithm 6.1 shows the pseudo-code of the algorithm used in the comparison phase of *GCNav*.

6.3.3 Optional Phases

The optional phases of *GCNav* are the pre-processing and post-processing phases as shown in the Fig. 6.4.

Pre-processing XML files: Large enterprise or ISP networks are highly heterogeneous consisting of config files that may have some redundant or irrelevant config blocks like timestamps, version number, device information etc. Diff computed on such redundant config blocks often prove to be distracting for the operators. Also evolving networks typically contain legacy devices that require some special handling before they can be processed. To address this requirement, we designed the characterization phase to optionally accept a set of pre-processing filters (using our filter language described below) as an external input from the operators. We discuss some of these aspects in detail in Sect. 6.4.

```
      input : Trees t1 and t2
      output: Annotated diff tree
 1  begin
 2  |   if t1.root.hash = t2.root.hash then
 3  |   |   return no diff;
 4  |   end
 5  |   while node ∈ BFS(t1, t2) do
 6  |   |   if node marked for process then
 7  |   |   |   (n1, n2) ← (nextNode(t1), nextNode(t2));
 8  |   |   |   (C1, C2) ← (n1.children, n2.children);
 9  |   |   |   for c1 ∈ C1 do
10  |   |   |   |   if c2 = match(c1, C2) then
11  |   |   |   |   |   if c1.hash = c2.hash then
12  |   |   |   |   |   |   c1, c2 equal;
13  |   |   |   |   |   |   for c upto c2 in C2 do
14  |   |   |   |   |   |   |   markAdded(c);
15  |   |   |   |   |   |   end
16  |   |   |   |   |   end
17  |   |   |   |   |   else
18  |   |   |   |   |   |   markModified(c1, c2);
19  |   |   |   |   |   end
20  |   |   |   |   end
21  |   |   |   |   else
22  |   |   |   |   |   markDeleted(c1);
23  |   |   |   |   end
24  |   |   |   end
25  |   |   |   if c ∈ C1seen then
26  |   |   |   |   markAdded(remainingnodes ∈ C2);
27  |   |   |   end
28  |   |   end
29  |   end
30  end
```

Algorithm 6.1: Compare

Post-processing XML files: As mentioned in Sect. 6.2.1, config files are large, complex and hard for human users to read and understand. It is therefore important for *GCNav* to have the ability to focus on certain sections of the config file that are important for the operators. For instance, network operators might want to view changes to the *interface* blocks alone and ignore any changes to the *description* blocks. To accommodate these requirements, we provide *GCNav* with a simple and intuitive filter language which uses *include* and *exclude* constructs to accept filtering queries from the operators as XPath [24] queries. A sample query expression for our example from Fig. 6.3 would look like *i-//interface:e-//description*, where multiple filter queries are separated by colon. The first half of the expression indicates whether it is an (i)nclude or (e)xclude construct and the second half of the expression gives the actual XPath query to be evaluated. For the above query, the filtering component would show *diff* sections that include *interface* nodes and excludes the *description* nodes from the results.

It is important to note that the pre and post processing phases are optional features that are provided to the operators to fine tune the system. These phases do not compromise the generality of our system and accepts a set of filter rules as its input and generates the *diff* reports accordingly. As a final note, *GCNav* is written completely in Python and uses *lxml* [21] for its XML library support.

6.4   Practical Considerations

In this section, we briefly discuss a few practical aspects that we encountered and needed to resolve while deploying *GCNav* on large ISP networks consisting of heterogeneous devices. This discussion, in particular, highlights the benefit of designing *GCNav* as a set of independent phases where the core phases remains well insulated from the quirks of the heterogeneous network.

Legacy devices only with CLI config files: Some legacy devices may not support XML config files. In such cases, *GCNav* can piggy-back on tools that can convert the CLI configs into structured XML configs [2]. For completeness, we include these solutions as a part of the pre-processing phase.

Errors in the XML files: From our initial experiments, we found that some config files collected from devices contained malformed XML constructs. These could have been due to manual configuration errors or even more systematic issues such as missing root nodes in the XML files. These issues can be ignored or fixed by custom or automated scripts in the pre-processing phase.

Vendor and device specific oddities: XML config files may have odd constructs that can mislead the comparison phase. For e.g., a certain config file that we processed had a timestamp attribute at the root node (wrapping the entire config file), which changes everyday. While this is a genuine modification in the config file, if we include that attribute in the *UID* and *HashValue* calculation (see Sect. 6.3.1), the root node would be always considered modified, which clearly is not the desired outcome. For this purpose, in *GCNav*, we provide the ability to specify filters or pre-processing rules in the characterization phase, so that we do not include such attributes as timestamp in the *UID* and *HashValue* calculation. These pre-processing rules can be provided by the operators (who have the domain knowledge) as a custom specification to *GCNav* as a static metadata. Our experience with *GCNav* on *IPNet* shows that these oddities can be easily addressed using a few (less than 5) simple filter queries.

6.5 Evaluation

We evaluated *GCNav* on a large, operational, customer facing IP network consisting of thousands of routers. These routers have varied functionality and come from a wide range of prominent vendors like Alcatel, Cisco and Juniper. All our evaluations are performed on the XML config files of these routers obtained for a period of 2 months (January–February, 2011).

We compare *GCNav* with the two prominent classes of existing generic diff solutions that are commonly used (see Sect. 6.2.2). We compare *GCNav* with (i) *GNUDiff* to highlight the lack of accuracy with the generic *diff* tools. (ii) GSAT [3] (a template auditing tool that uses structured XML diff) to show the benefit of *GCNav*'s insights in improving the performance while retaining its accuracy.

6.5.1 Vendor Neutrality of GCNav

Figure 6.5 shows an excerpt of the XML code used to configure an *interface* from the router config files of two prominent vendors, Cisco and Alcatel. It can be seen that though the code samples differ in syntax, they have very similar syntactic structure which is exploited by *GCNav*. In fact, the Alcatel code sample shown here was generated using a custom developed parser that generates XML from the CLI code. While we do not show here further details of configs from different vendors or different languages, we have extensively evaluated *GCNav* using router configurations from three major vendors – Alcatel, Cisco and Juniper. To emphasize this flexibility, in the following evaluations, we use config files from Alcatel devices in Sect. 6.5.2.1 and Cisco routers in Sect. 6.5.3.

```
<interface ID ="1">                    <interface ID ="1">
    <description>                          <address>
        description1                          address 11.111.11.111
    </description>                         </address>
    <ip>                                  <bfd>bfd text1 </bfd>
        <ip>                              <line>interface text2</line>
            address 11.111.11.111         <desc>
        </ip>                                 description1
        <ip>ip text2</ip>                 </desc>
    </ip>                                 <qos>qos3</qos>
    <service-policy>                  </interface>
        Service Policy1
    </service-policy>
</interface>
```

Fig. 6.5 Config snippet of an interface

(a) Cisco config sample   (b) Alcatel config sample

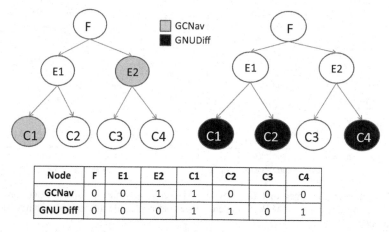

Node	F	E1	E2	C1	C2	C3	C4
GCNav	0	0	1	1	0	0	0
GNU Diff	0	0	0	1	1	0	1

Fig. 6.6 Measuring accuracy with symmetric difference

6.5.2   *Accuracy of* GCNav

In this section, we introduce a metric to measure the accuracy of *diff* tools when auditing router config files. We then evaluate the accuracy gained by *GCNav* by comparing it with the results produced by *GNUDiff* for over 3,500 field config files from the *IPNet* network.

6.5.2.1   Measuring Accuracy

The notion of accuracy while comparing config files is different from that of a traditional *diff*. A *diff* report is accurate if it is able to capture the context of the change reported. Consider the trees in Fig. 6.2. If the node $I1$ is considered *added* to the tree $T2$, then children of $I1$ (*desc* and *ip*) should also be considered implicitly as *added*. In other words, the impact of a change high up in the tree should be reflected in the entire sub-tree.

Since there is no standard measure of correctness of config *diff* reports, we verified *GCNav*'s accuracy based on operator expectations and feedback. However, we measure the accuracy gained by *GCNav* over *GNUDiff* by introducing a distance metric which represents the amount of dissimilarity between the *diff* results of the two tools. Since *GNUDiff* computes the diff by treating the XML config as flat file, we map its result back to the XML tree to ensure a fair measurement of the distance. Figure 6.6 shows the diff trees generated using the two *diff* methods. Intuitively, accuracy gained can be defined as the amount of dissimilarity between the two trees which can be computed using the symmetric distance (number of nodes which disagree in their results). The table in Fig. 6.6 shows how a simple symmetric distance is computed for the *diff* trees shown above it. Further, to capture the effect

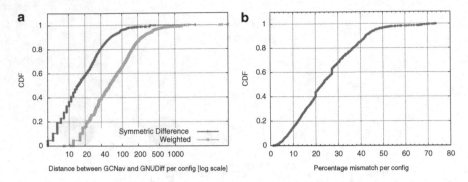

Fig. 6.7 Comparing accuracy of *GCNav* with *GNUDiff*. (**a**) Symmetric distance per config file between the two diff reports. (**b**) Percentage of nodes per config file that do not match across the two diff reports

of hierarchy, we associate weights based on the depth of the node in the config tree while computing the symmetric difference. The root should have the highest weight value (equal to the height of the tree) since it indicates a change in the entire config file, while the leaf would have the least value (a weight of one).

6.5.2.2 Comparing Accuracy of *GCNav* and *GNUDiff*

We evaluated the accuracy gained by *GCNav* over *GNUDiff* using the weighted symmetric difference scheme mentioned above. Figure 6.7a shows the CDF of the symmetric distance and weighted distance between the results of *GCNav* and *GNUDiff* for about 3,348 routers that had been modified across a period of 7 days. The graph shows that *GCNav* and *GNUDiff* differ at 20 nodes or more for 40 % of the config files (where at least one of the methods reported a change). An even more surprising observation is that among the routers that had some change reported, less than 5 % of the routers agreed completely on their *diff* results from the two tools. Figure 6.7b shows the CDF of the percentage of mismatch per config file between the *diff* reports of the two tools. It can be observed from the graph that about 40 % of the config files that reported some change had more than 25 % mismatch between the two methods. Our results show that traditional *diff* tools are very poorly suited for change-auditing config files. They also highlight the need for a system like *GCNav* which can provide *diff* reports that match operator expectations.

We now explain with an example why *GNUDiff* was inaccurate when comparing the config files. Consider Fig. 6.8 showing an excerpt from a XML field config file for 2 days (a) and (b). Figure 6.9 shows the comparison of the *GNUDiff* output (a) with the ideal (expected) output (b). *GNUDiff* is very different from the ideal diff result due to two reasons. First, it has no notion of structure in the config file and hence it is not able to associate a change at a node to its sub-tree. Second, it tries to compute the minimal edit distance which can lead to incorrect comparison.

```
<e ID ="1">                          <e ID ="1">
  <action>a1</action>                  <action>a3</action>
  <description>d1</description>        <description>d3</description>
  <line>e1 create</line>              <line>e1 create</line>
  <match ID ="p1">                     <match ID ="p3">
    <type>redirect</type>                <type>redirect</type>
    <line>match p1</line>                <line>match p3 </line>
  </match>                             </match>
</e>                                 </e>
                                    <e ID ="2">
                                      <action>a1</action>
                                      <description>d1</description>
                                      <line>e2 create</line>
                                      <match ID ="p1">
                                        <type>redirect</type>
                                        <line>match p1</line>
                                      </match>
                                    </e>

      (a) 17 Feb, 2011                          (b) 24 Feb, 2011
```

Fig. 6.8 Config from 2 days with relevant blocks

```
Add:<action>a3</action>              Del: <action>a1</action>
     <description>d3</description>        <description>d1</description>
     <line>e1 create</line>              <match ID ="p1">
     <match ID ="p3">                Add:<action>a3</action>
       <type>redirect</type>              <description>d3</description>
       <line>match p3 </line>             <match ID ="p3">
     </match>                        Add: <e ID ="2">
  </e>
  <e ID ="2">
Mod:<line>e1 create</line>
     <line>e2 create</line>

         (a) GNUDiff                            (b) Ideal
```

Fig. 6.9 Comparing *GNUDiff* with the ideal output

For instance, it matches node $e1$ from (a) with node $e2$ from (b) as they have a maximal match and reports the sub-tree of $e1$ from (a) as added. This phenomenon skews the *GNUDiff* output from the expectation as observed in the example.

6.5.3 *Response Time of* GCNav

We evaluated the performance of *GCNav* by comparing it with a template auditing tool called GSAT [3] where the goal of *gold standard* auditing is to ensure all field configs(XML) are equivalent to a certified gold config(XML) provided by the operators. We use *GCNav*'s filter queries to produce reports that matched GSAT's audit reports (i.e., both reports have the same accuracy) for a fair comparison of their performance. Though seemingly similar, *GCNav* is very different from GSAT in its design and approach. GSAT was developed as a point solution for a specific problem while *GCNav* is meant to be a generic and flexible solution that can cater

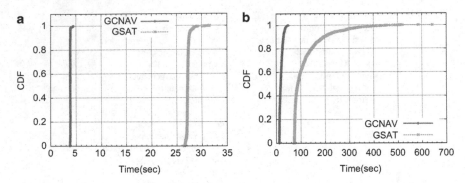

Fig. 6.10 CDF comparing the Total response time of *GCNav* vs. GSAT. (**a**) Template auditing. (**b**) Regular diff

to a variety of audit requirements. Also, GSAT (which makes use of a generic perl module called *SemanticDiff*) is not scalable and therefore has limited practical use as a more general tool. In contrast, *GCNav* is scalable and can be used for any change-auditing requirements without compromising on accuracy.

Figure 6.10a shows the CDF comparing the response time of *GCNav* and GSAT for computing the *diff* report for a set of 2,500 XML config files in the network. The Y-axis shows the CDF and X-axis represents time taken in seconds to obtain the *diff* (all phases including the pre and post processing phases) between the corresponding field config and the gold config. From the graph, it can be seen that *GCNav* is seven times faster than GSAT when computing the *diff*. Also the response time of *GCNav* is well within 5 s for all the config files making it a feasible tool for interactive auditing of router config files. On the other hand, GSAT takes more than 26 s for processing a *diff* making it too slow for interactive auditing. For this reason, GSAT was deployed as an offline tool.

We now evaluate the performance of *GCNav* and GSAT when comparing two versions of the same field config file across two successive days. Figure 6.10b shows the CDF comparing the response time of GSAT and *GCNav* to audit 2,500 XML config files across two successive days. The Y-axis shows the CDF and X-axis represents time taken for computing the *diff*(all phases). The graph shows that *GCNav* performs at least seven times better than GSAT. In particular, beyond the 50th percentile, GSAT shows exponential trends while the *GCNav*'s performance remains steady. Also, *GCNav* has a very short tail (and 95th percentile less than 20 s) compared to that of the GSAT (95th percentile greater than 300 s). Note that field configs are substantially larger in size than gold configs and therefore the problems with the scalability of GSAT becomes exacerbated. For this reason, GSAT was not practical for more general change-auditing requirements.

We compared the contribution of the various phases to the total time taken by *GCNav*. Our analysis showed that the *characterization* phase is the most expensive phase of *GCNav*, albeit taking less than 10 s for 60 % of the 2,500 files processed. A large of part of this time is spent on computing the *UID* (requiring traversal of the

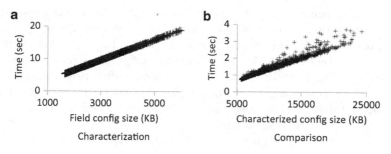

Fig. 6.11 Time vs. File size for the two key phases of *GCNav*

immediate child nodes) discussed in Sect. 6.3.1. However, characterization needs to be done exactly once for a given config file and can be performed offline as soon a new snapshot of the config files arrive. It is important to note that the rest of the phases in *GCNav* takes less than 2 s for 90 % of the files making it an effective tool even for online and interactive *diff* session.

We now perform a detailed evaluation on the scalability of *GCNav* by plotting the time taken by the characterization and comparison phases against different config file sizes. We make use of the XML field config files described in Sect. 6.5.3 for our evaluation of the scalability of *GCNav*.

Figure 6.11a shows the scatter plot representing the time taken by the characterization phase along the Y-axis and the input file size (field config) along the X-axis. Similarly, Fig. 6.11b shows the scatter plot with the time taken by the comparison phase along the Y-axis and the input file size (characterized file) along the X-axis. From the graphs, we see that the time taken by both the phases increases linearly with the increase in input file size indicating good scalability of *GCNav*. Comparing the file sizes across the two graphs also reveals the characterization overhead. Characterized files are approximately thrice the size of the corresponding field configs due to the annotations that are added as a part of the characterization phase. *GCNav* aims to reduce the audit time by adding annotations to the config files and as a consequence increases the size of the intermediate files generated. However, should space requirements become critical, characterization can be limited to specific sub-trees of the config file using the filter language described earlier.

6.6   Related Work

Change auditing is an important and frequent task performed in all enterprise networks. Many large enterprises have developed their own customized auditing solutions which is expensive and requires extensive modeling effort. Vendor specific solutions like [4] are another class of tools that have been used for auditing purposes. However, these solutions are either technology or vendor dependent and are not generic enough to be applicable for heterogeneous networks. *GCNav* on the other hand provides a generic methodology for change auditing in router configuration files. Configuration auditing has also been looked into from the perspective of solving problems like [3, 12, 18, 19]. Works like [14, 15] have looked at computing diff for Access Control Lists (ACLs) and firewall configuration. However, these are optimized and built to solve specific problems which often makes them slow or unsuitable to be used as a generic tool. On the other hand, *GCNav* adopts a more systematic and structured approach making use of the syntactic structure that is common to all router configuration files.

XML based router configuration has been explored in [22], and works like [6] have comprehensively studied the various algorithms that can be used for computing XML diff enumerating the features, advantages and disadvantages with each approach. Structured *diff* has been explored extensively in the field of version controlling [1, 8]. However, these solutions are again customized for versioning and optimized for merge operations making them unsuitable for auditing config files. Tools like XANADUE [13] have been used to detect changes in XML databases. However, unlike *GCNav* they are not context oriented, making them unsuitable for our purpose. *GCNav* differs from the generic XML *diff* tools [7, 23] in the following key design decisions. First, it does not compute the minimum edit distance which is fundamental to the accuracy of any config *diff*. Second, it does not match sub-trees across different parents which is key to both correctness and scalability of the solution.

6.7 Conclusions

In this paper, we presented *GCNav*, a configuration navigation system. Our design of *GCNav* focuses on a generic, accurate and scalable approach to change auditing in router configuration files. While existing solutions are customized towards solving specific problems, *GCNav* takes a first step towards developing a structured and general solution that retains the required accuracy and performance. *GCNav* uses the inherent syntactic structure common to all config files and thereby remains generic without compromising on the accuracy. *GCNav* takes advantage of key insights enforced by the syntactic structure of configuration files to optimize on performance of the algorithms, thereby making the system scalable. *GCNav*'s modular design renders it easily adaptable to a variety of audit requirements. Our evaluation shows that *GCNav* performs significantly better than the two prominent classes of generic diff solutions used by the operators. In the future, we also plan to compare the performance of *GCNav* with that of point solutions like semantically modeled or vendor specific tools.

GCNav has been an indispensable tool for change-auditing in a large operational customer-facing IP network for about a year and has catered to a variety of audit requirements. We believe that a system like *GCNav* which takes a general and structured approach to change-auditing in router configurations is a crucial first step that leads to an efficient and robust network management solution.

References

1. Apel, S., Liebig, J., Brandl, B., Lengauer, C., Kästner, C.: Semistructured merge: rethinking merge in revision control systems. In: ESEC/FSE, Amsterdam (2011)
2. Caldwell, D., Lee, S., Mandelbaum, Y.: Adaptive parsing of router configuration languages. In: INM, Orlando (2008)
3. Caldwell, D., Lee, S., Sen, S., Yates, J.: Gold standard auditing for router configurations. In: LANMAN, Long Branch (2010)
4. Cisco contextual configuration diff utility. http://www.cisco.com/en/US/docs/ios/fundamentals/configuration/guide/cf_config-diff.html (2003)
5. Cisco ios xml reference. http://www.cisco.com/en/US/docs/ios-xml/ios/xmlpi/configuration/12-4t/xml-pi-12-4t-book.pdf
6. Cobéna, G., Abdessalem, T., Hinnach, Y.: A comparative study for xml change detection. Research Report, INRIA Rocquencourt (2002)
7. Cobena, G., Abiteboul, S., Marian, A.: Xydiff tools detecting changes in xml documents. In: ICDE, San Jose (2002)
8. Elmougy, S., Al-Adrousy, W.: A structured-based differencing method for version control system for java codes. In: ISSPIT, Luxor (2010)
9. Feamster, N., Balakrishnan, H.: Detecting BGP configuration faults with static analysis. In: Proceedings of NSDI, Boston (2005)
10. Gnu diff. http://www.gnu.org/software/diffutils/diffutils.html
11. Junos xml reference. http://www.juniper.net/techpubs/software/junos/junos94/swconfig-automation/advantages-of-using-the-junoscript-and-junos-xml-apis.html
12. Le, F., Lee, S., Wong, T., Kim, H., Newcomb, D.: Detecting network-wide and router-specific misconfigurations through data mining. IEEE/ACM Trans. Netw. 17(1), 66–79 (2009)
13. Leonardi, E., Bhowmick, S.: Xanadue: a system for detecting changes to xml data in tree-unaware relational databases. In: SIGMOD, Beijing (2007)
14. Liu, A.: Firewall policy change-impact analysis. ACM Trans. Intern. Technol. (TOIT) 11(4), 1–24 (2012)
15. Liu, A., Gouda, M.: Diverse firewall design. IEEE Trans. Parallel Distrib. Syst. 19(9), 1237–1251 (2008)
16. Mahajan, R., Wetherall, D., Anderson, T.: Understanding BGP misconfiguration. In: Proceedings ACM SIGCOMM, Pittsburgh (2002)
17. Narain, S.: Network configuration management via model finding. In: Proceedings LISA, San Diego (2005)
18. Sung, Y., Lund, C., Lyn, M., Rao, S., Sen, S.: Modeling and understanding end-to-end class of service policies in operational networks. In: SIGCOMM, Barcelona (2009)
19. Sung, Y., Rao, S., Sen, S., Leggett, S.: Extracting network-wide correlated changes from longitudinal configuration data. In: PAM, Seoul (2009)
20. The alcatel cli reference. http://enterprise.alcatel-lucent.com/docs/?id=12979
21. The lxml python toolkit. http://lxml.de/
22. Vanbever, L., Pardoen, G., Bonaventure, O.: Towards validated network configurations with ncguard. In: INM, Orlando (2008)
23. Wang, Y., DeWitt, D. J., & Cai, J. Y. (2003, March). X-Diff: An effective change detection algorithm for XML documents. In Data Engineering, 2003. Proceedings. 19th International Conference on (pp. 519–530). IEEE.
24. Xpath query language. http://www.w3schools.com/xpath/default.asp

Chapter 7
The Right Files at the Right Time

Hayawardh Vijayakumar and Trent Jaeger

Abstract Programs fetch resources, such as files, from the operating system through the process of *name resolution*. However, name resolution can be subverted by adversaries to redirect victim processes to resources chosen by the adversaries, leading to a variety of attacks. These attacks are possible because traditional access control treats processes as black boxes, permitting all process permissions to all process system calls, enabling adversaries to trick victims into using resources that are not appropriate for particular system calls. Researchers have examined methods for enforcing distinct policies on individual system calls, but these methods are difficult to use because programmers must specify which permissions apply when manually. In this work, we examine the generation of system call-specific program policies to augment access control to defend against such name resolution attacks. Our insight in this paper is that system calls can be classified by the properties of the resources accessed to produce policies automatically. Given specific knowledge about name resolution attacks, such a classification may be refined further to prevent many name resolution attacks with little chance of false positives. In this paper, we produce a policy using runtime analysis for an Ubuntu 12.04 distribution, finding that 98.5 % of accesses can be restricted to prevent typical name resolution attacks and more than 65 % of accesses can be restricted to a single file without creating false positives. We also examine three programs in detail to evaluate the efficacy of using the provided package test suites to generate policies, finding that administrators can produce effective policies automatically.

H. Vijayakumar (✉) • T. Jaeger
SIIS Lab, The Pennsylvania State University, University Park, PA, USA
e-mail: hvijay@cse.psu.edu; tjaeger@cse.psu.edu

E. Al-Shaer et al. (eds.), *Automated Security Management*,
DOI 10.1007/978-3-319-01433-3_7, © Springer International Publishing Switzerland 2013

7.1 Introduction

Many vulnerabilities are caused because processes are tricked into using the wrong file for a particular task. In some cases, processes use adversary-controlled files when they expect protected files. For example, an untrusted search path vulnerability directs a process to an adversary-controlled file instead an expected library. In other cases, processes access trusted files when they expect unprivileged resources. Adversaries may redirect vulnerable processes to system files using links or maliciously-crafted file names using link and directory traversal attacks, respectively. We refer to these vulnerabilities collectively as *name resolution vulnerabilities*.

Authorization systems do not block access to name resolution vulnerabilities because they treat processes as black boxes. An authorization system restricts each process to perform only authorized operations on authorized objects given the process's subject, but any process system call can use any of these operations at any time. Processes are not homogenous entities, however. Each system call may have distinct expectations regarding the properties of the files used, as described above. For example, a process may require access to the password file for one system call (e.g., to authenticate users), but access to the password may not be appropriate for other system calls that retrieve content to be returned to a remote user. In general, if an access control policy permits access to any file that is inappropriate for even one system call, then the process may be vulnerable to attack.

Such problems cannot be prevented by proposed system defenses. Sandboxing [1–4] limits the permissions of a process, but cannot prevent one file from being accessible in one system call, but not another. A variety of system defenses have been proposed to prevent exploitation of race conditions in time-of-check-to-time-of-use (TOCTTOU) attacks [5–10]. However, researchers have found that systems defenses are fundamentally limited or incur false positives because they lack an understanding of process expectations [11].

As a result, the task falls to programmers to ensure that the files they use satisfy their requirements. However, this is a difficult task for programmers to get right. The fundamental problem for programmers is that they often do not know when their adversaries may have access to the files they request or the directories they use to retrieve files from names. This depends on the configuration of the system upon which the program is run. System call APIs have been extended to check file properties or for the following of links in name resolution, but these conditions are not always unsafe and are only useful in preventing some of these vulnerabilities. As a result, vulnerabilities are often present even when programmers use these APIs [12]. Capability systems [13] enable programmers to specify different permissions on different system calls, but capability systems are not commonly used in practice where programmers need to specify permissions manually, probably for the reasons above.

As a result, researchers are confident that many name resolution vulnerabilities could be prevented by enforcing system call policies, but no single system policy always applies and programmers are incapable of manually specifying policies correctly. As a result, we need methods to generate system call policies automatically. Such policies must be consistent with process expectations to prevent attacks without creating false positives [11]. Runtime analysis is now commonly used to produce access control policies [14–16]. However, runtime analysis is inherently unsound, so test cases must test enough of the program's behavior to avoid false positives and testing must distinguish safe from unsafe cases to avoid false negatives. Static analysis can be sound, but as described above, safe name resolution depends on both the system and the program, making tractable static analysis difficult.

Our insight in this paper is that programs often expect particular system calls to retrieve objects with the same properties on each use. We find that many name resolution system calls always retrieve the same file, files with the same security label, or files that are trusted by the program. For such system calls, invariants can be enforced that limit the files that may be accessed based on such classification. With further knowledge about name resolution attacks, classification may be refined further to prevent more attacks. For example, a single system call may only access trusted files, but if we know that the system call is prone to time-of-check-to-time-of-use (TOCTTOU) attacks [5, 17], then the files that may be accessed may be limited further (e.g., to those in a prior system call). Finally, knowledge that the program is run from the same configuration inputs may be used to further refine policy. For example, the same program run from two different configuration files may make distinct accesses as guided by the configuration file.

In this paper, we describe a method for generating system call policies automatically using runtime analysis. We produce system call policies for all programs the Ubuntu 12.04 distribution with a LAMP stack installed, finding that 98.5 % of accesses can be restricted to prevent typical name resolution attacks and more than 65 % of accesses can be restricted to a single file without creating false positives. As runtime analysis is unsound, we studied the use of package test suites for Apache, MySQL, and PHP. Results show how test suites can be helpful in covering more entrypoints and also exercising existing entrypoints in different ways. At the same time, we also find care must be taken to not allow test suites to generate false negatives for a particular deployment, and find that generating policies for a deployment can be automated.

7.2   Attacks

Once started, a process often needs additional system resources to complete any task (e.g., libraries, configuration files, logs, etc.) and may need to retrieve task-specific system resources (e.g., web content files, web requests via sockets, IPCs to worker processes, etc.). For convenience, resources are often retrieved by name, using a method known as *name resolution* [18, 19]. In a name resolution, a client (the process) provides a *name* to a name server (the OS), which uses *name bindings* managed by the name server to map the name to a *resource* managed by the OS.

Table 7.1 Table showing example attacks (with CWE classes) that occur due to unexpected adversarial control of name resolution components

Adversarial control of	Attack examples
Name	Directory traversal (CWE-22), external control of filename or path (CWE-73)
Binding	Link following (CWE-59), TOCTTOU (CWE-367)
Resource	Resource squatting (CWE-283), untrusted search path (CWE-426), TOCTTOU (CWE-367)

```
01  read(client_socket, filename);
02  extn = extension(filename);
03  if (extn requires module m) {
04        load_module(m);
05        process(m, filename);
06  } else {
07        stat(filename, &buf);
08        if (filename not found) {
09              write(client_socket, "404 Not Found");
10        } else {
11              fd = open(filename, O_RDONLY);
12              write(client_socket, "200 OK");
13              write(client_socket, contents(fd));
14        }
15  }
```

Fig. 7.1 Simplified processing cycle of a typical webserver

Various namespaces exist in operating systems, including the filesystem namespace, the signal namespace, and the System V IPC namespace in typical UNIX-based systems.

Name resolution attacks are possible because the names, name bindings, and resources used by the resolution mechanism may be controlled by adversaries. While programs may need to legitimately accept adversary interaction in certain name resolutions for functionality, problems arise when adversaries control name resolutions in ways the program does not expect. Table 7.1 shows examples of attacks that occur due to unexpected adversarial control of each of these components involved in name resolution.

As an example illustrating these attacks, consider a simplified version of the processing loop of a typical webserver (e.g., Apache) in Fig. 7.1. A remote client requests filename to be served. The webserver checks if a special module is required to serve the request (e.g., PHP for dynamic content), and loads it if required. Otherwise, it checks for the existence of the requested filename, and serves it if present. Possible adversaries of the webserver include both remote parties and local adversaries, such as dynamic content scripts supplied by untrusted parties. Only local adversaries are capable of modifying local information, such as name bindings and resources, whereas remote adversaries can modify names supplied to the server.

First, an adversary may attack the webserver by supplying malicious *names*. For example, `load_module` on line 4 searches for module files. Local adversaries have a variety of ways to affect the name used in such searches, using search path environment variables, insecure `RUNPATH` in binaries (CVE-2006-1564), and dynamic linker bugs. Remote adversaries may supply malicious names for the `filename`. For example, they may supply sequences of `../` to break out of the server's directory root and mount a directory traversal attack. If input filtering is not done properly, then the webserver may serve unauthorized files (line 14). While network filtering [20,21] may block some attacks of this type, malicious names may not always be filtered correctly. Handling names correctly has proven to be difficult for web application code (e.g., PHP inclusion attacks [22, 23]). Also, malicious names may obtained from local adversaries (e.g., untrusted configurations). Second, an adversary may attack the webserver by supplying malicious *name bindings*. Adversaries may supply symbolic links to redirect victims to sensitive resources, such as `/etc/shadow`. By default, Apache refuses to follow symbolic links in users' web directories to prevent this attack. This checking is done on line 7. However, a local adversary could change the name bindings corresponding to `filename` to a symbolic link to `/etc/shadow` between the check on line 7 and the use on line 11. Since the webserver is authorized to read `/etc/shadow`, this file will be opened on line 11, enabling leakage of secret data. This is an example of a classic time-of-check-to-time-of-use (TOCTTOU) attack [5, 17].

Third, an adversary may attack the webserver by controlling *resources* accessed by the webserver in unexpected ways. For example, if the webserver searches for modules in the user's document root directory, the user can supply a malicious library to gain control of the webserver process. Another example of unexpected control of a resource is IPC squatting, where the adversary creates a socket at a well-known location and masquerades as a legitimate server.

No current mechanism effectively prevents the myriad of name resolution attacks described above. Traditional access control is insufficient to prevent such attacks, as it views processes as a monolithic unit. In the example above, opening files in a user's web directory is valid on line 14, but invalid on line 4 while loading module libraries. Sandboxes [1–4] have a similar limitation, as they may reduce process permissions, but they still view processes monolithically. Prior defenses against such attacks [6–10, 24, 25] have been found to be flawed or only cover a subset of these attacks under limited conditions [11, 26].

7.3   Related Work

Relevant prior work has shown us that having policies that provide distinct permissions for some system calls is valuable and that useful security policies can be produced in a mostly-automated way. However, current methods for producing policies are inadequate for preventing attacks on system calls without creating too many false positives and negatives.

7.3.1 System Call Enforcement

Research has identified the need to mediate process access to system resources independently per system call to prevent vulnerabilities. Sekar et al. [27] presented an intrusion detection system that used the instruction that invokes the system call library (which we call *entrypoint* below) to parameterize automata models of programs. However, such models are not directed towards attacks and do not scale. In addition, program-only models in general cannot prevent name resolution vulnerabilities, because programs may still use the same name.

More recently, methods to approximate classical integrity are capable of reasoning about individual program system calls [28–32], judging whether the program will be able to upgrade or discard inputs safely as required by Clark-Wilson integrity [33]. Some systems provide limited integrity protection by identifying objects that may affect the processes' integrity [28, 29]. However, if the process is allowed to use adversary-controlled objects and uses them at the wrong time, then vulnerabilities are likely. Some system calls may require protected objects only, but others may accept a variety of inputs. Other research requires programmers to describe the permissions per system call using annotations [30, 31], analogous to capabilities. Such policies are complex for programmers to specify correctly, as evidenced by name resolution vulnerabilities. Researchers have shown that such annotations can be produced from constraints [34], although programmers must still specify such constraints manually.

Researchers have also explored methods to enable programs to enforce access control policies [35, 36]. Such methods depend on programmers labeling the system call invocations through which untrusted inputs may be received. To improve the accuracy of such enforcement, researchers have also examined integrating system and program MAC enforcement [37, 38]. In this case, system and program policies must be integrated. In some cases, it is possible to automate such integration [39], although program policies are still uncommon.

7.3.2 Policy Generation

Historically, MAC policies, such as Bell-LaPadula [40], IX [41], and Caernarvon [42], must be specified manually. In modern commodity systems, however, runtime analysis is now commonly used to produce mandatory access control (MAC) policies [14–16]. Runtime analysis is primarily used to prevent false positives in policies, as early commodity MAC enforcement was shunned due to too many false positives. In these runtime analyses, security-critical programs are run, and the permissions that they use are logged. Any permission request logged is then granted for the program since some real program operation required the permission. As a result, these MAC enforcement policies are designed to satisfy *least privilege* [43], where processes are only granted the permissions that they require to perform their function. Since such policies are not produced from a security goal some permissions may be unsafe for the process. In addition, as discussed in the Sect. 7.2, any process system call may use any of the permissions associated with the process, which causes the risks that adversaries leverage in name resolution attacks.

Runtime analysis is unsound, however, meaning that both false positives and false negatives are possible. False negatives may occur because even benign conditions may be unsafe. Suppose that the same system call is run in two different configurations where two different, but incompatible, files are accessed. Use of the wrong file may cause a vulnerability, which would be a false negative since both would be allowed. False positives may occur because of the lack of coverage in runtime test cases. If not enough cases are run, then the analysis may conclude that one file is accessed when in fact many may be accessed.

7.4   Approach

To prevent name resolution attacks, we must limit the files that may be retrieved as part of a name resolution system call. Thus, a system call policy consists of a set of files that may be retrieved for a particular system call.[1] The challenge is to define system call subjects and determine a method to find the files that such subjects may access safely. As with commodity MAC policies, the goal is to minimize false positives.

Starting with system calls, we uniquely identify each system call invocation by its program entrypoint. A *program entrypoint* is the program instruction calls a function in the system call library that results in a system call invocation [44]. For example, when a program wants to open a new file, it invokes the open function in the system call library (e.g., libc). As the program may have many different instructions that request the open system call, the program entrypoint differentiates among them enabling distinct policies to be applied based on each.

Each program entrypoint may request one or more different files. We identify four distinct classifications: (1) same file[2]; (2) same label; (3) same integrity; and (4) any file. An entrypoint that is classified as *same file* is thought to retrieve one file in all cases. An entrypoint that is classified as *same label* is thought to retrieve multiple files, but each file has the same MAC label. An entrypoint that is classified as *same integrity* either only retrieves files that are assigned labels that are trusted by the program or untrusted by the program. Note that many name resolution attacks can be prevented simply by ensuring that system calls only retrieve trusted or untrusted files. The finer classifications provide further assurance that adversaries cannot redirect victim processes in an exploitable manner. The fourth classification is for entrypoints that may retrieve arbitrary files.

---

[1] Name resolution attacks may be launched with any operation privilege to files, so we ignore the file operations requested in this work.

[2] This is actually the same inode, as inode is the unique identifier for file objects.

The classification of objects may be refined by knowledge about specific name resolution attacks, but we must be careful not to introduce false positives when using such knowledge. For example, TOCTTOU attacks change the file retrieved between a *check* system call and a corresponding *use* system call [24]. A check system call examines a file and the use system call enables the file to be processed. In general, a check-use pair is supposed to use the same file, so it is possible to restrict a use system call to a specific file (i.e., the one used in the check) even of the entrypoint was classified as any. Other attacks, such as PHP includes or directory traversal, may require limiting the file retrieved to a specific type and/or directory, although these restrictions are often represented in the MAC labeling of files.

Once the entrypoint is classified, then file access can be controlled per system call. While the approach above results in a low probably of false positives (depending on the analysis accuracy), some unnecessary false negatives may be created. The problem is that a single program may be run under multiple deployments. A program deployment may be influenced by a number of factors, such as its configuration files, environment variables, command line options, etc. The classifications may be refined further based on a specific program deployment, although the number of possible deployments for some programs may be large. Such deployment-specific policies are analogous to "booleans" in the SELinux policy, which specify different permissions when particular configuration options are selected. Note that booleans are set manually in SELinux policies, where we want find mappings between deployments and classifications automatically, if possible.

Finally, we use runtime analysis to produce the classification described above. As mentioned, runtime analysis may be error-prone because it is unsound, so it is important to find a method of producing runtime test cases with broad coverage of the functions performed by each program. Many program packages now include test suites used to test program functionality over a variety of configurations, so we explore the effectiveness of using such test suites for runtime analysis in this paper.

7.5 Design and Implementation

In this section, we discuss the design and implementation of our system to defend against name resolution attacks.

Our system is broadly divided into logging and enforcement phases. During the logging phase, our system logs accesses made by programs during name resolution calls, along with the entrypoint and security label of the final resource retrieved. Test suites for programs are run at this stage. These access logs are then used to classify entrypoints into four categories (Sect. 7.6), which are then enforced through rules that make sure that entrypoints obey their classification.

However, runtime coverage during the logging phase may not have captured all entrypoints possible, and test suites are not available for all programs. Thus, legitimate accesses may be blocked because they are not seen at runtime. This is a common problem amongst other runtime policy-generation approaches such as

SELinux as well. Our approach is to allow any operation at previously unseen entrypoints; thus, the program will continue to function, although attacks may be missed.

Our system is implemented for the Linux 3.2 kernel. It layers on top of the SELinux access control module, which is itself called on Linux Security Module (LSM) hooks. Thus, we intercept security-sensitive operations, and our enforcement is done on top of access control.

Obtaining the entrypoint is done in the kernel by unwinding the userspace stack. However, straightforward unwinding fails in modern distributions as programs are compiled without frame pointers. To overcome this, we parse the eh_frame section of the ELF binary, which contains the necessary information to obtain the stack trace, and is compiled by default on modern Fedora and Ubuntu distributions.

If the program is an interpreter, obtaining the stack will only give the interpreter's entrypoint, and not the script file or line number. In previous work [44], we devised methods to introspect into Bash and PHP interpreters to obtain this information. Finally, the entrypoint for processes launched from the Bash shell interpreter contains the parent shell script's filename and line number. This is because the entrypoints for programs like cp, mv should be considered in relation to their parent script and not solely as separate programs.

7.6   Evaluation

In this section, we first study the feasibility of using entrypoint classifications to restrict resource access. Our results suggest that most entrypoints can be classified as either accessing high or low integrity resources, leading to enforcement with few false positives. Next, test suites can help exercise programs to generate more accurate entrypoint resource mappings. We find that while test suites help significantly, they may also cause false negatives. Finally, we evaluate how effective our enforcement is in stopping attacks.

Our tests were carried out on an Ubuntu 12.04 Desktop distribution that also had the LAMP (Linux-Apache-MySQL-PHP) stack installed. The kernel had our module that layered on top of SELinux to perform logging and enforcement.

7.6.1   Entrypoint Classification

Table 7.2 shows the classification of entrypoints exercised system-wide at normal runtime. Most entrypoints access very specific resources, and only a few (around 1.4 %) of the total access resources of both high and low integrity. This was consistent even for programs run under the test suites – most entrypoints either accessed

Table 7.2 Different
entrypoint classifications.
It can be seen that only very
few entrypoints access both
high and low integrity
resources

Entrypoint class	Number	Percentage
Total	2,196	–
Single filename	1,486	67.6 %
Single label	1,716	78.1 %
Only high-integrity	1,910	86.9 %
Only low-integrity	254	11.5 %
Any integrity	32	1.5 %

Fig. 7.2 Histogram showing
the distribution of the number
of resources accessed by
entrypoints

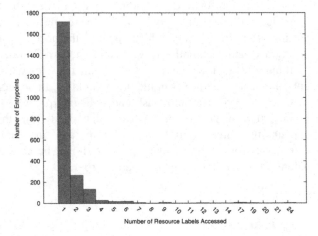

only high, or only low integrity. This suggests it is possible to constrain most
entrypoints to either high or low resources, thereby enabling effective enforcement
with low false positives.

Figure 7.2 shows the distribution of the number of resources accessed per
entrypoint. More than 90 % of entrypoints access 3 resources or less.

7.6.2   Test Suites

We first examine how test suites can help generate accurate entrypoint to resource
mappings by comparing normal runtime with test suites. Test suites contain test
cases created by developers and are primarily geared towards testing functionality,
although a few test suites also look for known security bugs. These test suites are
usually meant to test binaries compiled from the package's source code, although
many also support testing already deployed binaries. For example, test suites for the
Apache webserver, PHP and MySQL support testing existing deployments, whereas
the test suite for the OpenSSH server supports testing only a compiled binary.
For normal runtime of the LAMP server stack, we installed phpBB, a PHP-based
bulletin board system, and carried out tasks such as posting messages on the board.
PHP was setup through FastCGI so it runs as a process separate from Apache.

Table 7.3 Table showing the effect of test suites on programs. The first column shows the number of entrypoints exercised by a normal run, the second using the test suites. The last two columns show the number of entrypoints that changed classification after running the test suite, and whether they led to false positives, or negatives (identified manually)

Program	Normal run	Test suite	Class change	
			FP reduce	FN increase
Apache	32	36	2	2
MySQL	12	14	0	0
PHP	33	48	0	1

Table 7.3 shows how test suites are helpful in identifying additional behaviour. In all cases, we found the test suites uncovered additional entrypoints beyond normal runtime, thereby leading to more complete code coverage. In addition, the test suites may exercise already known entrypoints in ways normal runtime does not, thereby augmenting the set of accessed resources at this entrypoint. Thus, while test suites reduce false positives by exercising known entrypoints in different ways, they may also introduce false negatives by accessing resources not valid in the actual deployment of the program.

7.6.3   Factors Affecting Entrypoint Classification

We found that the sets of resources accessed by entrypoints in programs are affected by the several factors. Test suites both uncover new entrypoints and exercise entrypoints in different ways by varying these factors. However, some of these factors are fixed for a deployment, and varying them may result in false negatives. We discuss each factor below in relation to Table 7.3 with examples.

Configuration. Some entrypoints only operate under certain configurations. This was one reason why additional entrypoints were uncovered by the test suites. However, such entrypoints may not be enabled at all in normal runtime.

Other entrypoints exercise different configurations. However, these might result in false negatives. As an example, the Apache configuration option `AllowOverride` allows Apache to accept user-defined configuration files for user web pages. This may cause a security threat if such configuration files are not handled properly. it was tested by the test suite, thereby classifying the entrypoint reading configurations as accessing both high-integrity system-defined configuration and low-integrity user-defined configuration. However, our deployed configuration did not allow this option. Here, the test suite caused a false negative by making the entrypoint classification more generic than it should be.

Rules should thus be generated keeping for a particular deployment configuration. However, knowledge of how configuration options affect entrypoints is beneficial. We propose "tagging" generated rules with the corresponding configuration options, so a rule base appropriate for a deployment can be generated by simply examining target configuration.

Command line parameters and Environment Variables. Varying command-line parameters can both reduce false positives and increase false negatives, similar to configuration options. This depends on whether a program is launched with differing arguments, or with a fixed set of command-line parameters (e.g., startup scripts).

First, changing command line parameters reduces false positives. For example, the mount program takes as a command line parameter a mountpoint. If runtime sees only a single invocation with a single mountpoint, it can erroneously conclude that the mount entrypoint can only access that particular mountpoint. However, during normal system boot, several mountpoints are used, and the mount entrypoint is classified as accessing both high- and low-integrity directories. Other utilities such as cp, mv, cat also exhibit similar behavior.

However, note that such programs are often launched from scripts where they have to access very particular files (e.g., redirect output to a temporary file). Thus, if a program is launched from a shell script, we take its entrypoint to be the parent interpreter's script, and can enforce such resource access.

Second, changing command line parameters increases false negatives. This behaviour is observed when command line parameters indicate configuration options that are not used. For example, the Apache test suite specifies a configuration file using a command line parameter, and runtime erroneously concludes that entrypoints accessing the log file are more generic than they should be.

Environment variables also have effects similar to command line parameters.

Working Directory. The working directory may affect the resources accessed if relative pathnames are specified. These again mainly affect utility programs.

7.6.4 Effectiveness of Enforcement

To evaluate the effectiveness of our enforcement on known bugs, we selected a few previously known vulnerabilities and a previously unknown and unpatched name resolution vulnerability [12] at entrypoints uncovered by our runtime analysis. Table 7.4 shows the exact attacks we tried. We found that all the exploits that we tested were blocked.

Firefox and Apache searched for library files in the current working directory, which could lead to compromise if they were launched in an adversary-accessible directory. The entrypoint that reads library files was associated only with high-integrity files and so adversary supplied libraries at this entrypoint were blocked.

PHP is vulnerable to a directory traversal attack due to a parsing error in the filename of uploaded files (CVE-2011–2202). We tried to force a vulnerable version of PHP to store our uploaded file at an arbitrary location. This attack was also blocked because this entrypoint was associated only with resources in /tmp. This entrypoint was actually covered by the test suite and not normal runtime (as we did not upload any file during normal runtime), and is an example of how test suites help in covering program entrypoints. Finally, a shell script that initializes

Table 7.4 The exploits we tested our process firewall against

Program	Reference	Class
Firefox	CVE-2010-3,182	Untrusted search
Apache	CVE-2006-1,564	Untrusted search
Php	CVE-2006-5,178	TOCTTOU
Init script	Prev. unknown	Link following
Php	CVE-2011-2,202	Directory traversal
Mysql	CVE-2010-1,848	Directory traversal

the avahi-daemon is vulnerable to link following due to insecurely writing to a temporary file. We created a symbolic link in /tmp to /etc/passwd. This attack was also blocked, because the script entrypoint was again associated with only /tmp, and access to /etc was disallowed. This demonstrates how our enforcement mechanism stops attacks, even though it aims for low false positives.

7.7 Conclusions

The class of name resolution attacks is a difficult problem to solve, because it involves both program context and system knowledge. Thus, adversaries have been able to keep taking advantage of these vulnerabilities to compromise systems. We identify how adversarial control of the name, binding and resources used in name resolution can lead to a variety of attacks. We propose a uniform solution for these problems by restricting program entrypoints to only appropriate resources. We find that program entrypoints fall under classes which can be easily enforced to stop these attacks with little or no false positives. We find over 98 % of name resolution accesses can be restricted to rule out name resolution attacks. Since our classification of entrypoints is based on a runtime analysis for which coverage is a challenge, we examine how test suites help to generate policies, and steps towards automation of policy generation. Finally, we demonstrate how our system can defend against instances of name resolution attacks, showing the promise of our system to protect programs against this class of attacks, while not unduly producing false positives. In future work, we aim to explore how static analysis can be used to generate rules.

References

1. Berman, A., et al.: TRON: process-specific file protection for the UNIX operating system. In: USENIX TC '95, Framingham (1995)
2. Goldberg, et al.: A secure environment for untrusted helper applications. In: USENIX Security '96, San Jose (1996)
3. Acharya, et al.: MAPbox: using parameterized behavior classes to confine untrusted applications. In: USENIX SSYM, Denver (2000)

4. Garfinkel, et al.: Ostia: a delegating architecture for secure system call interposition. In: NDSS '04, San Diego (2004)
5. Bishop, M., Digler, M.: Checking for race conditions in file accesses. Comput. Syst. **9**(2), Spring 131–152 (1996)
6. Cowan, C., et al.: Raceguard: kernel protection from temporary file race vulnerabilities. In: USENIX Security Symposium, Washington, DC (2001)
7. Tsyrklevich, et al.: Dynamic detection and prevention of race conditions in file accesses. In: USENIX Security, Washington, DC (2003)
8. Dean, et al.: Fixing races for fun and profit. In: USENIX SSYM, San Diego (2004)
9. Tsafrir, D., et al.: Portably solving file tocttou races with hardness amplification. In: USENIX FAST, San Jose (2008)
10. Chari, S., et al.: Where do you want to go today? Escalating privileges by pathname manipulation. In: NDSS '10, San Diego (2010)
11. Cai, X., et al.: Exploiting unix file-system races via algorithmic complexity attacks. In: IEEE SSP '09, Cardiff (2009)
12. Vijayakumar, H., Schiffman, J., Jaeger, T.: Sting: finding name resolution vulnerabilities in programs. In: Proceedings of the 21st USENIX Security Symposium (USENIX Security 2012), Bellevue (2012)
13. Levy, H.M.: Capability-Based Computer Systems. Digital Press, Bedford (1984). Available at http://www.cs.washington.edu/homes/levy/capabook/
14. Provos, N.: Improving host security with system call policies. In: USENIX Security '03, Washington, DC. USENIX Association, Berkeley (2003)
15. AppArmor Linux application security, http://www.novell.com/linux/security/apparmor/ (2008)
16. audit2allow, http://fedoraproject.org/wiki/SELinux/audit2allow (2013)
17. McPhee, W.S.: Operating system integrity in OS/VS2. IBM Syst. J. **13**, 230–252 (1974) [Online]. Available: http://dx.doi.org/10.1147/sj.133.0230
18. Needham, R.: Chapter: names. In: Mullender, S. (ed) Distributed Systems. Addison-Wesley, Boston (1989)
19. Domain Names – Implementation and Specification, http://www.ietf.org/rfc/rfc1035.txt (1987)
20. Vigna, et al.: Testing network-based intrusion detection signatures using mutant exploits. In: ACM CCS, Washington, DC (2004)
21. What is "Deep Inspection"? http://www.ranum.com/security/computer_security/editorials/deepinspect/ (2013)
22. PHP LFI to arbitrary code execution. http://www.exploit-db.com/download_pdf/17010/ (2011)
23. Balzarotti, et al.: Saner: composing static and dynamic analysis to validate sanitization in web applications. In: IEEE SSP, Oakland (2008)
24. Wei, et al.: Tocttou vulnerabilities in unix-style file systems: an anatomical study. In: USENIX FAST '05, San Francisco (2005)
25. Suk Lhee, K., Chapin, S.J.: Detection of file-based race conditions. Int. J. Inf. Secur. **4**(1–2), 105–119 (2005)
26. Borisov, et al.: Fixing races for fun and profit: how to abuse atime. In: USENIX Security '06, Baltimore (2005)
27. Sekar, R., Venkatakrishnan, V., Basu, S., Bhatkar, S., DuVarney, D.C.: Model-carrying code: a practical approach for safe execution of untrusted applications. In: Proceedings of the Nineteenth ACM Symposium on Operating Systems Principles, ser. SOSP '03, Bolton Landing, pp. 15–28. ACM, New York (2003) [Online]. Available: http://doi.acm.org/10.1145/945445.945448
28. Li, et al.: Usable mandatory integrity protection for operating systems. In: IEEE SSP, Madison (2007)
29. Sun, W., Sekar, R., Poothia, G., Karandikar, T.: Practical proactive integrity protection: a basis for malware defense. In: Proceedings of the 2008 IEEE Symposium on Security and Privacy, Oakland (2008)

30. Shankar, U., Jaeger, T., Sailer, R.: Toward automated information-flow integrity verification for security-critical applications. In: Proceedings of the 2006 ISOC Networked and Distributed Systems Security Symposium (NDSS'06), San Diego (2006)
31. Krohn, M.N., Yip, A., Brodsky, M., Cliffer, N., Kaashoek, M.F., Kohler, E., Morris, R.: Information flow control for standard OS abstractions. In: Proceedings of the 21st ACM Symposium on Operating Systems Principles, Stevenson, pp. 321–334 (2007)
32. Zeldovich, N., Boyd-Wickizer, S., Kohler, E., Mazières, D.: Making information flow explicit in HiStar. In: Proceedings of the Seventh Symposium on Operating System Design and Implementation, Seattle, pp. 263–278 (2006)
33. Clark, D.D., Wilson, D.: A comparison of military and commercial security policies. In: 1987 IEEE Symposium on Security and Privacy, Oakland (1987)
34. Harris, W., Jha, S., Reps, T.: Difc programs by automatic instrumentation. In: Proceedings of Computer and Communications Security (CCS), Chicago (2010)
35. Denning, D.: A lattice model of secure information flow. Commun. ACM **19**(5), 236–242 (1976)
36. Myers, A.C., Liskov, B.: A decentralized model for information flow control. In: Proceedings of the 16th ACM Symposium on Operating System Principles, Saint Malo (1997)
37. Hicks, S., Boniface, Jaeger, T., McDaniel, P.: From trusted to secure: building and executing applications that enforce system security. In: Proceedings of the USENIX Annual Technical Conference, Santa Clara. USENIX Association, Berkeley (2007)
38. Liu, J., George, M.D., Vikram, K., Qi, X., Waye, L., Myers, A.C.: Fabric: a platform for secure distributed computation and storage. In: In Proceedings ACM Symposium on Operating Systems Principles, Big Sky, pp. 321–334 (2009)
39. Rueda, S., King, D., Jaeger, T.: Verifying compliance of trusted programs. In: Proceedings of the 17th USENIX Security Symposium, San Jose (2008)
40. Bell, D.E., LaPadula, L.J.: Secure computer system: Unified exposition and Multics interpretation, Deputy for Command and Management Systems, HQ Electronic Systems Division (AFSC), L. G. Hanscom Field, Bedford, MA, Technical Report ESD-TR-75-306, March 1976, also, MITRE Technical Report MTR-2997
41. McIlroy, D., Reeds, J.: Multilevel windows on a single-level terminal. In: Proceedings of the (First) USENIX Security Workshop, Portland (1988)
42. Toll, D.C., Karger, P.A., Palmer, E.R., McIntosh, S.K., Weber, S.: The caernarvon secure embedded operating system. SIGOPS Oper. Syst. Rev. **42**(1), 32–39 (2008) [Online]. Available: http://doi.acm.org/10.1145/1341312.1341320
43. Saltzer, J.H., Schroeder, M.D.: The protection of information in computer systems. Proc. IEEE **63**(9), 1278–1308 (1975)
44. Vijayakumar, H., Jakka, G., Rueda, S., Schiffman, J., Jaeger, T.: Integrity walls: finding attack surfaces from mandatory access control policies. In: Proceedings of the Seventh ACM Symposium on Information, Computer, and Communications Security (ASIACCS 2012), Hangzhou (2012)

Chapter 8
Rule Configuration Checking in Secure Cooperative Data Access

Meixing Le, Krishna Kant, and Sushil Jajodia

Abstract In this paper, we consider an environment where a group of parties have their own relational databases and provide restricted access to other parties. In order to implement desired business services, each party defines a set of authorization rules over the join of basic relations, and these rules can be viewed as the configurations of the accessible information in the cooperative data access environment. However, authorization rules are likely to be developed by each enterprise somewhat independently based on their business needs and may not be sufficiently well defined to be enforceable. That is, the rules may be missing some crucial access capabilities that are essential for implementing the desired restrictions. In this paper, we propose a mechanism to check the rule enforceability for each given authorization rule.

8.1 Introduction

Providing rich services to clients with minimal manual intervention or paper documents requires the enterprises involved in the service path to collaborate and share data in an orderly manner. For instance, an automated determination of patient coverage and costs requires that a hospital and insurance company be able to make certain queries against each others' databases. Similarly, to arrange for automated shipping of merchandise and to enable automated status checking, the e-commerce vendor and shipping company should be able to exchange relevant information, perhaps in form of database queries. In such environments, data must be released only in a controlled way among cooperative parties, subject to the authorization policies established by them. The authorization policies are the configurations for

M. Le (✉) • K. Kant • S. Jajodia
Center for Secure Information Systems, George Mason University, 4400 University Drive
Fairfax, VA 22030, USA
e-mail: mlep@gmu.edu; kkant@gmu.edu; jajodia@gmu.edu

E. Al-Shaer et al. (eds.), *Automated Security Management*,
DOI 10.1007/978-3-319-01433-3_8, © Springer International Publishing Switzerland 2013

the accessible information in such an environment. In this paper, we expose and study the accuracy and enforceability of such configurations in a collaboration setting.

In general, enterprise data may appear in a variety of forms, including the simplistic key-value forms like Google's BigTable. However, for concreteness, we assume that all data is stored in relational form, with all tables in a standard form such as BCNF. In such a model, data access privileges are given by a set of authorization rules, each of which is defined either on original tables belonging to an enterprise or over the lossless join of two or more of these. The join operations, coupled with appropriate projection and selection operations define the access restrictions; although in order to enable working with only the schemas, we do not consider selection operation. The authorization rules must be enforceable, and each incoming query should be efficiently verifiable against them.

Although the problem is rather straightforward, there are many hurdles in properly specifying and implementing the authorization rules. First, since the enterprises are allowed to specify an arbitrary set of authorization rules, it is possible that there is no way to derive a safe execution plan for certain rules. The simplest way to illustrate this problem is by considering the following situation: a rule specifies access to $R \bowtie S$ (where R and S are relations owned by two different parties); however, no party has access to both R and S individually and thus no party is able to do the join operation! Thus, a basic problem is to determine enforceability of the given rules. If a rule is not enforceable, we should either remove it or make it enforceable. If not, this will cause problems for the queries. For instance, a query for the information of $R \bowtie S$ is authorized by the rule configuration, but cannot be properly answered.

We address the configuration checking problem in two steps. First, we examine the enforceability of each authorization rule in a constructive bottom-up manner, and build a graph structure that captures the relationships among the rules. In a collaborative environment, a rule can be enforced with not only the locally available information but also the remote information from the cooperative parties. If a rule is not totally enforceable, we remove the unenforceable part of the rule, so that only enforceable rules are retained.

The rest of the paper is organized as follows. Section 8.2 briefly discusses the related work. Section 8.3 defines the problem of cooperative access formally, introduces a number of definitions and concepts, which are illustrated via a running example. Section 8.4 discusses the mechanism to check rule enforceability. Finally, Sect. 8.5 concludes the discussion.

8.2   Related Work

The problem of controlled data release among collaborating parties has been studied in [8]. The basic model in this paper is identical to ours and provides the motivation for our work. Its main contribution is an algorithm to check if a query with a given query plan tree can be safely executed. However, it does not address the problem of rule enforceability. Without a trusted third party, the unenforceable rules are inaccurate configurations and need to be revised, and we address that in this work. In another work [7], the same authors evaluate whether the information release the query entails is allowed by all the authorization rules given to a particular user, which considers the possible combinations of rules and assumes that the rules are defined in an implicit way. In our work, we assume authorizations are explicitly given, and data release is prohibited if there is no explicit authorization. As they focus on the problem of query authorization, we emphasize the executability of the authorized queries.

Processing distributed queries under protection requirements has been studied in [6, 13]. In these works, data access is constrained by a limited access pattern called binding pattern, and the goal is to identify the classes of queries that a given set of access patterns can support. We have a very different authorization model involves independent parties who may cooperate in the execution of a query. There are also classical works on distributed query processing [5, 12], but they do not deal with constraints made by the data owners.

Answering queries using views [10, 11, 14] has been extensively studied, and the technique is useful for query optimization, data integration and so on. The given view definitions is these works can be similar constraints to our authorization rules. However, these works usually consider the queries and views in the form of conjunctive queries, and they do not consider the collaboration relationships among different parties. These make our problem different from their works.

In the area of outsourced database services, some works [1, 9] discuss how to secure the data in such environments, and there are also services like Sovereign joins [2]. It gets encrypted relations from the participating data providers, and sends the encrypted results to the recipients. These methods are useful to enforce our authorization rules, but we discuss the problem without any involvement of third parties.

The given authorization rules is also similar to the firewall rules, which indicates what types of queries can go through. As firewall rules are need to be enforceable and accurate [4, 15], we have the same requirements in our situation.

8.3 Problem and Definitions

We consider a group of cooperating parties, each of which maintains its data in a standard relational form such as BCNF. (It is possible to consider more complex normal forms than BCNF, but we do not consider them here.) We assume simple select-project-join queries (e.g., no cyclic join schemas or queries). The query may be answered by any of the parties that has the required permissions. We assume that the join schema is given – i.e., all the possible join attributes between relations are known. Each join in the schema is lossless so a join attribute is always a key attribute of some relations. We assume the rules to be **"upwards closed"** which is the same as [8]. That is, if two rules expressly grant permission to access two different relations, say R and S, then there also exists a rule providing access to

Fig. 8.1 The given join
schema for the example

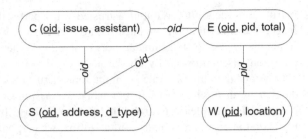

their join result $R \bowtie S$. We study the problems only involving existing cooperative
parties, without any third parties.

The basic problems considered here are as follows: Given a set of authorization
rules R on N cooperating parties, identifies the subset of R that can be enforced,
and determines the maximal portion of the rules that can be enforced.

8.3.1 A Running Example

Our running example for illustration models an e-commerce scenario with four
parties: (a) *E-commerce*, denoted as E, is a company that sells products online,
(b) *Customer_Service*, denoted C, that provides customer services (potentially for
more than one Company), (c) *Shipping*, denoted S, provides shipping services
(again, potentially to multiple companies), and (d) *Warehouse*, denoted W, is the
party that provides storage services. To keep the example simple, we assume that
each party owns but one relation described as follows:

1. E-commerce (*order_id*, product_id, total) as E
2. Customer_Service (*order_id*, issue, assistant) as C
3. Shipping (*order_id*, address, delivery_type) as S
4. Warehouse (*product_id*, location) as W

In the following, we use oid to denote $order\_id$ for short, pid stands for
$product\_id$, and $delivery$ stands for $delivery\_type$. The possible join schema
is also given in Fig. 8.1. Relations E, C, S can join over their common attribute oid;
relation E can join with W over the attribute pid. In the example, relations are in
BCNF, and the only FD (Functional Dependency) in each relation is the underlined
key attribute determines the non-key attributes.

8.3.2 Authorization Model and Definitions

Following the definition of authorization model in [8], an **authorization rule** r_t is
a triple$[A_t, J_t, P_t]$, where J_t is called the join path of the rule, A_t is the authorized
attribute set, and P_t is the party authorized to access the data.

Table 8.1 Authorization rules for e-commerce cooperative data access

Rule no.	Authorized attribute set	Join path	Party
1	{pid, location}	W	P_W
2	{oid, pid}	E	P_W
3	{oid, pid, location}	$E \bowtie_{pid} W$	P_W
4	{oid, pid, total}	E	P_E
5	{oid, pid, total, issue}	$E \bowtie_{oid} C$	P_E
6	{oid, pid, total, issue, address}	$S \bowtie_{oid} E \bowtie_{oid} C$	P_E
7	{oid, pid, location, total, address}	$S \bowtie_{oid} E \bowtie_{pid} W$	P_E
8	{oid, pid, issue, assistant, total, address, delivery}	$S \bowtie_{oid} E \bowtie_{oid} C \bowtie_{pid} W$	P_E
9	{oid, address, delivery}	S	P_S
10	{oid, pid, total}	E	P_S
11	{oid, pid, total, address, delivery}	$E \bowtie_{oid} S$	P_S
12	{oid, pid, total, location}	$E \bowtie_{pid} W$	P_S
13	{oid, location, pid, total, address, delivery}	$S \bowtie_{oid} E \bowtie_{pid} W$	P_S
14	{oid, pid}	E	P_C
15	{oid, issue, assistant}	C	P_C
16	{oid, pid, issue, assistant}	$E \bowtie_{oid} C$	P_C
17	{oid, pid, issue, assistant, total, address, location}	$S \bowtie_{oid} C \bowtie_{oid} E \bowtie_{pid} W$	P_C

Definition 1. *A **join path** is the result of a series of join operations over a set of relations $R_1, R_2 \ldots R_n$ with the specified equi-join predicates $(A_{l1}, A_{r1}), (A_{l2}, A_{r2}) \ldots (A_{ln}, A_{rn})$ among them, where (A_{li}, A_{ri}) are the join attributes from two relations. We use the notation J_t to indicate the join path of rule r_t. We use JR_t to indicate the set of relations in a join path J_t. The **length** of a join path is the cardinality of JR_t.*

We can consider a join path as the result of join operations without limitations on the attributes. Thus, A_t is the set of attributes projection on the join path that is authorized to be accessed by party P_t. Table 8.1 shows the set of rules given to these parties. The first column is the rule number, the second column gives the attribute set of the rules, join paths of the rules are shown in the third column, and the last column shows the authorized parties of the rules. We make one more assumption regarding the rules we are considering. We assume that each given authorization rule always includes *all of the key attributes of the relations that appear in the rule join path*. In other words, a rule has all the join attributes on its join path. We argue that this is a reasonable assumption as in many cases when the information is released, it is always released along with the key attributes.

When a query is given, it should be answered by one of the parties that have the authorization. Since our authorization model is based on attributes, any attribute appearing in the Selection predicate in an SQL query is treated as a Projection attribute. In other words, the authorization of a PSJ(Project, Select, Join) query is transformed into an equivalent Projection-Join query authorization. Therefore, a query q can be represented by a pair $[A_q, J_q]$, where A_q is the set of attributes

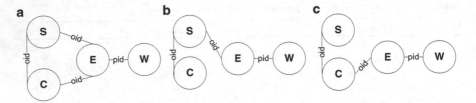

Fig. 8.2 Join path equivalence

appearing in the Selection and Projection predicates, and the query join path J_q is the FROM clause of an SQL query. For instance, there is an SQL query Q_1:

"Select $oid, total, address$ From E Join S On $E.oid = S.oid$ Where $delivery = $ 'ground'"

The query can be represented as the pair $[A_q, J_q]$, where A_q is the set $\{oid, total, address, delivery\}$; J_q is the join path $E \bowtie_{oid} S$.

In fact, each join path defines a new relation/view. To better understand the authorization relationships between the queries and the rules, we give the definition for join path equivalence.

Definition 2. *Two join path J_i and J_j are equivalent, noted as $J_i \cong J_j$, if any tuple in J_i appears in J_j and any tuple in J_j appears in J_i.*

For two join paths to be equivalent, a necessary condition is $JR_i = JR_j$. However, if several relations joins over the same attributes, then the join predicates among the join paths can be different, but they are still equivalent. To decide join path equivalence, we put join paths into join graphs. A **join graph** is a graph where each node indicates a relation, and each edge is the join attribute for the possible join between two nodes. The given join schema is an example of join graph. For a given join path, we also put its relations and join predicates into a graph. A valid join path is a spanning tree of a join graph, and two join paths are equivalent if they are both spanning trees of the same join graph. Figure 8.2a shows the join graph of the given join schema, (b) is the graph representation of the join path of example rule r_8, and (c) is for the join path of rule r_{17}. Since Fig. 8.2b, c are both spanning trees of (a), these two join paths are equivalent.

8.3.3   Query Authorization and Rule Enforcement

Authorization rules define the set of queries that are authorized to retrieve information from the parties. A query q is called **authorized** if there exists a rule r_t such that $J_t \cong J_q$ and $A_q \subseteq A_t$. The join paths must be equivalent. Otherwise, the relation/view defined by the rule will have fewer or more tuples than the query asks for. Here we don't consider the situation where the projections on two different join paths get the same result (e.g., by joining on foreign keys) since data coming from different parties usually does not have foreign key constrains. For instance, the example query Q_1 is authorized by r_{11}, but it cannot be authorized by r_{13}. Although all the required attributes are authorized by r_{13}, the information regulated by such a rule usually authorizes fewer tuples than the correct answer of Q_1, since the pid attribute in relation W filters some tuples in the join results.

On the other hand, "authorized" is only a necessary condition for a query to be answered but not sufficient. To actually answer a query, we need at least one query execution plan. A **query execution plan** or "query plan" for short, includes several ordered steps of operations over authorized and obtainable information and provides the composed results to a party. The result of a query execution plan pl is also relational, and it can also be presented with the triple $[A_{pl}, J_{pl}, P_{pl}]$. A valid query plan should be authorized by a given authorization rule r_t. Therefore, a plan pl answers a query q, if $J_{pl} \cong J_q \cong J_t$, $A_q = A_{pl} \subseteq A_t$ and $P_{pl} = P_t$. An authorization rule defines the maximal set of attributes that a query on the equivalent join path can retrieve. Therefore, a rule can also be viewed as a query. We call the query plan to enforce a rule as an **enforcement plan** or "plan" for short below.

Definition 3. *A rule r_t can be* totally enforced, *if there exists a plan pl such that $J_t \cong J_{pl}$, $A_t = A_{pl}$, $P_t = P_{pl}$. r_t is* partially enforceable, *if it is not totally enforceable and there is a plan pl that $J_t \cong J_{pl}$, $A_t \supset A_{pl}$, $P_t = P_{pl}$. Otherwise, r_t is not enforceable. A join path J_t is enforceable if there is a plan pl that $J_t \cong J_{pl}$.*

At the very beginning, only the rules indicating the data owners have their own data are known to be totally enforceable. As a plan contains steps bringing information together to enforce a rule, an enforcement plan can have following three operations over the enforceable information: A projection (π) is performed on a single party to select attributes; A join ($\bowtie$) operation is also performed at a single party, and it combines two pieces of information and generates information on a longer join path; Data transmission ($\rightarrow$) is an operation that happens between two parties, and one party sends information to the other. It is required that the two parties have two rules on the equivalent join paths and the information transmitted is based on such join path. In addition, the rule on the receiving party should have an attribute set that includes all the attributes of the information being transmitted. Otherwise, the transmission is not safe. For instance, P_S can send information on r_{13} to P_E as $J_{13} \cong J_7$, but it cannot send attribute $delivery$ to P_E. Such information cannot be sent to P_C because P_C does not have rule on join path equivalent to r_{13}.

It is obvious that a rule defined on basic relation is totally enforceable as a data transmission operation will give the enforcement plan. However, a rule with longer join path is not always enforceable. Whether an enforcement plan exists depends on whether pieces of enforceable information on shorter join paths are available at the same party and whether they can be joined losslessly. Besides, the enforceable information on remote cooperative parties may also be helpful to construct an enforcement plan. Overall, in the cooperative scenario, a rule can have many enforcement plans.

8.4   Checking Rule Enforcement

In this section, we first introduce some concepts and results, then we present the algorithm that works from bottom-up to check the enforceability of each given authorization rule.

8.4.1   Key Attributes Hierarchy

Given the BCNF form, there is only one possible lossless join between any two relations. It is known that for a lossless join, the join attribute in at least one of the two joining relations must be a key attribute [3]. Therefore, for any pair of joins, the key attribute of one relation is also the key of the join result. For instance, relations W and E can do a lossless join over the attribute pid, and pid is the key attribute of W. Let $K(X)$ denote the key attributes of the relation X, and $\overset{*}{\to}$ the functional dependency. Then, $K(E) \overset{*}{\to} K(W)$ for the resulting relation, and $K(E)$ becomes the key for it. We call this situation as *key hierarchy*, since the key simply extends over the joined relation. In some cases such as relations E and S, they join over oid, which is the key for both relations. Since $K(E) = K(S)$, there is no hierarchy. The key attributes from basic relations in a join path also form a hierarchal structure. Otherwise, there will be a relation in the join path that is determined by two or more different upper level key attributes. In such case, relations with upper level keys join with each other over the non-key attribute, and this creates a forbidden graph [3], so the join path is lossy. Based on these conditions, there always exists a key attribute from one basic relation that is also the key attribute of a join path. We call this attribute as the key attribute of the join path (or the key of the rules defined on such join path). If the join result of two join paths forms a valid longer join path, the join operation is always lossless. We call a plan as **joinable plan** if such a plan contains all the key attributes of the basic relations in its join path.

Lemma 1. *If a join path J_t is enforceable, there exists a joinable plan pl that $J_t \cong J_{pl}$.*

Proof. As we assume all the rule definitions contain the key attributes of the relations in its join path, these attributes are always authorized in data transmission operations. All the plans start from the rules on basic relations which are totally enforceable, and a longer join path is enforced by join operations over plans on shorter join paths. Therefore, if there is a plan for join path J_t, there always exist one plan that never project out any of these key attributes through the different operations in the entire plan, and such plan is joinable.

In some cases, a rule does not have a total enforcement plan, but only some partial plans. A partial plan only enforces a rule with an attribute set that is a proper subset of the rule attribute set. We say that an attribute set is a **maximal enforceable attribute set** for a rule, if it is enforced by a plan of the rule, and there is no other plan of the same rule that can enforce a superset of these attributes. If a rule is totally enforceable, its maximal enforceable attribute set is the rule attribute set, and we have the following lemma.

Lemma 2. *A rule has only one maximal enforceable attribute set.*

Proof. Firstly, a totally enforceable rule only has one maximal enforceable attribute set. Thus, a rule defined on basic relation only has one such set. To get the maximal attribute set, we do not eliminate any attributes via projections of plans, and maximal information is exchanged in data transmission operations, and such plans are always joinable. Therefore, if a rule is not totally enforceable, even it has several partial plans, these joinable plans are on the same join path and can always be merged by joining over the key attributes of the join path. Consequently, a partially enforceable rule have one maximal enforceable attribute set. At last, if a rule is not enforceable, its enforceable attribute set is empty.

8.4.2 Enforcement Checking Mechanism

As discussed above, it is desired to have a mechanism to check the rule enforceability for given set of rules. Such a mechanism can tell which rules can be enforced and what are their maximal enforceable attribute sets, and that also gives the answer of what are the set of authorized queries that can be safely answered according to the given configurations of the rules. We have two options with the given rules that are not enforceable. The first choice is that we keep only the found enforceable rules with their maximal enforceable attribute sets, and rules that are not enforceable as well as the unenforceable attributes are removed from the rule configurations. In other words, the algorithm finds all the information that can be safely retrieved according to the given set of rules, and all inaccurate and unenforceable configurations are removed. This solution can be thought as a conservative one since it prohibits some authorized information to be released because of the enforceability. In contrast, we can also modify the rule configurations in an aggressive way. In such scenario, we think all the information regulated by the rules are authorized, and authorized information should be retrievable. Therefore, whenever any information in the defined rules cannot be enforced, we change the rule configurations by granting more privileges so as to make these information enforceable. However, this releases more information, and such situation may not be desired by the cooperative parties. In this paper, we adopt the first option, so we propose a constructive mechanism that checks the rules in a bottom-up manner. In general, an enforcement plan for a rule combines pieces of information available and generates the information authorized by the rule. For each rule, the mechanism checks its relevant information locally and remotely and indicates if it can be enforced and what is its maximal enforceable attribute set. The set of unenforceable attributes and the unenforceable rules are removed from the rule set. We describe the mechanism in detail below.

8.4.3 Finding Enforceable Information

When examining a rule $[A_t, J_t, P_t]$, we call such a rule r_t as *Target Rule*, the attribute set A_t as *Target Set*, the join path J_t as *Target Join Path*, and the party P_t in the rule as *Target Party*. All the other parties are *Remote Parties*. To check the enforceability of r_t, we first find the relevant information that can be obtained locally at P_t. If this is not enough, we check the information from remote parties.

Rules can be enforced by performing consistent operations over the information that is already enforceable. In addition, it is always the case that information from short join paths is put together to enforce a rule of longer join path. Therefore, we propose the algorithm to work in a bottom-up way in the order of join path length, and it begins with rules on basic relations (length of 1 rules). As the mechanism works bottom-up, when examining a target rule with join path of length n, we can assume that all the rules on join paths with shorter lengths have already been examined, and only the maximal enforceable attribute sets of the rules are preserved.

Since the first task is to identify relevant information locally, we check the rules relevant to r_t at P_t. We call a join path as a **Sub-Join Path** of J_t if it is a join path which contains a proper set of relations of JR_t. Rules not on the sub-join paths are not relevant to r_t since any composition with these rules will contain information more than what r_t authorizes. At party P_t, a joinable plan that is on a sub-join path of J_t is a **Relevant Plan**, and a rule defined on a sub-join path of J_t is a **Relevant Rule** to the target rule. Parties that have rules defined on the equivalent join path of J_t are called J_t-**cooperative parties**, and information on J_t is allowed to be exchanged only among these parties by data transmission operations. For instance, P_E and P_S are J_{13}-cooperative parties since $J_{13} \cong J_7$. We assume that each inspected rule is represented by an enforcement plan. When inspecting the target rule, we consider using these plans to enforce it. We say "join among rules" below, which means their enforcement plans.

The checking process iterates in the order of the join path lengths beginning with the rules defined on the basic relations on various parties. These rules can be totally enforced as the data owners sending their data to the authorized parties. From then on, the algorithm checks for rules defined on longer join paths. At the same time examining the rules, the algorithm also builds a graph structure. Each node in such structure is a rule with its maximal enforceable attribute set. The nodes in the graph are put in different levels based on their join path lengths. Two nodes on the same party are connected if one is the relevant rule of the other. Among different parties, nodes can be connected if they have the equivalent join paths. Such a structure captures the relevance and cooperation relationships among the enforceable rules. Figure 8.3 shows the built structure for our running example. The different parties are separated vertically. The bold boxes show the basic relations owned by different parties. The algorithm starts the iteration with the rules on basic relations r_1, r_2, r_4, r_{10}, and so on.

As the algorithm iteratively checks all the rules, when a target rule r_t is examined, the algorithm first checks whether the join path J_t can be enforced using relevant

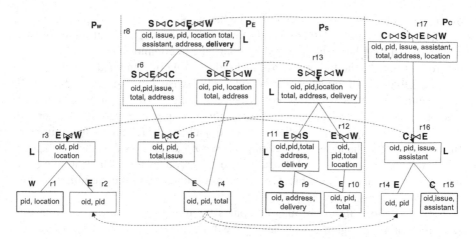

Fig. 8.3 Graph structure built for the example

rules on P_t. After that, all the rules with equivalent join path of J_t are checked respectively at J_t-cooperative parties. Then the algorithm checks the possible enforcement by exchanging information among these parties. In Fig. 8.3, on the level of join path length 2, the algorithm checks the rules with the order of r_3, r_{12}, r_5, r_{16}, r_{11} because $J_3 \cong J_{12}$ and $J_5 \cong J_{16}$. J_t-cooperative parties such as P_W and P_S on J_3 will check the remote enforcement between r_3 and r_{12}, which will be described later.

To check local enforceability, the algorithm finds its local relevant rules in the currently built graph structure since all its relevant rules have already been examined and added to the graph. It only checks with the top level relevant rules in the current graph, where top level rules are the nodes not connected to any higher level nodes (rules with longer join paths) in the currently built graph during the bottom-up procedure. For example, in Fig. 8.3, when the algorithm examines r_{13} on P_S, only r_{11}, r_{12} are top level rules. And when checking r_8, r_7 and r_5 are top level rules since r_6 is not enforceable. Here, we take advantage of the upwards closed property of the rules, so that the top level rules cover all possible join results among the lower level rules. If these top level rules cannot be composed to enforce the J_t, there is no need to check lower level rules. When examining r_{13}, there is no need to consider the join between r_9 and r_{10}. Among the rules in the graph on P_t, a relevant rule r_r of r_t can be efficiently decided, if $JR_r \subset JR_t$.

The following step is to check whether the join path J_t can be enforced locally by performing joins among these top level relevant rules. The algorithm basically checks each pair of these rules. We check it pairwise because if a pair of them can join, the result must be able to enforce J_t. Otherwise, there must exist another relevant rule of r_t authorizing the join result, and such a rule is on higher level of the pair of rules being inspected, which is contradict to the fact that the pair of rules are top level rules. When checking whether a pair of rules (r_s, r_r) can join, the algorithm first tests their relation sets to see if $JR_s \cap JR_r = \emptyset$. If these two join paths have overlapped relations, they can join over the key attribute of the overlap part, and J_t can always be enforced. Otherwise, we need to further check the attributes of two rules to see if they have the required join attribute in common. If J_t can be locally enforced, we mark the target rule as **local enforceable** rule and add it to the graph by connecting it with top level relevant rules. Otherwise, it has to wait and see if J_t can be enforced on other parties. For instance, when checking r_3 in our example, it has top level relevant rules r_1 and r_2, since there is no overlapped relation for the pair of rules, the algorithm checks whether join attribute pid can be found in both rules. On the other hand, when checking the pair r_{11} and r_{12}, as E is the overlapped relation, the join path J_{13} can be locally enforced. r_{17} does not has a valid join pair, and it is not locally enforceable. Once a pair is found to enforce the join path, the algorithm proceeds to next steps.

Meanwhile, the algorithm also computes the union of the attributes from top level relevant rules regardless of the enforceability of J_t. The resulting attribute set A_r includes all attributes that can be obtained from party P_t if J_t can be enforced. It is always the case that $A_r \subseteq A_t$ as rules are upwards closed. If A_r not equals to A_t, we call the set of attributes $A_t \setminus A_r$ as **missing attribute set** A_m. The attributes in A_m are potentially obtainable from the J_t-cooperative parties. In the example, the attribute $delivery$ in r_8 cannot be found in its top level rules r_7 and r_5, and it is a missing attribute after the local checking.

Next, the algorithm checks the remote information that a party can use to enforce a rule, and only J_t-cooperative parties are checked. As the previous steps of the algorithm tell which parties can locally enforce the join path J_t, if there exists any party that can enforce J_t, then all the J_t-cooperative parties can have joinable plans for their rules on J_t. Thus, the party P_t is able to get attributes from all its J_t-cooperative parties to enforce r_t. For instance, r_{17} is not locally enforceable, but J_8 can be enforced with a joinable plan at P_E. Thus, we can add a data transmission operation to such plan, and r_{17} also has a joinable plan. This plan can join with r_{16}, so that attributes $issue, assistant$ in r_{17} can be enforced. Consequently, these attributes in r_8 can also be enforced. Therefore, we take the union of the attribute sets from all J_t-cooperative parties to check if r_t can be totally enforced. If the missing attribute set $A_m \subset A_{r_1} \bigcup A_{r_2} \dots A_{r_k}$ (where A_{r_i} is the relevant attribute set of a J_t-cooperative party P_i), then r_t can be totally enforced. Otherwise, A_m is updated by removing the attributes appear in any A_{r_i}. In such case, r_t has a maximal enforceable attribute set on J_t without the attributes in A_m. The node r_t in the graph structure is presented with the attribute set $A_t \setminus A_m$. Meanwhile, **connection edges** are added among the J_t-cooperative rules in the graph structure. For example, attribute $delivery$ of r_8 also cannot be found in its J_t-cooperative party P_C, so it cannot be enforced. r_8 in the graph is represented with the attribute set without $delivery$. We use bold font in Fig. 8.3 to indicate this attribute is not enforceable. Also, since join path J_6 cannot be enforced at any party, r_6 is not enforceable, and it will not be included in the graph structure. In Fig. 8.3, we use the dashed box to show r_6 is removed. The local enforceable rules are marked with "L". The detailed algorithm is described in Algorithm 8.1.

```
   Data: All given authorization rule set R on all parties
   Result: Find enforceable rules and build graph
 1 Mark rules with length 1 as total enforceable rules;
 2 Get the maximal length of join path length N;
 3 for Join path of length 2 to N do
 4     for Each join path J_t length equal to i do
 5         AJ_t ← ∅, the set of shared attributes on J_t;
 6         for Each party P_t has a rule r_t on J_t do
 7             Obtain the set of top level relevant rules R_v;
 8             Add the node and connections to R_v in graph;
 9             A_v ← the union of attributes in R_v;
10             Missing attribute set A_m ← A_t;
11             for Each pair of relevant rule (r_s, r_r) do
12                 if The pair can locally enforce J_t then
13                     | A_m ← A_m \ A_v and break;
14                 end
15             end
16             if A_m ≠ ∅ then
17                 | Put r_t with A_m into the Queue of J_t;
18             end
19             AJ_t ← AJ_t ∪ A_v;
20         end
21         for Each rule r_t in the Queue of J_t do
22             if J_t can be enforced on some party then
23                 Add connections among J_t-cooperative parties in graph;
24                 A_m ← A_m \ AJ_t;
25                 if A_m ≠ ∅ then
26                     | Replace A_t with A_t \ A_m in graph;
27                 end
28             else
29                 | r_t cannot be enforced, remove rules on J_t from graph;
30             end
31         end
32     end
33     Join path length i++;
34 end
35 end
```

Algorithm 8.1: Rule enforcement checking algorithm

In algorithm 8.1, each rule will be examined at most twice, with one local enforceability check and another one in checking the queue of J_t. In the step of local enforcement checking, only the top level relevant rules on party P_t are checked. Suppose that the total number of rules is N_t, the maximal number of relevant rules of a rule is N_o, and checking join condition takes constant C. Then the worst case complexity for algorithm 8.1 is $O(N_t * N_o^2 * C)$, where N_o is usually very small. In addition, this algorithm can be used as a pre-compute step once all the rules are given.

Theorem 1. *The **Rule Enforcement Checking Algorithm** finds all enforceable information among cooperative parties.*

Proof. As all the information can be obtained on join results comes from the basic relations, the algorithm works in bottom-up manner to capture the operation results. If the join path of a rule cannot be enforced, then all the rules on this join path cannot be enforced and can be discarded. The algorithm first finds a way to enforce the join path of the rule r_t. The check on local relevant rules explores all possible ways to compose useful information on P_t. Since the only other information can be used to enforce r_t must come from J_t-cooperative parties, the algorithm also considers all the attributes that r_t can get from them. There is no other way to enforce more attribute for r_t.

8.5 Conclusions and Future Work

In previous research work, a flexible data authorization model has been proposed to meet the security requirements for collaboration among different data owners in a distributed environment. Since authorization rules are made based on business requirements, it is possible that some rules cannot be enforced among the cooperative parties. In this work, we propose an algorithm to check the enforceability of the given rules among cooperative parties.

For future works, we will study the problem of enforcing the join paths by adding new rules to the existing configurations. In addition, we will also study the problem where a trusted third party is available. In such a scenario, we will investigate the problems of how to enforce the rules without modifications and what are the optimal ways to enforce such rules. Moreover, we will implement the algorithms to evaluate them under practical scenarios, and we will also explore the possibility of implementing the algorithms in Datalog.

References

1. Aggarwal, G., Bawa, M., Ganesan, P.: Two can keep A secret: a distributed architecture for secure database services. In: CIDR, Asilomar, pp. 186–199 (2005)
2. Agrawal, R., Asonov, D., Kantarcioglu, M., Li, Y.: Sovereign joins. In: ICDE 2006, Atlanta, p. 26 (2006)
3. Aho, A.V., Beeri, C., Ullman, J.D.: The theory of joins in relational databases. ACM Trans. Database Syst. 4(3), 297–314 (1979)
4. Al-Shaer, E., El-Atawy, A., Samak, T.: Automated pseudo-live testing of firewall config-uration enforcement. IEEE J. Sel. Areas Commun. 27(3), 302–314 (2009)
5. Bernstein, P.A., Goodman, N., Wong, E., Reeve, C.L., Rothnie, J. B. Jr.: Query processing in a system for distributed databases (SDD-1). ACM Trans. Database Syst. 6(4), 602–625 (1981)
6. Cali, A., Martinenghi, D.: Querying data under access limitations. In: ICDE 2008, Cancun, pp. 50–59 (2008)

7. De Capitani di Vimercati, S., Foresti, S., Jajodia, S., Paraboschi, S., Samarati, P.: Assessing query privileges via safe and efficient permission composition. In: CCS 2008, Virginia (2008)
8. De Capitani di Vimercati, S., Foresti, S., Jajodia, S., Paraboschi, S., Samarati, P.: Controlled information sharing in collaborative distributed query processing. In: ICDCS 2008, Beijing (2008)
9. De Capitani di Vimercati, S., Foresti, S., Jajodia, S., Paraboschi, S., Samarati, P.: Keep a few: outsourcing data while maintaining confidentiality. In: ESORICS, Saint Malo, pp. 440–455 (2009)
10. Goldstein, J., Larson, P.: Optimizing queries using materialized views: a practical, scalable solution. In: SIGMOD, Santa Barbara, pp. 331–342 (2001)
11. Halevy, A.Y.: Answering queries using views: a survey. VLDB J. 10(4), 270–294 (2001)
12. Kossmann, D.: The state of the art in distributed query processing. ACM Comput. Surv. 32(4), 422–469 (2000)
13. Li, C.: Computing complete answers to queries in the presence of limited access patterns. VLDB J. 12(3), 211–227 (2003)
14. Pottinger, R., Halevy, A.Y.: Minicon: a scalable algorithm for answering queries using views. VLDB J. 10(2–3), 182–198 (2001)
15. Wool, A.: A quantitative study of firewall configuration errors. IEEE Comput. 37(6), 62–67 (2004)

Part IV
Diagnostics and Discovery

Chapter 9
Programmable Diagnostic Network Measurement with Localization and Traffic Observation

Michael R. Clement and Dennis Volpano

Abstract As networks become increasingly complex and pervasive, understanding and evaluating their running behavior and diagnosing configuration problems becomes more challenging and yet more important. This motivates a need to craft new diagnostic measurements suited to particular network environments and applications. However, once measurement protocols are in place on network devices it becomes difficult to modify them to new needs. Others have explored programmatic approaches that allow executing custom code at otherwise "unintelligent" network devices in order to provide configuration management and define new services. This approach can also be used to make meta-level observations from within a running network. We introduce a programmatic approach to diagnostic network measurement that offers such observation. It gives users a language in which to express measurements succinctly and an execution platform that enables network observation and localization of measurement. The design of the language and its platform are sketched with an example application.

9.1 Introduction

Networks are at once becoming more complex and more pervasive. An increasing user population is finding itself overwhelmed in trying to effectively manage these networks. The software defined networking community has offered respite from tedious network configuration by making every network device not only configurable but programmable (e.g., [2, 5, 9, 14]). Users can then specify a higher-level configuration that is translated into runnable code and executed across all devices. Likewise, work has been done historically to programmatically extend protocols and services (e.g., [8, 22]). Programmatic approaches not only allow

M.R. Clement (✉) • D. Volpano
Naval Postgraduate School, Monterey, CA 93940, USA
e-mail: mrclemen@nps.edu; volpano@nps.edu

E. Al-Shaer et al. (eds.), *Automated Security Management*,
DOI 10.1007/978-3-319-01433-3_9, © Springer International Publishing Switzerland 2013

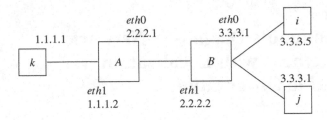

Fig. 9.1 Network with a duplicated IP address at client j

simplified specification but also flexibility as network technologies and applications evolve. Presuming all network devices support an appropriate execution platform, new services can be deployed merely by localizing custom code at devices. No firmware or hardware changes are necessary to support a new capability.

A programmatic approach can also be applied to diagnostic network measurement. Whereas programmatic configuration management simplifies the task of specifying desired network behavior, programmatic network measurement simplifies the task of observing, diagnosing, and verifying expected network behavior. It complements offline configuration specification and debugging with a flexible online capability to quickly understand and evaluate a running network. Flexibility is key as identifying a standard tool set for every kind of measurement in any type of network seems hopeless.

Consider the simple network in Fig. 9.1. It consists of two routers, A and B, and three edge devices, i, j, and k. Edge device k is attached to interface $eth1$ at router A; i and j are attached to interface $eth0$ at router B. Observe that the network interface at j duplicates the IP address of interface $eth0$ at B. Now suppose a network application situated at k attempts to access a service at i. Assuming the routing tables of A and B are configured correctly, the request packet will arrive successfully at i. However, when i issues an Address Resolution Protocol (ARP) [16] request for gateway address 3.3.3.1, j may answer before B. In this case, i will send its response through j, which will drop the packet since it is not configured for packet forwarding. From the perspective of k, this is indistinguishable from i being offline or misconfigured.

Without some means of diagnosing this problem remotely, the network operator at k would have to manually (and often physically) inspect each device along the path to determine the location and nature of the issue. Tools such as Traceroute [12] cannot fully diagnose this problem since they can only leverage the support (such as Time-To-Live handling) already available at every network device. Even the detection techniques described in [3] rely on fixed protocols and only make information available locally at the offending device, not to a remote operator. *We posit that if custom code that performs specific measurements by injecting and observing traffic could be initiated locally to an operator, relocated and executed locally at a specific network device (such as B), and the results made available locally to the operator, then this problem could be diagnosed remotely.*

The contribution of this paper is a proposed approach to network measurement that can address the specific problem above, and the more general problem of providing flexible, resilient, and efficient measurement and diagnosis. Our approach is targeted at small to medium-sized networks consisting of dozens of switches and routers in a single administrative domain. These are networks where it is feasible to deploy programmable measurement on an open switch platform. This work has culminated in a para-network facility we call the XPLANE (eXplanatory PLANE). It consists of a language for succinct expression of measurements, a transformation that handles tedious details such as localization and observation scheduling, and an execution platform on each network device to perform computation, observation, and localization. In practice, the platform would reside on an open switch platform in order to take advantage of computing resources available there without burdening the forwarding plane.

The remainder of the paper is organized as follows. The next section discusses the challenges in designing a programmable measurement framework. Section 9.3 introduces a new domain-specific language. Then in Sect. 9.4, we demonstrate the utility of our approach with a nontrivial application that addresses the problem described above. This is followed by a brief discussion of our current implementation in Sect. 9.5. Finally, Sect. 9.6 discusses related work.

9.2 Design Challenges

The argument laid out above calls for a programmatic approach to diagnostic measurement that allows the creation of new measurements from a set of well-understood primitives. As it turns out, however, the design of such a solution is fraught with subtleties that are largely unaddressed in the current literature.

Since the set of operations each measurement will entail may vary, a solution cannot rely solely on predefined device attributes as the Simple Network Management Protocol (SNMP) [1] and others (e.g., [7, 11, 18, 24]) do. A wide variety of useful measurements can be derived by injecting and observing traffic at various network devices; network problems that are difficult or impossible to detect at a distance on a live running network can be uncovered by targeted observations made at nearby devices. Since the idiosyncrasies of device network stacks can affect observations, the observation facility must exist outside the network stack. Moreover, since network devices have limited processing and memory resources and thus cannot continuously observe all traffic, observations must be coordinated with demand so that packet capture only occurs when needed for a specific measurement.

An important aspect of any measurement is where it is taken. Many routing problems for example cannot be diagnosed solely from an endpoint; it is necessary to make observations at nearby devices to isolate the problem. Hence the ability to localize a measurement is key. Common methods of localizing computation include Remote Procedure Calls (RPC) and Remote Evaluation [20]. These approaches require the device requesting localization to maintain state about the request and subsequent local computation. This is not robust to momentary network glitches, especially if each relocated computation spawns yet another along some path. Another method is to use linearized threads that carry with them all remaining computation so that only one device maintains the computation state at any given time. Though more robust, it requires the programmer to make explicit the relocation back to the requesting device. This extra code is an additional burden and is prone to error. A better solution is to allow the programmer to write programs assuming RPC-like localization and then compile them, synthesizing code to relocate the result back to the requesting device.

Localization also requires a means of transferring code between devices. But, applications may need to relocate in a *misconfigured* network in order to diagnose a routing or addressing problem. If the network topology is unknown, applications may need to relocate to *all* immediate neighbors to find the problem. The localization facility must then coexist on the physical network but live entirely outside the logical organization of the network by being "underneath" the addressing, routing, and firewall configurations of devices. It must further allow flooding to immediate neighbors in order to explore unknown topologies.

9.3 Language Overview

The XPLANE Programming Language (XPL) allows programmers to succinctly express custom network measurements. Programmers build up measurements from attributes and network traffic observations using standard language constructs. These measurements are expressed at a high level without specifying how localization or observation occur.

To illustrate, consider the XPL code in Fig. 9.2. It discovers from a given client, all physical paths to every server on the network by localizing from device to device looking for devices labeled as servers. For this application, only *device attributes* are used. The XPLANE interpreter on each device exposes three device attributes: a unique identifier (*node*), type (*node.type*), and a list of device interfaces (*node.ifaces*). We currently constrain devices to have a single type such as Router, Server, or Client; however, since these are arbitrary values they can be extended or replaced for other deployments. Each interface k in *node.ifaces* provides its

```
letfun f path =
  if node.type = Server then
    path ++ [node]
  else let n = node in
    if not (member n path) then
      OnFlood {f (path ++ [n])}
in f []
```

Fig. 9.2 Server discovery

Fig. 9.3 Notional execution
timeline of
print (OnFlood {1 + 2} + 4)

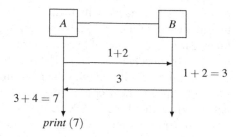

hardware address (*node.k.ethaddr*) and its IP address (*node.k.ip*). The interpreter also exposes one *code attribute* as part of each localization: *ai*, the interface at which the code arrives.

Recursive function *f* takes as its argument a list of device identifiers (*path*) that is accumulated as the code localizes from device to device . This list serves two purposes: first, it contains the path being explored. If the computation eventually arrives at a server via several localizations, the list will contain the full path from the originating device to that server. Second, it is used to prevent the computation from localizing in a loop as explained below.

At each new non-Server device, the code localizes to *all* its immediate neighbors. For this, it uses *On Flood {e}* where *e* is an expression to be evaluated at the remote device. Any occurrence of a device or code attribute in *e* is bound at the remote device since attributes are device-specific; likewise, packet injection and capture (explained further below) contained in *e* will be performed at the remote device. The value of *On Flood {e}* is the value of *e* as computed at the remote device; however, the value is actually produced at the device that evaluated *On Flood {e}*, which we call the local device. Hence, a programmer can write expressions like *print (On Flood {1 + 2} + 4)* where 1 + 2 is evaluated remotely yet the result (3) is produced at the local device where it is summed with 4 and printed (see Fig. 9.3). The expression inside *OnFlood* can be code that inspects device attributes, performs network observation, or relocates the computation yet again. Since there may be multiple neighbors, *OnFlood* may spawn multiple threads, each producing its own value at the local device. There is a second localization primitive, *On {e} e′* where *e* is evaluated only at neighbor *e′*. Otherwise it is identical to *OnFlood*.

Each time the application floods to its neighbors, it recursively evaluates *f* and appends the current device identifier to its list (++ stands for list concatenation and : : for construction). If the current device has already been visited by the same thread of computation, then its identifier will be in the list. In this case, there is no need to continue processing since it would loop between those devices indefinitely. XPL includes a one-armed conditional to handle cases such as this; the implied else clause terminates execution without producing a value. Notice that copies of a computation generated by *OnFlood* do not communicate, hence sibling copies cannot detect whether each other has already visited a particular device. Intuitively this seems like a significant drawback to XPL, but for topologies that are unknown or that may contain multiple paths between endpoints, this feature allows broader network exploration to take place than if the XPLANE forced "duplicate" computation to be discarded.

If a Server is reached, its identifier is appended to the list, and that list becomes the final value of the computation. Although the computation may relocate several times during the course of execution, the value is produced at the originating device by relocating back along the path it took to the server as described below.

The design of XPL enables the programmer to articulate a measurement without having to specify how computation is localized and how observations are coordinated. While the design of XPL applications may remain the job of experienced programmers, new applications can be added to an ever-growing library, the entirety of which can be executed on any XPLANE-enabled network without modification.

9.3.1 CPS Transformation

As discussed earlier, it is desirable to run an application as a totally self-contained computation on a single network device at any given time. In order to do this, the code must be "linearized" so that whenever localization occurs, all remaining computation is localized along with the code to be evaluated remotely. This is unlike RPC, where the local device would keep state to the effect of *print* (? + 4) while $1 + 2$ was being evaluated remotely. However, the semantics of *On Flood* (and *On*) requires that its value be made accessible at the device where it was initially executed. One cannot rewrite *print* (*On Flood* $\{1 + 2\}$ + 4) as *On Flood* $\{print(1 + 2 + 4)\}$ because the result will be printed at the remote device rather than the local device. Returning the value to the local device is *implicit* computation that follows execution of *On Flood*. It is made explicit, not by the programmer, but rather automatically by a continuation-passing style (CPS) transform [6,23].

CPS makes remaining computation explicit by packaging it in a *continuation* that can be passed as an argument and applied as a function to an evaluated expression. When CPS encounters an instance of *On* or *OnFlood*, it extends the continuation with a new instance of *On* to transfer the result back to the local device. This continuation is relocated along with a transformed version of the expression inside the *On* or *OnFlood*. Once that expression is evaluated, the continuation is applied to the value. It relocates the value back to the local device and proceeds with the rest of the computation. Hence the CPS form of *print* (*On Flood* $\{1 + 2\}$ + 4) would be *On Flood* $\{(lambda\ v\ On\ \{print(v + 4)\}\ n)\ (1 + 2)\}$ where n is the identifier of the local device and *lambda* denotes an anonymous function (here with a single argument v). Once the remote device evaluates $1 + 2$, it applies the continuation to 3 yielding the expression *On* $\{print(3 + 4)\}$ n. The expression inside the *On* is relocated to device n where the final calculation and print take place.

Figure 9.4 shows the result of putting the server discovery application of Fig. 9.2 into CPS form. Here function f is transformed to expect a continuation. As f is called recursively, the continuation returning the value to the originating device is computed. When a server is reached, the continuation is applied to the composed path. Had we been forced to write linear code from the start then our application may have looked like that in Fig. 9.5 where code is provided to return the result of

Fig. 9.4 Server discovery
following CPS

```
letfun f path k =
  if node.type = Server
    then k (path ++ [node])
  else let n = node in
    if not (member n path) then
      OnFlood {f (path ++ [n])
                 (lambda v On {k v} n)}
  in f [] (lambda u u)
```

Fig. 9.5 Server discovery
with explicit return relocation

```
letfun goback path route =
  if null (tl path) then node::route
  else On {goback (tl path)
               (hd path)::route
          } hd (tl path)
in letfun f path =
  if node.type = Server then
    let m = node in
      if null path then [m]
      else On {goback path [m]
              } (hd path)
  else let n = node in
    if not (member n path) then
      OnFlood {f n::path}
in f []
```

discovery back to the originating device, done there with function *goback*. This code
is unnecessary using CPS.

It is well known that CPS can code size to grow. Experience thus far however
suggests there is a rich set of measurements and observations that can be performed
by applications that do not exhibit this type of growth under CPS. Moreover, the
CPS of each application in this set is linear, meaning each can run in space bounded
by the length of its input. For many diagnostic applications, input length is the length
of the longest acyclic path between any two devices in the network. So for these, the
CPS can execute completely within the space of a single Ethernet MTU in practice
for network paths consisting of dozens of devices [4].

9.3.2 Packet Observation and Injection

Packet capture and injection are integrated into the design of XPL. This is a major
point of departure from related work. The challenge is to introduce these in a way
that provides programming flexibility yet can be compiled efficiently. Obviously
we do not want large packet captures transmitted around the network so we exploit
the support XPL provides for localizing computation by requiring that whenever
an application reaches a capture point in its execution, the execution must be local
to the device where the capture is to occur. Similarly, we do not want to explicitly
represent the entire set of packets as an XPL value in device memory. Capture is
parameterized on a primitive recursive function that processes packets as they are

captured and produces a value. This is the value of the entire capture expression, rather than the set of packets captured.

A packet capture expression has the form $pcap\ e_1\ e_2\ e_3$ where e_1 is an interface at the current device, e_2 a capture timeout in seconds, and e_3 a primitive recursive function that processes packets and produces a value; $pcap$ applies e_3 to a list of packets observed at e_1 over at most e_2 seconds. Function e_3 may inspect these packets and perform simple computations. Its value is the value of the whole $pcap$ expression. A packet is injected using $send\ e_1\ e_2;\ e_3$ where e_1 is a local interface, e_2 a packet descriptor, and e_3 an arbitrary XPL expression. Packet descriptors are lists containing a packet type, source and destination address, and type-specific options. The value of $send\ e_1\ e_2;\ e_3$ is the value of e_3 after the packet has been sent. Semantically, any instances of $pcap$ should be in e_3 if the capture is intended to look for the packets injected by $send$, even if the capture takes place at a different device interface or even a different device.

Since execution must be local to the device where injection occurs and local to the device where capture occurs, relocation via On may be necessary. The advantage of XPL is the abstraction provided to accomplish this. One merely sends some packets and then localizes execution to capture them. The steps taken in the network to realize it are far more complex. It is not viable to observe traffic continuously at all interfaces on every device, so interfaces should observe on demand only. An interface typically must be initialized to capture before any packets are sent which is inconsistent with XPL's send-then-capture semantics. The approach we take is to fork a packet send when a $pcap$ is reached. That way the interface can be initialized before the packet is sent and the computation can remain at the capturing device where it can be signaled by the forked send after the packet is sent. Which packet gets sent can be determined at compile time because the scope of $send$ is static. In other words, for each $pcap$ instance, all instances of $send$ that could ever inject packets that might be captured by it can be determined statically. Further, the code needed to place their injection on the correct device can be gleaned from the current continuation. Static scoping can also be exploited to initialize a packet capture with a filter based on the packet descriptors of $send$ instances in scope.

Each instance of $pcap$ is transformed into instances of primitives $pcap\_sched$ and $pcap\_stop$ to make explicit the coordination of capture with any preceding injections. $pcap\_sched$ takes four arguments, the first three of which are those of $pcap$. The fourth is a "send continuation" that contains all instances of $send$ that are in scope with all interface and descriptor arguments pre-evaluated, along with any necessary localization code. This is synthesized during the conversion; it localizes as necessary and performs all injections in scope, finally returning to the capturing device and evaluating $pcap\_stop$ with a capture handle argument. It in turn produces the packets captured and provides them to processing function e_3, the value of which is the value of $pcap\_sched$ just like $pcap$.

As an illustration of this along with CPS, consider the XPL expression

```
send eth0 pd; On {pcap eth1 15 f} B
```

that begins at device A, injects a packet described by pd at A's $eth0$, relocates to device B, then captures packets for 15 s at B's $eth1$. We desire to first initialize capture at B, then perform the injection at A, process the resulting capture at B, and finally produce the result at A. This is accomplished by the transformed code

```
On {(lambda v On {v} A)
       (pcap_sched eth1 15 f
          (lambda h On {send eth0 pd;
                        On {pcap_stop h} B
                   } A))
    } B
```

The code relocated to device B consists of the continuation generated by the CPS transform applied to an instance of *pcap_sched*. Since no computation remains after the capture, the continuation simply relocates the result to A. Inside *pcap_sched*, the capture is initialized at $eth1$ for 15 s. Then the send continuation is applied to a unique handle (bound to h) generated by *pcap_sched*. It executes in its own thread while the main code continues to capture. The send continuation localizes at A, sends a packet from $eth0$, and returns to B where it results in the list of captured packets. Once this completes, *pcap_sched* evaluates function f with the captured packets, yielding that value as its result.

Although both *pcap* and *pcap_sched* accept a timeout, this is not strictly needed. The processing function could stop observation early based on encountering a particular packet. In this case, the implementation would begin processing captured packets immediately rather than await the completion of the send continuation. This transformation also allows multiple instances of *send* followed by a single *pcap*, even if they span multiple devices. We are currently extending it to allow one or more *send* followed by multiple instances of *pcap*.

9.4 Application

We now present an example application of XPL to illustrate its use. This application is tailored to a networking environment operating under certain assumptions. Because we anticipate the XPLANE being deployed in a variety of networks, our aim is to allow programmers to write measurement applications suited to their environment.

9.4.1 Duplicate IP Detection

This application performs simple duplicate IP address detection across all routers in a network, using gratuitous ARP requests [21]. We assumes that all routers in this network are properly configured, but edge devices are allowed to attach to the network with arbitrary configurations. Further, all routers support the XPLANE

Fig. 9.6 Duplicate IP check

```
letfun finddupes iflist =
  if null iflist then []
  else let i = hd iflist in
    letfun f pkts =
      if null pkts then False
      else if match (hd pkts)
             [ARPReply, any,
               node.i.ethaddr, node.i.ip]
           then True
           else f (tl pkts)
    in send i [ARPRequest, node.i.ethaddr,
           FF:FF:FF:FF:FF:FF, node.i.ip];
    if pcap i 5 f then
       node.i.ip :: finddupes(tl iflist)
    else finddupes(tl iflist)
  in letfun dupecheck path =
    if not (member node visited) and
           (node.type = Router) then
    let d = finddupes(node.ifaces) in
      if null d then let n = node in
        OnFlood {dupecheck n::path}
      else [node, d]
  in dupecheck []
```

but edge devices may or may not. Hence applications cannot rely on inspecting attributes or making observations at arbitrary edge devices.

The code is given in Fig. 9.6. It primarily consists of two functions, *finddupes* and *dupecheck*. Function *finddupes* recursively iterates through a list of device interfaces, checking each for the presence of a device connected to it that duplicates its address. It does so by injecting an ARP request frame from that interface, then observing traffic for a few seconds looking for an ARP reply with the same IP address as that interface. The function produces a list of router IP addresses that are duplicated. Function *dupecheck* performs this check at each router it encounters. If it finds duplicates at a router, it immediately returns a list containing the device identifier and the list produced by *finddupes*. Otherwise, it floods to all neighbors, repeating the check only if the neighbor has not already been visited and if the neighbor is a router. Observe that we make two assumptions. First, there are no loops in the network; otherwise a router may be checked by multiple threads arriving via different paths. Second, it is acceptable not to detect all duplicates in a single execution; each thread stops with the first device where duplicates are found. Since network assumptions will vary, each programmer can choose how best to write this application.

9.4.2 Example Execution

Suppose we ran this application on the network shown in Fig. 9.1. The application starts at k. We highlight a few salient points about its execution.

Since no devices duplicate an address of k, the application will flood to its only neighbor A. Likewise, after not detecting duplicates at A, it floods to all neighbors; here, both k and B. The expression inside *OnFlood* is *dupecheck n :: path* but the definitions of *dupecheck*, *n*, and *path* (and *finddupes* since it is referenced by *dupecheck*) are also localized along with the current continuation. Since dynamically-bound variable *node* is rebound upon localization, n is used to preserve its value.

At k the first conditional in *dupecheck* fails since k is already in *path*. At B, the code continues by evaluating *finddupes* with the interface list [*eth0, eth1*]. Function *finddupes* sends an ARP request out *eth0* and observes subsequent traffic. Instances of *send* and *pcap* are transformed prior to execution, so first observation is initiated at *eth0*, then the ARP request is injected. The packet descriptor given to *send* represents the ARP message "Who has 3.3.3.1? Tell 3.3.3.1". All packets observed during the 5 s interval are given as a list to function f. It checks each packet using the *match* predicate and a packet descriptor. Fields are ignored using *any*.

Here the IP address of *eth0* is duplicated by j, so f should find a matching packet and result in $True$. Since this is the only interface with a duplicated address at B, *dupecheck* will result in $[B, [3.3.3.1]]$. At this point, the result must be returned to k, so the continuation built up during execution is now evaluated. Since two localizations occurred for this particular thread, one from k to A and another from A to B, and no other computation remains, the continuation would be

```
(lambda u On {(lambda v On {v} k) u} A)
```

Applying this to the result will cause the result to be produced at the originating device; in this case, k.

9.5 Implementation

We have developed a prototype implementation of the XPLANE on top of TinyScheme [19]. All software runs in userspace on an unmodified Linux kernel with a compiled footprint under 320 KB. Whenever a localization primitive is evaluated, the expression inside is marshaled and transferred to one or more remote devices. Then the local device releases its state. The interior expression can be directly serialized; however, it may reference exterior variables and functions that must be transferred with it along with the current continuation. Here static and dynamic bindings are treated differently. Static bindings may be exported from the local environment and localized along with the interior expression, or substituted directly into the interior expression. Dynamically bound identifiers (namely, device and code attributes) are bound at the remote device, so their local definitions are not exported.

Once the expression is fully marshaled, it is transferred to one or more neighboring devices. The XPLANE is meant to support diagnosing misconfigured networks, so the transfer mechanism cannot rely on the logical network. Therefore all transfers are by default sent as link-layer broadcasts out all device interfaces using the Linux

Fig. 9.7 XPLANE packet
format

Marker	Version	Packet Length
Sender ID		Receiver ID
Sequence Number		
Fragmentation		Checksum
Authentication (20 bytes)		
Marshaled Code ...		

packet socket interface. There is limited support for an ARP-like facility so that known neighbors can be reached by unicast. Otherwise, in the case of *On*, transfers are filtered at each receiving device by a receiver identifier field in the message header.

The XPLANE message format is shown in Fig. 9.7. Currently, only the *Marker*, *Version*, *Packet Length*, *Receiver ID*, and *Checksum* fields in the header are utilized. *Sender ID*, *Sequence Number*, and *Fragmentation* are provided to support larger code sizes if necessary. The 160-bit message authentication field is a placeholder for future security extensions.

Implementation of coordinated observation and injection is underway. The currently implemented *pcap* is not transformed but instead queries a separate process built on top of libpcap [13], which runs continuously in the background and stores a predefined set of packet attributes. These are made accessible to the packet processing function as list data. *send* is a wrapper for existing software such as ping, and packet descriptors are lists of command line arguments.

9.6 Related Work

The need to address managing complex networks is evident from recent attention in programmable networks. In addition to the work identified above, others have considered programmatic approaches to querying networks. Many approaches treat the network as a distributed database and emphasize query decomposition and execution (e.g., [18, 24]). These generally rely on known topologies and require a reliable logical configuration to convey queries and results. Others have examined programmable scheduling of probes or data collection, either at individual devices (e.g., [25]) or across an entire network (e.g., [10,15]). All of these approaches rely on devices already supporting a fixed set of attributes used to compute measurements; they cannot be easily extended to support new attributes once deployed.

An example of more closely related work is PLAN [8]. Their language and platform allow creation of measurements such as traceroute. Rather than defining a set of primitives for a measurement domain, they rely on deployable "service routines" to provide additional support at devices. They also rely on a known topology for localization and require the programmer to make explicit all relocations.

Localization techniques have also been well explored (e.g., [17, 20]). Where the XPLANE differs is in its easy to program semantics and novel transformation which preserves those semantics while linearizing execution and localization. This is a significant difference from other work including PLAN.

9.7 Conclusion

The XPLANE is an ongoing project aimed at a facility for enabling succinct expression of custom network measurements that can be executed efficiently in a network and without reliance on logical network sanity. Reducing the size of computations is important as the facility should not adversely impact the network's performance. To this end, we strive to enforce, through language design and clever compilation techniques, applications that can run completely within the space of a single 1,500-byte Ethernet frame and do not burden network devices with maintaining any control or communication state for them. Depending on where in the stack the XPLANE lives, running times of useful applications might be governed more by transfer delay than by router processing delay. This is an enormous challenge for programmatic approaches to measurement such as ours since measurements can be quite complex. However, techniques and other restrictions exist that when applied can lead to significantly smaller applications and a more efficient XPLANE. For instance, higher-order binding time analysis, partial evaluation and threading at XPLANE devices all show promise and are being investigated.

Thus far we have not addressed concerns regarding security for two reasons. First, until we arrived at a design that provided the flexibility, robustness, and efficiency necessary to realize programmable network measurement, there was nothing to secure. The design aspects treated in this paper present subtle challenges that must be properly addressed for programmable measurement to be viable in the first place. Second, and more importantly, the security requirements of such a system can only be adequately addressed in the context of a specific threat model. The current design leaves open the option of signing every XPL application when it localizes. If the XPLANE is deployed in an environment where trusted devices are given signing keys, then this addresses the threat of unauthorized execution. However, if eavesdroppers are a primary concern, then encryption should be utilized. Further, trust relationships when operating beyond a single administrative domain quickly become complicated. These challenges are best addressed once the threat model for a particular environment is understood.

A final aspect that is a subject of ongoing work is establishing the upper resource bounds on XPL applications. Given the ability to inject traffic, perform packet capture, and flood computation with unbounded recursion, even in a secure environment running an application containing a subtle bug could result in overwhelming the network with traffic or processing. It appears intuitively that network measurement applications may fall into distinct classes in terms of computation complexity and code growth, and that formal analysis techniques can be applied at compilation time to ensure that an application falls within a certain class before executing it.

References

1. Case, J.D., Fedor, M., Schoffstall, M.L., Davin, J.: Simple Network Management Protocol (SNMP). RFC 1157 (Historic) (1990)
2. Chen, X., Mao, Y., Mao, Z.M., Van der Merwe, J.: Declarative configuration management for complex and dynamic networks. In: Proceedings of the 6th International Conference, CoNEXT'10, Philadelphia, pp. 6:1–6:12. ACM, New York (2010)
3. Cheshire, S.: IPv4 Address Conflict Detection. RFC 5227 (Proposed Standard) (2008)
4. Clement, M., Volpano, D.: XPLANE: real-time awareness of tactical networks. Technical report, Naval Postgraduate School (2012)
5. Foster, N., Harrison, R., Freedman, M.J., Monsanto, C., Rexford, J., Story, A., Walker, D.: Frenetic: a network programming language. In: Proceedings 16th ACM SIGPLAN International Conference on Functional Programming, Tokyo. ACM, New York (2011)
6. Friedman, D.P., Wand, M.: Essentials of Programming Languages, 3rd edn., pp. 203–224. MIT, Cambridge (2008)
7. Gude, N., Koponen, T., Pettit, J., Pfaff, B., Casado, M., McKeown, N., Shenker, S.: NOX: towards an operating system for networks. SIGCOMM Comput. Commun. Rev. **38**(3), 105–110 (2008)
8. Hicks, M., Kakkar, P., Moore, J.T., Gunter, C.A., Nettles, S.: PLAN: a packet language for active networks. In: Proceedings 3rd ACM SIGPLAN International Conference on Functional Programming, Baltimore. ACM, New York (1998)
9. Hinrichs, T., Gude, N.S., Casado, M., Mitchell, J.C., Shenker, S.: Practical declarative network management. In: Proceedings of the 1st ACM Workshop on Research on Enterprise Networking, Barcelona, pp. 1–10. ACM, New York (2009)
10. Kompella, R.R., Snoeren, A.C., Varghese, G.: mPlane: an architecture for scalable fault localization. In: Proceedings of the 2009 Workshop on Re-architecting the Internet, ReArch'09, Rome, pp. 31–36. ACM, New York (2009)
11. Loo, B.T., Condie, T., Garofalakis, M., Gay, D.E., Hellerstein, J.M., Maniatis, P., Ramakrishnan, R., Roscoe, T., Stoica, I.: Declarative networking: language, execution and optimization. In: Proceedings of the 2006 ACM SIGMOD International Conference on Management of Data, SIGMOD'06, Chicago, pp. 97–108. ACM, New York (2006)
12. Linux man page. traceroute(8). http://linux.die.net/man/8/traceroute. Accessed 5 Aug 2012
13. Linux man page. pcap(3). www.tcpdump.org/pcap3_man.html. Accessed 13 July 2013
14. Narain, S., Levin, G., Malik, S., Kaul, V.: Declarative infrastructure configuration synthesis and debugging. J. Netw. Syst. Manag. **16**(3), 235–258 (2008)
15. Natu, M., Sethi, A.S.: Efficient probing techniques for fault diagnosis. In: Second International Conference on Internet Monitoring and Protection, ICIMP'07, San Jose, p. 20 (2007)
16. Plummer, D.: Ethernet Address Resolution Protocol: Or Converting Network Protocol Addresses to 48.bit Ethernet Address for Transmission on Ethernet Hardware. RFC 826 (Standard) (1982)
17. Sewell, P., Leifer, J.J., Wansbrough, K., Nardelli, F.Z., M. Allen-Williams, Habouzit, P., Vafeiadis, V.: Acute: high-level programming language design for distributed computation. In: Proceedings of the Tenth ACM SIGPLAN International Conference on Functional Programming, ICFP'05, Tallinn, pp. 15–26. ACM, New York (2005)
18. Shieh, A., Sirer, E.G., Schneider, F.B.: NetQuery: a knowledge plane for reasoning about network properties. In: Proceedings of the ACM CoNEXT Student Workshop, CoNEXT'10 Student Workshop, Philadelphia, pp. 23:1–23:2. ACM, New York (2010)
19. Souflis, D., Cozens, K., Shapiro, J.S.: TinyScheme. http://tinyscheme.sourceforge.net/home.html. Accessed 5 Aug 2012
20. Stamos, J.W., Gifford, D.K.: Remote evaluation. ACM Trans. Program. Lang. Syst. **12**(4), 537–564 (1990)
21. Stevens, W.R.: TCP/IP Illustrated. Vol 1: The Protocols, 1st edn., pp. 503–506. Addison-Wesley, Reading (1994)

22. Tennenhouse, D., Smith, J.M., Sincoskie, W.D., Wetherall, D.J., Minden, G.: A survey of active network research. IEEE Commun. Mag. **35**, 80–86 (1997)
23. Wand, M., Friedman, D.P.: Compiling lambda-expressions using continuations and factorizations. Comput. Lang. **3**(4), 241–263 (1978)
24. Wawrzoniak, M., Peterson, L., Roscoe, T.: Sophia: an information plane for networked systems. SIGCOMM Comput. Commun. Rev. **34**, 15–20 (2004)
25. Yuan, L., Chuah, C.-N., Mohapatra, P.: ProgME: towards programmable network measurement. IEEE/ACM Trans. Netw. **19**(1), 115–128 (2011)

Chapter 10
Discovery of Unexpected Services and Communication Paths in Networked Systems

Ichita Higurashi, Akira Kanaoka, Masahiko Kato, and Eiji Okamoto

Abstract Gaining a complete understanding of the active services and open communication paths present in recently created networked systems consisting of various servers and network devices is often difficult because of the rapidly expanding complexity of those services and their wide-ranging functions. Furthermore, the IT administrators of hand-designed systems often lack ways to identify and close unnecessary services and communication pathways. In this paper, we propose an automated approach to identifying and understanding the active services and the permitted communications on all servers and network devices. We then show how hand-designed networked systems containing such devices are prone to contain numerous unnecessary active services and communication paths, which exposes them to malicious actions such a service denial, information theft, and/or cyber espionage. An evaluation result shows the effectiveness of our proposed approach.

10.1 Introduction

The evolving services available on the Internet are causing numerous other systems to become increasingly complex. The present systems providing such services are also complex. As a result, many recent systems are composed of multiple small

I. Higurashi (✉) • M. Kato
Internet Initiative Japan Inc., 1-105 Kanda jinbo-cho, Chiyoda-ku, Tokyo, Japan
e-mail: higurashi@iij.ad.jp; masa@iij.ad.jp

A. Kanaoka,
University of Tsukuba, 1-1-1 Tennodai, Tsukuba, Ibaraki 305-8573, Japan
e-mail: kanaoka@risk.tsukuba.ac.jp

E. Okamoto
University of Tsukuba, 1-1-1 Tennodai, Tsukuba, Ibaraki, Japan
e-mail: okamoto@risk.tsukuba.ac.jp

E. Al-Shaer et al. (eds.), *Automated Security Management*,
DOI 10.1007/978-3-319-01433-3_10, © Springer International Publishing Switzerland 2013

networks and often consist of several servers and numerous network devices. We call such systems "networked systems (NSs)".

Management of vulnerabilities and the prevention of attack damage on a NS are achieved through the proper configuration of multiple aspects including servers, routers, switches, firewalls, and load balancers. Security is achieved by considering the interactions among each server and network device. Single point security is insufficient for achieving safety on an entire system, so the creation of compound points over multiple layers is required. Even though a NS consisting of tens of servers and devices may not be considered a large system, its complexity in security terms can be quite high.

Designing NSs that ensure essential communications are always available to the primary service users is crucial. Thus, unnecessary communication paths and services on each server and network device in a NS should be closed to achieve system security. To close unnecessary communication paths and services against the ever-increasing number of threats, a complete understanding of the functions and vulnerabilities of each server and network device is required.

However, it is difficult to gain a complete understanding of the active services and communications on every server and network device on present operating systems and network devices, because recently they have wide variety of complex functions. This means it is probable that unexpected communication paths, which are unnecessary for achieving the primary service, exist in such NSs. Furthermore, it is especially difficult to shut down all unnecessary services and communication paths in hand-designed network systems. If we allow such unnecessary open communication paths and services to exist in a NS, we make it possible for sophisticated attackers to access the system for malicious purposes such as service denial, information theft, and/or cyber espionage.

To prevent these threats, it is necessary to detect all active services and communication paths in a NS. Typically, active services that operate without the knowledge of IT systems administrators are found in software products that have not been updated to the latest version, even if those vulnerabilities were found and reported by the manufacturer. Then, such unnecessarily services cause the various threads.

On the other hand, several tools are available for use in assessing the vulnerabilities of a host. Such vulnerability assessment tools include NMAP, which can assess a target host in detail. However, such tools cannot merge gathered information from a number of assessed hosts in a coordinated fashion. There have also been several studies aimed at discovering networked topologies [1–3]. However, these studies discover only single or double layers.

We propose an automated approach to understanding active services and allowed communication on servers and network devices. We then show how many hand-designed systems are likely to possess numerous unnecessary services and communication paths, which exposes them to threats such as service denial, information theft, and/or cyber espionage. Our proposed approach consists of two stages: The first involves gathering configuration information from each server and network device in a NS. In the second stage, we connect and estimate available communication paths between the servers and network devices in multi-layer manner.

As a proof of concept, we developed a script for gathering configuration information from servers and devices, as well as a tool for connecting to and estimating the available communication paths identified from information gathered by our script. To discover multi-layered network topology, we use information obtained from management information base (MIB) objects and estimate the missing information. Additionally, the NS security quantification model (NSQ model) proposed by Kanaoka et al. [4] is used to evaluate information from multi-layered systems.

Then, to evaluate our proposed approach, we apply our developed script and tool to a NS with a three-tiered architecture, and a NS with a demilitarized zone (DMZ) architecture. The results of our evaluations indicate the level of understanding related to the services and communication paths, as well as the execution performance, of our proposed approach.

10.2 Related Works

10.2.1 Networked System Security Quantification Model

The NSQ model was proposed by Kanaoka et al. [4] as a new multifunctional NS representation model for quantifying NS reliability. The NSQ model contains the "layer" concept and classifies various network device functions into five layers (Fig. 11.1).

In the NSQ model, network devices and services are represented by *module*. Modules are constructed by nodes and links corresponded to the vertex and edge in graph theory. The nodes represent communication endpoints or relay points in each layer and contain information such as a IP address which is used as an ID. The relay nodes pass on communication data from endpoint to endpoint. The links represent dependency, relay, or communications between nodes.

There are seven module types: *Internet (I), Service (S), Layer 1 Relay (L1R), Layer 2 Relay (L2R), Layer 3 Relay (L3R), Layer 4 Relay (L4R)*, and *Layer 5 Relay (L5R)*. The Internet module represents the Internet and is the source of communication with the NS. A service module provides services such as World Wide Web (WWW). Relay modules represent network devices and network functions.

10.2.2 Topology Discovery

10.2.2.1 Method of Breitbart et al. [1]

A method for layer 2 and layer 3 topology discovery in heterogeneous IP networks has been proposed by Breitbart et al. [1]. This method exploits the simple network management protocol (SNMP), MIB objects, and the address forwarding table

Fig. 10.1 Layer definition

Layer5 : Abstracted services [WWW, DNS, etc]	●
Layer4 : TCP/UDP [port number, software]	●
Layer3 : IP [IP address]	●
Layer2 : Ethernet [Mac address]	●
Layer1 : Physical object	●

(AFT). The basic idea behind this algorithm is as follows: First, the neighboring routers of a known router are discovered using routing information in MIB-II, and the connectivity between routers is mapped. Next, they discover the connectivity between switches, and between routers and switches, using AFTs. They then implemented their algorithm and demonstrated its ability to fully discover all paths on the target network.

10.3 Topology Discovery Algorithm

10.3.1 Relationship Between MIB and NSQ Model

Since our approach is primarily based on SNMP, we first show how MIB objects are used to build a discovery algorithm in a multi-layered network. Table 10.1 shows the relationship between the NSQ model and MIB objects. As can be seen in the table, we are unable to obtain MIB information that corresponds to portion of the nodes of layers 4 and 5, or the links of layers 1, 2, 4 and 5. Such information deficits are resolved via MIB estimations in the next step. Details on that process will be provided in the following sections.

Even though we were unable to obtain the information of layer 1 links from the MIB object, layer 1 links are basically decided by layer 2 links. Therefore, we do not need to obtain information on layer 1 links directly.

10.3.2 Overview

In this section, we describe a topology discovery algorithm that operates under the following assumptions: (1) All devices support SNMP; (2) There is no hub; (3) There is no Virtual Local Area Networks (VLANs); (4) The AFTs are complete.

Our topology discovery algorithm is divided into two phases, *Phase 1: Information Extraction* and *Phase 2: Nodes and Links Estimation*. In phase 1, we discover the connectivity between devices using the work of Breitbart et al. [1] to obtain the configuration information of all devices. With this information, we can construct

Table 10.1 Relationship between the NSQ model and the MIB object

NSQ model	MIB object
L1 Node	sysName
L2 Node	ifPhysAddress
L3 Node	ipAdEntAddr
L4 Node (listen port)	tcplocalport, udplocalport
L4 Node (transmit port)	–
L5 Node	–
L1 Link	not required
L2 Link	ipNetToNediaPhysAddress
L3 Link	ipRouteNextHop
L4 Link	–
L5 Link	–
Module type	sysServices
Routing information	ipForwarding

an overview of the modules and the communication links between the modules in layers 2 and 3. After information extraction, we can then estimate any missing nodes and links in layers 1, 4 and 5 in phase 2. As mentioned earlier, since it is impossible to obtain information on all nodes and links using MIB, estimations are made instead.

10.3.3 Phase 1: Information Extraction

In this phase, we discover the device information and connectivities between devices simultaneously. The basic idea behind this phase is to repeatedly find the neighboring devices of the currently known devices until no new devices can be discovered, and then to obtain configuration information from all known devices.

The initial input in our method is the IP address of a known gateway router. At the beginning, the device itself decides whether to be L3R, L4R, L5R or S using *sysServices* of MIB. If a device has sysServices (0000100) – its third bit is set. We then decide the device L3R. Depending on the device type, the relevant MIB objects are retrieved from SNMP. For example, if the device type is S, we obtain the layer 1 node that corresponds to *sysName*, the layer 2 node that corresponds to *ifPhyAddress*, the layer 3 node that corresponds to *ipAdEntAddr*, the layer 4 node that corresponds to *tcplocalport* and *udplocalport*. The services of the layer 5 node are determined from the port numbers of the layer 4 node. However, we cannot determine the layer 4 nodes that correspond to transmit ports at this juncture, so it is necessary to estimate them.

Second, to discover the neighboring devices from a known device, we use *ipForwarding*, which is a routing information used to discover connectivities between L3R and L3R/L4R and L4R and L4R. We then scan the subnet to discover connectivities between L3R and L5R/S, L4R and L5R/S and S and S.

After we have discovered all connectivities between devices, which include L3R, L4R, L5R and S, and have obtained the configuration information for all devices, we can then discover the configuration information of the switch that corresponds to L2R, and the connectivity between switch and router as well as the switch and switch. To discover this connectivity, we apply the method of Breitbart et al.

In this way, we can recursively determine the connectivity between devices and obtain their configuration information.

10.3.4 Phase 2: Nodes and Links Estimation

In phase 2, we estimate links for the links of layers 1 and 4, layer 4 nodes, and layer 5 links, in that order, using modules and layer 3 links.

First, we estimate layer 1 links. Since we have already discovered the connectivities between the devices in layer 2, we are now able to estimate the layer 1 links between modules. If layer 2 nodes a and b are connected, we can then presume that layer 1 nodes x and y, which are connected to a and b, are connected.

Next, we estimate layer 4 nodes and layer 4 links. The process used to estimate layer 4 nodes and links differs from the one used to estimate links for layers 1. Because it is necessary to estimate nodes in addition to links. The basic scheme used to estimate layer 4 nodes and links is as follows: If module A and module B, which are either L4R, L5R, S or I are connected with layer 3 links and communicate with each other, those modules will have a pair of layer 4 nodes that correspond to a listen port and a layer 4 node that corresponds to a transmit port. More specifically, if module B has a layer 4 node such as 80, module A must also have a layer 4 node that corresponds to a transmit port.

In the third step, we estimate layer 5 links. If layer 4 nodes a and b are connected, we can presume that layer 5 nodes x and y, which are connected to a and b, are connected as well.

In this manner, all missing nodes and links are estimated.

10.4 Implementation and Experimental Results

10.4.1 Implementation and Experimental Environment

We implemented our information extraction and estimation methods in the Java 1.6. environment. When implementing the information extraction method, we cannot use the previously discussed method for discovering the switches and the connectivities between switches and the switch and router because that method requires *complete AFTs*. That is why we estimate the switches and connectivities between the switch and router, and then implement the method used to estimate layer 2 links and L2R.

Fig. 10.2 Three-tiered
architecture

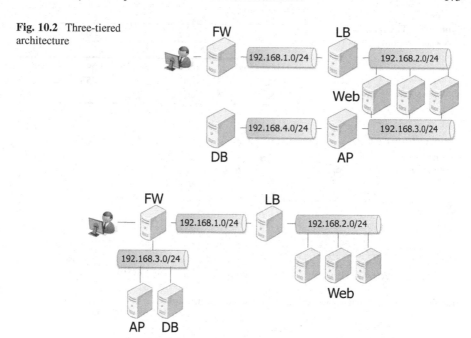

Fig. 10.3 DMZ architecture

Fig. 10.4 IRS architecture

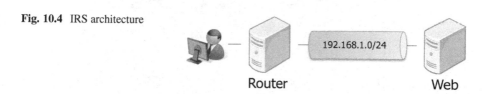

Prior to testing our proposed method, we constructed three types of NSs: three-tiered architecture, DMZ architecture and, internet-router-server (IRS) architecture. Figures 10.2–10.4 show the three types of NSs. SSH service was employed to control the devices. In addition, we also installed the software that implemented our method. However, note that we did not run any other services, nor did we change the configurations of these NSs.

Configuration of each servers is based on initially installed OS related services and applications and specific service (like Apache HTTPD, Apache Tomcat, MySQL). Initially OS installed services and applications sometimes run unnecessary services required to original purpose of the server. The aim of configuration is to expose that initially installed services cause the difficulty of complete understanding of a NS, and might be a big threat to sophisticated attacks.

Table 10.2 The number of
nodes and links in phases 1, 2

	Phase 1		Phase 2	
	Node	Link	Node	Link
Three-tired	305	312	644	5899
DMZ	204	207	453	4181
IRS	34	33	39	69

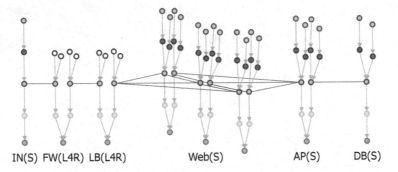

Fig. 10.5 Phase 1 visualization results: three-tiered architecture

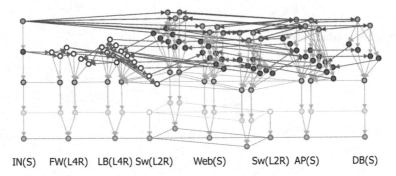

Fig. 10.6 Phase 2 visualization results: three-tiered architecture

10.4.2 Evaluation of the Proposed Method

Table 10.2 shows the number of nodes and links discovered during information
extraction along with the estimated node and links. We observed that a significant
number of nodes and links were estimated. Almost all node increments were layer
4 nodes that corresponded to transmit ports. Similarity, almost all link increments
belonged to layers 4 and 5, or the links between the layer 4 and layer 5 networks.
These node and link increments informed us that the modules have a significant
number of active services, and that each module can communicate with each of the
other modules.

Finally, we will show a visualization of the experimental result of three-tiered
architecture in phase 1 (Fig. 10.5) and phase 2 (Fig. 10.6). Note that in this

representation, we only visualize two nodes in each module, specifically FW, LB, Web, AP or DB in layer 4 and layer 5, even though it is possible to retrieve information on 13 nodes for layer 4 from each module.

10.5   Consideration

Using our method, we can detect unnecessary active services for IT system administrators. Recently, various forms of malicious software including Trojan horses, backdoors, computer viruses, worms, and other malware have been used to steal important information such as passwords.

To prevent information leakage, it is necessary to detect all active services in a NS and to stop any that are unnecessary. Typically, active services that operate without the knowledge of IT systems administrators are found in software products that have not been updated to the latest version, even if those vulnerabilities were found and reported by the manufacturer. Such exposed services degrade the security of NSs.

Table 10.3 shows the services that our method extracted from the Web server used in the experiment. The services of *sshd*, *httpd*, *our software* and *snmpd* are those we intended to use and expected to find. However, we detected the unexpected but active services of *portmap*, *rpc.stad*, *cupsd* and *avashi-daemon*. Thus, as discussed in the sections above, our method enabled us to detect unnecessary active services.

10.6   Conclusion

A NS consists of servers and network devices, and it is important for IT systems administrators to understand all the active services and communication paths that are operating in their NSs. Recently, malware is often employed to steal important information from NSs. Active services and communication paths that are operating on NSs without the knowledge of the administrator can cause actualization of such threats. Thus, gaining a total understanding of the active services and open communication paths in a NS is necessary for every IT systems administrator.

Table 10.3 Results of Web server service detection

Port	Pro	Service	Port	Pro	Service
22	TCP	sshd	111	UDP	portmap
80	TCP	httpd	161	UDP	snmpd
111	TCP	portmap	631	UDP	cupsd
932	TCP	rpc.stad	926	UDP	rpc.statd
32123	TCP	our software	929	UDP	rpc.statd
57911	UDP	avashi-daemon	5353	UDP	avashi-daemon

In this paper, we proposed an approach that can be used to discover and understand all the active services and open communications on every server and device in a NS. We then showed how numerous unnecessary services and communication paths are typically left open in a hand-designed NS, which increases system vulnerabilities to threats like service denial, information theft, and/or cyber espionage. The results of an evaluation of our approach demonstrated its effectiveness.

References

1. Breitbart, Y., Garofalakis, M., et al.: Topology discovery in heterogeneous IP networks: the NetInventory system. IEEE ACM Trans. Netw. **12**(3), 401–414 (2004)
2. Black, R., Donnelly, A., et al.: Ethernet topology discovery without network assistance. In: ICNP, Berlin, pp. 328–339 (2004)
3. Chen, X., Zhang, M., et al.: Automating network application dependency discovery: experiences, limitations, and new solutions. In: OSDI, San Diego, pp. 117–130 (2008)
4. Kanaoka, A., Katoh, M., et al.: Extraction of parameters from well managed networked system in access control. In: ICIMP, Venice/Mestre, pp. 56–61 (2009)

Chapter 11
Tracing Advanced Persistent Threats in Networked Systems

Masahiko Kato, Takumi Matsunami, Akira Kanaoka, Hiroshi Koide, and Eiji Okamoto

Abstract We herein discuss the modeling of target information systems as well as various attacks, in order to clarify the impact of Advanced Persistent Threats (APTs) and to enable efficient planning of defense strategies to counter APTs.

11.1 Introduction

Information systems structures are becoming increasingly complex and larger in scale. Since the number of services provided through the Internet is growing, the amount of data continues to increase in order to support multiple functions and diversity. On the other hand, thefts of confidential information have also increased in recent years. In particular, a new type of threat referred to as Advanced Persistent Threat (APT) has become a major threat. Attackers have strong purpose in APT. Attackers attack a specific information system repeatedly over a long period of

M. Kato (✉)
Internet Initiative Japan Inc., 1-105 Kanda jinbo-cho, Chiyoda-ku, Tokyo 101-0051, Japan
e-mail: masa@iij.ad.jp

T. Matsunami
Kyushu Institute of Technology, 680-4 Kawazu, Iizuka-shi, Fukuoka 820-8502, Japan
e-mail: tgv@klab.ai.kyutech.ac.jp

A. Kanaoka • E. Okamoto
University of Tsukuba, 1-1-1 Tennodai, Tsukuba, Ibaraki 305-8573, Japan
e-mail: kanaoka@risk.tsukuba.ac.jp; okamoto@risk.tsukuba.ac.jp

H. Koide
Information-technology Promotion Agency Japan, 16th Floor, Bunkyo Green Court, 2-28-8, Hon-Komagome, Bunkyo-ku, Tokyo 113-6591, Japan
e-mail: koide@ai.kyutech.ac.jp

E. Al-Shaer et al. (eds.), *Automated Security Management*,
DOI 10.1007/978-3-319-01433-3_11, © Springer International Publishing Switzerland 2013

time until finally obtaining confidential information. There have been a number of incidence in which confidential information has been stolen from enterprises and government agencies. We have previously protected such confidential information using several defense methods that are suitable for individual attacks. Before the emergence of APT, we were able to detect attacks by observing anomalies on the security boundary. In existing methods, we can simplify security design for an information system even if the network is growing in scale and becoming more complex, because we can assume that the attackers cannot break into the safety zone through the security boundary. Therefore, it is difficult to defend against APT attacks that break into the internal zone. Since attacks often occur in the safety zone, the above assumption is not feasible.

In the present study, we propose a method by which to trace APT attacks in an information system, especially a system that consists of several servers and network equipment. We refer to such information systems as Networked Systems. We first propose and develop a data model for each APT attack technique and a networked system under APT. We then simulate attacks using the proposed model.

There are two approaches by which to counter APTs. The first involves increasing the sophistication of security devices, and the second involves the development of a system design methodology for complex networked systems to enable detection and reaction after an intrusion. We chose the latter. The proposed method focuses on tracing APT attacks. In addition, the proposed method can be used during system design. As mentioned earlier, APT attacks are complex and persistent. The impact of an APT usually cannot be measured at the start of the intrusion.

We have to measure the total threat, and carefully determine the overall influence of attacks inside a networked system. Since measuring the total threat on a running system is difficult, measurement requires data that express a networked system and attacks based on data models. We first apply a data model to a networked system that consists of a wide variety of components, including several servers (such as Web, E-mail, DNS, LDAP, and Proxy servers), switches, routers, firewalls, load balancers, and operation terminals, using XML. The data model is used as a snapshot of a networked system. We then propose a data model for the behavior of malware on a network as well as a domain specific language (DSL) for expressing snapshots of networked system and malware behavior on the network. Furthermore, we develop Threat Tracer, which simulates the behavior of malware based on the proposed DSL. Threat Tracer was developed using Scala.

We then demonstrate the impact of an APT in a networked system. Comparison of the proposed method with an existing method, which experts and/or designers of an information system analyzes the attacks as a desk plan, reveals that the proposed method provides excellent reproducibility and exhaustively. In addition, the proposed method is expected to reduce the load of human security analysts.

The remainder of the present paper is organized as follows. We describe a network model and research related to a malware working model in Sect. 11.2. In Sect. 11.3, we present the proposed approach. Section 11.4 describes the development of the proposed method. Finally, we conclude the paper in Sect. 11.5.

11.2 Related Research

11.2.1 Networked System Security Quantification Model

The NSQ model was proposed by Kanaoka et al. [1] as a new multifunctional networked system representation model for quantifying the reliability of a networked system. The NSQ model contains the layer concept and classifies various network device functions into five layers (Fig. 11.1).

In the NSQ model, network devices and servers are represented by the *module*. Modules are constructed of nodes, and links correspond to vertexes and edges in graph theory. There are seven module types: *Internet (I), Service (S), Layer 1 Relay (L1R), Layer 2 Relay (L2R), Layer 3 Relay (L3R), Layer 4 Relay (L4R),* and *Layer 5 Relay (L5R).* The Internet module represents the Internet and is the source of communication with the networked system. A service module provides services, such as the World Wide Web (WWW), secure shell (SSH), or domain name service (DNS). Relay modules represent network devices and network functions. For example, L1R is a hub, L2R is a switch, L3R is a router, L4R is a firewall, and L5R is a proxy.

Nodes represent communication endpoints or relay points in each layer and contain information such as a MAC address, an IP address, or a port number, which is used as an ID. Relay nodes pass on communication data from endpoint (source) to endpoint (destination). Vertical links represent dependency, and horizontal links indicate access between nodes.

Figure 11.2 shows an example of a networked system. The use of the NSQ model allows us to explain the components of various networked systems as modules without losing sight of their functional characteristics.

11.2.2 Malware Attribute Enumeration and Characterization

Malware attribute enumeration and characterization (MAEC) is a standard language for attribute-based malware characterization. Malware attribute enumeration and characterization was developed and is maintained by the MITRE Corporation [2].

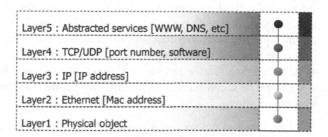

Fig. 11.1 Layer definition

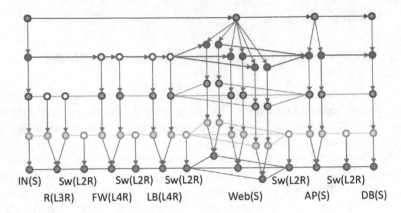

Fig. 11.2 Example of a networked system

Malware attribute enumeration and characterization is suitable for exchanging malware information and can describe slight differences in malware behavior, structure, and details on addressing various types of malware. Vocabulary is used for malware enumerations and is composed three levels of abstraction (high-level taxonomy, mid-level behavior, and low-level attribute).

Malware attribute enumeration and characterization is very useful for malware enumerations and information exchange because the purpose of MAEC is to come up with a standard format for malware information and to construct a malware DB. However, how the malware communicates on a networked system must be determined, and to describe about action more than two computers on a networked system influence each other. Thus, MAEC seems like over-spec for what we do.

11.3 Threat Trace Framework

11.3.1 Modeling of Malware Behavior on Network Modeling

Advanced persistent threat attacks consist of two steps in order to invade a networked system and achieve the goal of the attack [3]. The first step is intrusion into a networked system. Intrusion methods are diverse and include phishing attacks by e-mail with a malware, SSH login brute force attacks, or other social engineering methods. In order to defend against such intrusions, the improvement of existing countermeasures, such as anti-virus software and intrusion detection systems (IDSs), and education on moral issues in information technology, is desirable. The second step involves building a platform of an attack in the networked system as follows:

1. Searching the network configuration, sending the obtained information to the attacker using a backdoor, and connecting to the C&C server.

Fig. 11.3 An example of a simple network written in DSL

```
object Sample extends MalwareSimulationLibrary {
  val pc1, pc2 = PCterminal
  val router1 = Router
  val malware1 = Conficker
  val rtable1 = RoutingTable
  pc1 has a networkCard ''192.168.0.2/24''
  pc2 has a networkCard ''192.168.1.2/24''
  pc1 opens tcpPort (22, 80)
  pc2 opens tcpPort (22, 80, 443)
  router1 has a networkCard ''192.168.0.1/24''
  router1 has a networkCard ''192.168.1.1/24''
  router1 has a rtable1
  pc1 connects to router1
  pc2 connects to router1
  pc1 is infectedWith malware1
  run
}
```

Fig. 11.4 An example of simple malware that builds an attack platform written in DSL

```
class Sample extends SimpleMalwareLibrary {
  initialize {
    makeBackDoor()
    communicatesWith(cncServer)
  }
  control {
    case Invoke => invokeMalwareCode()
    case GetNetInfo => getsNetworkInfo()
    case HttpMsgCom => communicatesWith(cncServer)
    case Updates => updatesMyselfBy(cncServer)
    case Infection => infectsTo(pc2)
  }
}
```

2. Spreading same malware by copying itself, updating itself by command from C&C server.

After these steps, attackers accomplish the goal of the attack using the constructed platform. The final purpose includes obtaining confidential information on a target, authentication information of users, falsification of a Web site of a target, and further attacks on other organizations.

11.3.2 Domain Specific Language

The NSQ model has a data structure of a statically networked system. Koide et al. proposed DSL for modeling the action of malware on a networked system described by a NSQ model. This DSL defines the information system and the malware's action to do abstraction reasonably. For example, a simple information system, which is constructed of two PCs, is connected through one router written in DSL, as shown in Fig. 11.3. Action when malware build attacking platform is written Fig. 11.4 by DSL. Initialize section says initial action when PC is infected, control section describe running the method by C&C control message.

11.3.3   Threat Tracer

Threat Tracer interprets the modeling system and modeling malware written in DSL and then simulates the actions of malware. Malware initially makes a backdoor and connects to a C&C server. Then, exceed the attack by changing network configuration or copying malware itself to other hosts. The system status is changed by the malware. Since there is absolute in discreteness, we can determine how malware will influence an information system by searching.

11.3.4   Parallel Distributed Processing by Task Scheduling Method

The complexity of Threat Tracing is decided by the number of nodes and edges on a network and the number of malware functions. In addition, Threat Tracing must handle multiple malware applications in one information system. Threat Tracing also affects the complexity.

The nodes of the network are the PC, the router, the switching hub, the load balancer, the firewall, the IDS, the anti-virus appliance, and various types of servers. In the present paper, the edge of a network indicates a network cable connecting nodes. In order to analyze a layered network using the NSQ model, logical network connection is sometime dense, even though physical network connections are sparse. The density does not depend on the physical network topology. In order to simulate a malware attack, it is necessary to take into consideration the access control structure divided by the logical layer.

When we consider situations in which intrusions have occurred as a result of multiple malware applications on large-scale information systems such as large enterprise systems or government systems, the simulation of tracing requires a very long time for calculation. Calculation must be performed using high-powered machines or parallel distributed processing using a number of machines. If the workload is shared among a number of CPUs by parallel distributed processing, various techniques can be considered using the task scheduling method for parallel distributed processing. By considering each node as a task and each edge as the dependence of a task, a network model can be regarded as a task interaction graph that have dependence each other. A network model that expresses a task interaction graph is only once translated Task Flow Graph before calculating dynamically to trace threats. This processing is the same as that of a compiling program and involves automatic interpretation and translation. As such, by clearly assigning the flow of tasks sets, the preload of the scheduler decreases and the efficiency of calculation is improved. However, the network configuration is changed by renewal and so on, we need to create Task Flow Graph again with remodeling and statically processing. Dynamic threat tracing requires task assignment under dynamic management of PCs and calculation by the task scheduler. The task scheduler refers to the task flow graph processing statically and manages computer assignment.

11.4   Prototype System Development

Threat Tracer was developed using Scala. Threat Tracer is suitable for a domain specific language and can use XML to easily describe networks and malware. In the case of simulating an information system having several function (e.g., routing, malware behavior, whether software is run), we can collect into one after mix-in composition automatically by arranging for every function called Trait. Finally, large-scale software or complex parallel distribution software can be implemented, can use the Java library, and has good performance.

11.4.1   Internal Description of an Information System

Threat Tracer simulates the state of link structures with regard to nodes and the system status, as follows:

Basic node: This node contains basic information as an information system. Accessor methods is implemented about sequential number, identified label, layer, type of nodes, MAC address, IP address, TCP port, UDP port, service and so on.

Infected node: This node simulates of malware infection and has a list of malware intrusions. Implemented methods involve malware infection (getsInfectWith), malware removal (removeMalware), and malware invocation (invokeMalware).

Network node: This node simulates the behavior of the IP layer and has a list of network interface connected nodes, a default route, a routing table, and firewall rules.

Communication node: This node confirms the connectivity of the other communication node and sends a message if the node is connectable. This node is implemented by inheritance of scala.actors.Actor.

11.4.2   Discrete Event Simulation

Discrete event simulation is newly implemented based on the versatile discrete event simulator. We performed a test implementation in order to facilitate the design a DSL or Threat Tracer. We put test information system (Fig. 11.5) in test implementation, and PC1 is infected simple malware. Figures 11.6–11.8 indicate that the infection spreads from PC1 to PC2 and from PC2 to PC3.

1. In the initial state, the information system has a router and a PC. PC1 is infected (Fig. 11.6).
2. The malware of PC1 searches for the next infectable device. The malware then finds PC2, which is infectable. Therefore, PC2 is infected. The network status is shown below print in the log and indicates that PC2 is newly infected (Fig. 11.7).

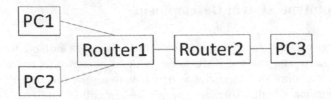

Fig. 11.5 A sample of a network used for testing

Fig. 11.6 An example of
testing (initial state)

```
$ java -jar MalwareSimulator.jar
PCTerminal(pc1)
PCTerminal(pc2)
Router(router1)
PCTerminal(pc3)
Router(router2)
Malware(PCTerminal(pc1))
```

Fig. 11.7 An example of
testing (after PC2 has been
infected)

```
Malware(PCTerminal(pc1)):action
PCTerminal(pc1):send Router(router1)
Router(router1):send PCTerminal(pc1)
PCTerminal(pc1):send Router(router1)
Router(router1):send PCTerminal(pc2)
PCTerminal(pc2):send Router(router1)
Router(router1):send PCTerminal(pc1)
PCTerminal(pc2):call isInfectable true
print
PCTerminal(pc1)
PCTerminal(pc2)
Router(router1)
PCTerminal(pc3)
Router(router2)
Malware(PCTerminal(pc1))
Malware(PCTerminal(pc2))
```

3. The malware of PC1 and PC2 search for the next infectable device at the same
   time. Since PC3 is detected and is infectable, PC3 is infected according to the
   log (Fig. 11.8).

11.5   Conclusion

Advanced persistent threat attacks have steps inside security boundary. Moreover,
since attack methods change dynamically, countermeasures on the perimeter are
ineffective. Thus, recent system structures have become more complex. Designing
an information system that has the capability to defend against various APT attacks
requires the use of computer aided design. In the present paper, we modeled APT

Fig. 11.8 An example of
testing (after PC3 has been
infected)

```
Malware(PCTerminal(pc1)):action
Malware(PCTerminal(pc2)):action
PCTerminal(pc2):send Router(router1)
....cut...
Router(router1):send PCTerminal(pc2)
PCTerminal(pc2):call isInfectable false
PCTerminal(pc1):send Router(router1)
PCTerminal(pc1):call isInfectable false
Router(router1):send Router(router2)
....cut...
Router(router1):send Router(router2)
PCTerminal(pc3):call isInfectable true
Router(router2):send PCTerminal(pc3)
PCTerminal(pc3):send Router(router2)
Router(router2):send Router(router1)
Router(router1):send PCTerminal(pc2)
PCTerminal(pc3):call isInfectable false
print
PCTerminal(pc1)
PCTerminal(pc2)
Router(router1)
PCTerminal(pc3)
Router(router2)
Malware(PCTerminal(pc1))
Malware(PCTerminal(pc2))
Malware(PCTerminal(pc3))
```

attacks using DSL. In addition, we simulated the behavior of APT attacks using the NSQ model and proposed a malware model. As a result, we demonstrated that the influence of an APT may be able to be clarified by calculation. In the future, we intend to simulate existing malware (such as Conficker) on a more complex system and refine the proposed model. We will simulate a large-scale system at high-speed. In addition, we will discuss linking with MAEC.

References

1. Kanaoka, A., Katoh, M., Toudou, N., Okamoto, E.: Extraction of parameters from well managed networked system in access control. In: Proceedings of the ICIMP, Venice/Mestre, pp. 56–61 (2009)
2. The MITRE Corporation: Malware attribute enumeration and characterization. http://maec.mitre.org (2011)
3. Information-technology Promotion Agency Japan: Design and operational guide to protect against "Advanced Persistent Threats", revised 2nd edn. http://www.ipa.go.jp/security/vuln/documents/eg_newattack.pdf (2011)

Printed in the United States
By Bookmasters